STEP 2

WORD
Bridge
3600

Intro

Word Bridge 3600의 수준별 학습
중학교 필수 단어에서 특목고 대비를 위한 단어까지 총 3,600 단어가 단계별로 레벨업되어 있습니다. 자신의 수준에 맞추어서 차근차근 어휘력을 다져나갈 수 있도록 하였습니다.

귀로 듣고, 입으로 따라하기
단어마다 문법과 구문법칙이 응용된 모범예문을 원어민의 정확한 발음으로 듣고 따라하다 보면 암기 효과를 두 배로 올릴 수 있도록 하였습니다.

영영정의를 통한 의미 이해
단어의 주요 의미를 영영으로 정의해 놓고 연관된 예문을 제시함으로써 그 의미를 더욱 정확하게 이해할 수 있도록 하였습니다.

반복, 반복 쏙쏙 암기
눈으로 암기하는 단어는 오래 기억되지 못합니다. 듣기, 말하기, 쓰기 등을 활용한 다양한 연습 형태를 통해 반복적으로 단어를 학습할 수 있도록 하였습니다.

교재의 구성

본 교재는 단계별로 총 5권으로 구성되어 있습니다.

각 권은 10 Part로, 각 Part는 모두 4 unit으로 구성되어 있습니다.

Listen and repeat
주요 학습 파트로 새로운 단어 18개와 단어를 활용한 모범예문이 수록되어 있으며 듣기 학습이 포함되어 있습니다.

Exercise / Review
주요 학습에서 익힌 단어와 예문을 활용하여 문제를 풀어보고 암기합니다.

▼ Step 1
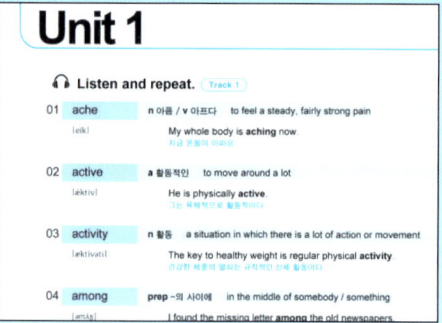

▼ Step 2
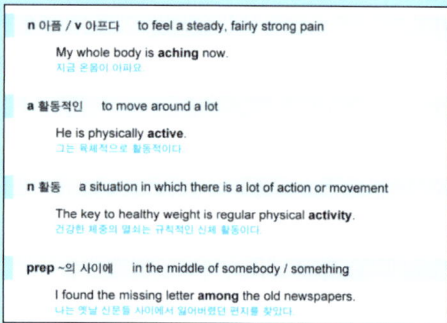

▼ Step 3
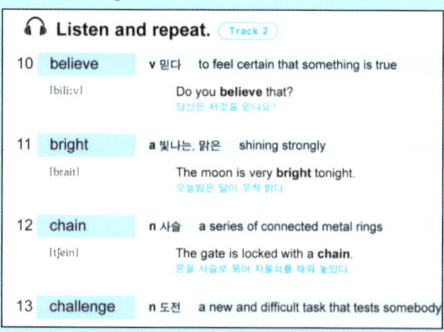

▼ Step 4

▼ Step 5

B. Fill in the word and meaning.

Word	Meaning		Meaning	Word
01 activity		01	아픔, 아프다	
02 basis		02	활동적인	
03 chain		03	활동	
04 bright		04	~의 사이에	
05 ache		05	기본적인	
06 become		06	기초, 근거	
07 chance		07	아름다움	
08 active		08	~ 때문에	
09 believe		09	~이 되다	
10 character		10	믿다	
11 basic		11	빛나는, 밝은	
12 chart		12	사슬	
13 challenge		13	도전	
14 because		14	우연, 기회	

▼ Step 6

🎧 **C. Listen, write the word and meaning.** (Track 3)

Word	Meaning		Word
01		10	
02		11	
03		12	
04		13	
05		14	
06		15	
07		16	
08		17	
09		18	

▼ Step 7

A. Read and fill in the word and meaning.

word	definition	meaning
	to start to be something	
	to feel certain that something is true	
	stating the reason for something	
	a series of connected metal rings	
	to feel a steady, fairly strong pain	
	shining strongly	
	the quality of being pleasing to the mind	
	a new and difficult task that tests somebody's skill	
	a situation in which there is a lot of action or movement	
	an opportunity	

교재의 학습방법

- **Step 1 - 새 단어 귀로 들으며 익히기**
  새 단어와 예문을 원어민의 발음으로 들으며 익힌다.

- **Step 2 - 단어 뜻 암기하기**
  영영 정의를 익히면서 단어의 정확한 의미를 이해하고, 예문을 해석하면서 예문 속에서 단어의 쓰임을 학습합니다.

- **Step 3 - 입으로 따라하며 암기하기**
  다시 한 번 CD를 들으면서 큰 소리로 따라합니다. 예문을 따라하면서 통째로 암기합니다.

- **Step 4 - 문장 완성하기**
  주어진 단어 힌트를 이용하여 암기한 예문을 완성합니다.

- **Step 5 - 단어와 뜻 채우기**
  제시된 영어 단어는 뜻을 우리 말로 쓰고, 단어의 뜻이 제시되어 있으면 영어 단어를 쓰면서 복습합니다.

- **Step 6 - 듣고 단어와 뜻 채우기**
  CD를 듣고 정확한 발음을 익히며 영어 단어와 뜻을 쓰면서 반복 학습합니다.

- **Step 7 - 단어 암기 확인**
  영영 정의를 읽고 암기한 영어 단어와 뜻을 쓰면서 확인 학습을 합니다.

Contents

part 1

Unit 1 ········· 6
Unit 2 ········· 10
Review 1 ········· 14

Unit 3 ········· 16
Unit 4 ········· 20
Review 2 ········· 24

part 2

Unit 5 ········· 26
Unit 6 ········· 30
Review 3 ········· 34

Unit 7 ········· 36
Unit 8 ········· 40
Review 4 ········· 44

part 3

Unit 9 ········· 46
Unit 10 ········· 50
Review 5 ········· 54

part 4

Unit 11 ········· 56
Unit 12 ········· 60
Review 6 ········· 64

Unit 13 ········· 66
Unit 14 ········· 70
Review 7 ········· 74

Unit 15 ········· 76
Unit 16 ········· 80
Review 8 ········· 84

part 5

Unit 17 ········· 86
Unit 18 ········· 90
Review 9 ········· 94

Unit 19 ········· 96
Unit 20 ········· 100
Review 10 ········· 104

WORD BRIDGE 3600

part 6

Unit 21	106
Unit 22	110
Review 11	114
Unit 23	116
Unit 24	120
Review 12	124

part 7

Unit 25	126
Unit 26	130
Review 13	134
Unit 27	136
Unit 28	140
Review 14	144

part 8

Unit 29	146
Unit 30	150
Review 15	154

Unit 31	156
Unit 32	160
Review 16	164

part 9

Unit 33	166
Unit 34	170
Review 17	174
Unit 35	176
Unit 36	180
Review 18	184

part 10

Unit 37	186
Unit 38	190
Review 19	194
Unit 39	196
Unit 40	200
Review 20	204
Total Test	207
Answer Key	229

Unit 1

🎧 Listen and repeat. (Track 1)

01 ache [eik]
n 아픔 / v 아프다   to feel a steady, fairly strong pain
My whole body is **aching** now.
지금 온몸이 아파요.

02 active [ǽktiv]
a 활동적인   to move around a lot
He is physically **active**.
그는 육체적으로 활동적이다.

03 activity [æktívəti]
n 활동   a situation in which there is a lot of action or movement
The key to healthy weight is regular physical **activity**.
건강한 체중의 열쇠는 규칙적인 신체 활동이다.

04 among [əmʌ́ŋ]
prep ~의 사이에   in the middle of somebody / something
I found the missing letter **among** the old newspapers.
나는 옛날 신문들 사이에서 잃어버렸던 편지를 찾았다.

05 basic [béisik]
a 기본적인   forming the part of something that is most necessary
The family is the **basic** unit of society.
가정은 사회의 기본 단위이다.

06 basis [béisis]
n 기초, 근거   the principle or reason which lies behind
We made our decision on the **basis** of the reports.
우리는 그 보고들에 기초해서 결정을 내렸다.

07 beauty [bjúːti]
n 아름다움   the quality of being pleasing to the mind
A thing of **beauty** is a joy forever.
아름다운 것은 영원한 기쁨이다.

08 because [bikɔ́ːz]
conj ~때문에   stating the reason for something
He is upset **because** she got a very good grade.
그녀가 높은 점수를 받았기 때문에 그는 속이 상했다.

09 become [bikʌ́m]
v ~이 되다   to start to be something
You will **become** a good artist.
당신은 훌륭한 예술가가 될 것 입니다.

key words
steady a 끊임없이 / fairly ad 상당히 / whole a 전부의
society n 사회 / forever a 영원한 / upset a 근심되는 / grade n 등급, 성적

🎧 Listen and repeat. Track 2

10 believe [bilíːv]
v 믿다   to feel certain that something is true
Do you **believe** that?
당신은 저것을 믿나요?

11 bright [brait]
a 빛나는, 맑은   shining strongly
The moon is very **bright** tonight.
오늘밤 달이 무척 밝다.

12 chain [tʃein]
n 사슬   a series of connected metal rings
The gate is locked with a **chain**.
문을 사슬로 묶어 자물쇠를 채워 놓았다.

13 challenge [tʃǽlindʒ]
n 도전   a new and difficult task that tests somebody's skill
The company will be faced with many **challenges** in this month.
그 회사는 이번 달에 많은 도전에 직면하게 될 것이다.

14 chance [tʃæns]
n 우연, 기회   an opportunity
I will give you one more **chance**.
내가 한 번 더 기회를 주지.

15 change [tʃeindʒ]
v 바꾸다   to become different
The woman is **changing** the sheets.
여자가 시트를 바꾸고 있다.

16 character [kǽriktər]
n 특성, 성격   all the features that make a person
Every mother and father wants to raise a child with a strong moral **character**.
모든 부모들은 자녀를 도덕성을 잘 갖춘 아이로 양육하기를 바란다.

17 chart [tʃɑːrt]
n 차트, 도표   a page of information in the form of lists
What is this **chart** for?
이 도표는 무엇을 나타내는 것인가?

18 clear [kliər]
a 분명한, 맑은   easy to understand
His voice wasn't very **clear** on the telephone.
전화상의 그의 목소리는 분명하지 않았다.

key words
shine v 빛나다 / lock v 잠그다 / task n 일, 작업 / feature n 특징
raise v 기르다, 키우다 / moral a 도덕을 지키는

Exercise

A. Complete the sentence.

1. The key to healthy weight is regular physical _____.
   건강한 체중의 열쇠는 규칙적인 신체 활동이다.
2. What is this _____ for?
   이 도표는 무엇을 나타내는 것인가?
3. I found the missing letter _____ the old newspapers.
   나는 옛날 신문들 사이에서 잃어버렸던 편지를 찾았다.
4. A thing of _____ is a joy forever.
   아름다운 것은 영원한 기쁨이다.
5. The woman is _____ the sheets.
   여자가 시트를 바꾸고 있다.
6. The family is the _____ unit of society.
   가정은 사회의 기본 단위이다.
7. We made our decision on the _____ of the reports.
   우리는 그 보고들에 기초해서 결정을 내렸다.
8. He is upset _____ she got a very good grade.
   그녀가 높은 점수를 받았기 때문에 그는 속이 상했다.
9. The company will be faced with many _____ in this month.
   그 회사는 이번 달에 많은 도전에 직면하게 될 것이다.
10. I will give you one more _____.
    내가 한 번 더 기회를 주지.
11. You will _____ a good artist.
    당신은 훌륭한 예술가가 될 것 입니다.
12. My whole body is _____ now.
    지금 온몸이 아파요.
13. Do you _____ that?
    당신은 저것을 믿나요?
14. The moon is very _____ tonight.
    오늘밤은 달이 무척 밝다.
15. The gate is locked with a _____.
    문을 사슬로 묶어 자물쇠를 채워 놓았다.
16. Every mother and father wants to raise a child with a strong moral _____.
    모든 부모들은 자녀를 도덕성을 잘 갖춘 아이로 양육하기를 바란다.
17. He is physically _____.
    그는 육체적으로 활동적이다.
18. His voice wasn't very _____ on the telephone.
    전화상의 그의 목소리는 분명하지 않았다.

Hint

| character | because | change | among | basis | ache | chart | bright | chance |
| believe | challenge | active | basic | chain | activity | beauty | become | clear |

Exercise

B. Fill in the word and meaning.

	Word	Meaning
01	activity	
02	basis	
03	chain	
04	bright	
05	ache	
06	become	
07	chance	
08	active	
09	believe	
10	character	
11	basic	
12	chart	
13	challenge	
14	because	
15	clear	
16	among	
17	change	
18	beauty	

	Meaning	Word
01	아픔, 아프다	
02	활동적인	
03	활동	
04	~의 사이에	
05	기본적인	
06	기초, 근거	
07	아름다움	
08	~ 때문에	
09	~이 되다	
10	믿다	
11	빛나는, 맑은	
12	사슬	
13	도전	
14	우연, 기회	
15	바꾸다	
16	특성, 성격	
17	차트, 도표	
18	분명한, 맑은	

C. Listen, write the word and meaning. (Track 3)

	Word	Meaning		Word	Meaning
01			10		
02			11		
03			12		
04			13		
05			14		
06			15		
07			16		
08			17		
09			18		

Unit 1

Unit 2

🎧 Listen and repeat. (Track 4)

01 culture [kʌ́ltʃər]
n 문화, 교양   the customs and beliefs of particular country
Greece is the source of European **cultures**.
그리스는 유럽 문화의 근원이다.

02 custom [kʌ́stəm]
n 풍습, 관습   an accepted way of behaving in a society
It's the **custom** in Britain for a bride to throw her bouquet.
신부가 부케를 던지는 것은 영국의 풍습이다.

03 dangerous [déindʒərəs]
a 위험한   likely to hurt or harm you
These cars are fast but **dangerous**.
이 차들은 속력은 빠르지만 그만큼 위험하다.

04 dead [ded]
a 죽은   no longer alive
The man pretended to be **dead**.
그 사람은 죽은 시늉을 했다.

05 degree [digríː]
n 도, 정도, 계급   a measurement of temperature
It's minus 10 **degrees**.
영하 10도입니다.

06 diligent [dílədʒənt]
a 근면한, 부지런한   to effort in your work or duties
On the whole Koreans are **diligent**.
대체로 한국인은 부지런하다.

07 else [els]
ad 그밖에, 달리   in addition to something already mentioned
I want to meet you somewhere **else**.
다른 장소에서 봤으면 좋겠어요.

08 empty [émpti]
a 속이 빈, 비어 있는   with no people or things inside
The glass is completely **empty**.
잔은 텅 비어 있다.

09 energy [énərdʒi]
n 에너지   the power that comes from coal, electricity, gas, etc
Almost every country is interested in the uses of atomic **energy**.
거의 모든 나라가 핵에너지 사용에 관심이 있다.

---

key words
source n 근원, 원천 / bouquet n 부케 / pretend v ~인 체하다
duty n 임무 / already ad 이미 / atomic a 원자의

🎧 Listen and repeat. Track 5

10 engineer
[èndʒəníər]
n 기술자, 기사   a person whose job is to repair engines, machines, etc
What did you say to the new **engineer**?
새 기술자에게 뭐라고 했나요?

11 enough
[inʌ́f]
a 충분한   as much as you need or as much as is necessary
However, she doesn't have **enough** money.
하지만 그녀는 돈이 충분하지가 않다.

12 enter
[éntər]
v 들어가다   to come or go into something
They **entered** a fast food restaurant.
그들은 패스트푸드 식당에 들어갔다.

13 fight
[fait]
v 싸우다 / n 싸움   to use physical strength, guns, etc against somebody / something
He was afraid of **fighting** with an enemy.
그는 적군과 싸우는 것을 두려워했다.

14 final
[fáinəl]
a 마지막의   being at the end of a series of events
What is the train's **final** destination?
열차의 마지막 역은 어디입니까?

15 first
[fə:rst]
a 최초의, 처음의   coming before all other similar things
His team was from Brazil and won for the **first** time that year.
그의 팀은 브라질에서 왔고 이 팀은 그해 처음 승리했다.

16 fit
[fit]
a 건강이 좋은, 알맞은   with the right qualities or skills
I was very happy because the shirt **fit** perfectly.
그 셔츠가 꼭 맞아서 나는 매우 행복했다.

17 flick
[flik]
v 탁치다   to hit something lightly and quickly
She **flicked** the dust off her jacket.
그녀는 재킷의 먼지를 탁 쳐냈다.

18 flu
[flu:]
n 독감   an illness which is similar to a bad cold but more serious
He called in sick with the **flu**.
그는 독감 때문에 아프다고 전화했어요.

key words
necessary a 필요한 / strength n 힘 / destination n 목적지 / similar a 유사한 / serious a 심각한

Unit 2 11

Exercise

A. Complete the sentence.

1. It's the _____ in Britain for a bride to throw her bouquet.
   신부가 부케를 던지는 것은 영국의 풍습이다.

2. The glass is completely _____.
   잔은 텅 비어 있다.

3. On the whole Koreans are _____.
   대체로 한국인은 부지런하다.

4. The man pretended to be _____.
   그 사람은 죽은 시늉을 했다.

5. Greece is the source of European _____.
   그리스는 유럽 문화의 근원이다.

6. It's minus 10 _____.
   영하 10도입니다.

7. I want to meet you somewhere _____.
   다른 장소에서 봤으면 좋겠어요.

8. Almost every country is interested in the uses of atomic _____.
   거의 모든 나라가 핵에너지 사용에 관심이 있다.

9. I was very happy because the shirt _____ perfectly.
   그 셔츠가 꼭 맞아서 나는 매우 행복했다.

10. However, she doesn't have _____ money.
    하지만 그녀는 돈이 충분하지가 않다.

11. They _____ a fast food restaurant.
    그들은 패스트푸드 식당에 들어갔다.

12. He was afraid of _____ with an enemy.
    그는 적군과 싸우는 것을 두려워했다.

13. He called in sick with the _____.
    그는 독감 때문에 아프다고 전화했어요.

14. These cars are fast but _____.
    이 차들은 속력은 빠르지만 그만큼 위험하다.

15. What did you say to the new _____?
    새 기술자에게 뭐라고 했나요?

16. What is the train's _____ destination?
    열차의 마지막 역은 어디입니까?

17. His team was from Brazil and won for the _____ time that year.
    그의 팀은 브라질에서 왔고 이 팀은 그 해 처음 승리했다.

18. She _____ the dust off her jacket.
    그녀는 재킷의 먼지를 탁 쳐냈다.

Hint

| else | flick | dangerous | empty | final | culture | enter | dead | first |
| energy | fit | custom | enough | degree | diligent | flu | engineer | fight |

Unit 2

Exercise

B. Fill in the word and meaning.

	Word	Meaning
01	dead	
02	else	
03	diligent	
04	first	
05	enough	
06	custom	
07	energy	
08	final	
09	flick	
10	dangerous	
11	enter	
12	flu	
13	empty	
14	fit	
15	fight	
16	culture	
17	engineer	
18	degree	

	Meaning	Word
01	문화, 교양	
02	풍습, 관습	
03	위험한	
04	죽은	
05	도, 정도, 계급	
06	근면한, 부지런한	
07	그밖에, 달리	
08	속이 빈, 비어 있는	
09	에너지	
10	기술자, 기사	
11	충분한	
12	들어가다	
13	싸우다, 싸움	
14	마지막의	
15	최초의, 처음의	
16	건강이 좋은, 알맞은	
17	탁치다	
18	독감	

C. Listen, write the word and meaning. (Track 6)

	Word	Meaning		Word	Meaning
01			10		
02			11		
03			12		
04			13		
05			14		
06			15		
07			16		
08			17		
09			18		

Review 1

A. Read and fill in the word and meaning.

word	definition	meaning
	to start to be something	
	to feel certain that something is true	
	stating the reason for something	
	a series of connected metal rings	
	to feel a steady, fairly strong pain	
	shining strongly	
	the quality of being pleasing to the mind	
	a new and difficult task that tests somebody's skill	
	a situation in which there is a lot of action or movement	
	an opportunity	
	the principle or reason which lies behind	
	to become different	
	a situation in which there is a lot of action or movement	
	all the features that make a person	
	forming the part of something that is most necessary	
	a page of information in the form of lists	
	in the middle of somebody / something	
	easy to understand	

Hint

chance   clear   basic   among   basis   chain   chart   challenge   character
believe   bright   active   change   ache   activity   beauty   become   because

B. Read and fill in the word and meaning.

word	definition	meaning
	a measurement of temperature	
	to come or go into something	
	no longer alive	
	as much as you need or as much as is necessary	
	to use physical strength, guns, etc against somebody / something	
	likely to hurt or harm you	
	in addition to something already mentioned	
	to effort in your work or duties	
	an accepted way of behaving in a society	
	being at the end of a series of events	
	the customs and beliefs of particular country	
	the power that comes from coal, electricity, gas, etc	
	to hit something lightly and quickly	
	coming before all other similar things	
	with no people or things inside	
	an illness which is similar to a bad cold but more serious	
	with the right qualities or skills	
	a person whose job is to repair engines, machines, etc	

Hint

else   flick   dangerous   empty   final   culture   enter   dead   first
energy   fit   custom   enough   degree   diligent   flu   engineer fight

Unit 3

🎧 Listen and repeat. Track 7

01 happen v 일어나다   to take place, especially without being planned
[hǽpən]
It **happened** three years ago.
그것은 3년 전에 일어났다.

02 heavy a 무거운   weighing a lot; difficult to lift or move
[hévi]
Isn't it too **heavy**?
너무 무겁지는 않니?

03 hero n 영웅   a man who is admired for doing something brave
[híərou]
Everybody cannot be a **hero**.
누구나 다 영웅이 될 수 있는 것은 아니다.

04 hide v 숨다, 숨기다   to put something in a place where they cannot be seen
[haid]
The little goats **hide** around the house.
새끼 염소들이 집안 여기저기로 숨는다.

05 hobby n 취미   an activity that you enjoy doing in your spare time
[hábi]
Riding a bicycle is my **hobby**.
자전거 타기는 내 취미이다.

06 if conj 만약 ~라면   to say that a thing will happen or can be true
[if]
If I were you, I would apologize to her.
만약 내가 너라면 그녀에게 사과할 텐데.

07 lose v 잃다, 놓치다   to be unable to find something / somebody
[lu:z]
She doesn't want to **lose** her flute.
그녀는 자신의 플루트를 잃고 싶지 않아.

08 magazine n 잡지   a publication with a paper cover containing articles, photographs, etc
[mæ̀gəzíːn]
I want to buy a movie **magazine**.
영화 잡지를 하나 사고 싶어요.

09 magic n 마법   the power to use supernatural forces
[mǽdʒik]
Let me touch the **magic** lamp only once.
한번만 마법 램프를 만질 수 있게 해 주세요.

key words
admire v 칭찬하다 / spare a 한가한 / apologize v 사과하다
publication n 출판물 / supernatural a 초자연의

🎧 Listen and repeat. Track 8

10 main
[mein]
a 주요한 being the most important of its kind
What's the **main** difference between the two offices?
두 사무실 사이에 주요한 차이점이 뭔가요?

11 mark
[ma:rk]
n 점수, 기호 a written or printed symbol
I got an excellent **mark** on the last test.
지난번 시험에서 훌륭한 점수를 받았다.

12 marry
[mǽri]
v 결혼하다 to become the husband or wife of somebody
You will **marry** and have many children.
당신은 결혼을 하고 많은 아이들을 갖게 될 거에요.

13 Olympic
[əlímpik]
n 올림픽 a set of international sports competitions
Where were the **Olympics** held in 1988?
1988년에 올림픽이 어디서 개최되었지?

14 order
[ɔ́:rdər]
n 명령, 순서 in authority to tell somebody to do something
It's an urgent **order**.
긴급한 명령이다.

15 own
[oun]
a 자기 자신의 to indicate that something belongs to a person
I have my **own** car.
나에게는 내 차가 있다.

16 pack
[pæk]
v 싸다, 꾸리다 put clothes and other things into a bag
We are **packing** sleeping bags.
우리는 침낭을 꾸리고 있다.

17 pair
[pɛər]
n 한 쌍, 한 벌 two things of the same type
She puts on a new **pair** of shoes.
그녀는 새 신발 한 켤레를 신고 있습니다.

18 parents
[pɛ́ərənts]
n 부모 your mother and father
You should respect your **parents**.
너는 부모님을 공경해야 한다.

---

key words
international **a** 국제적인 / competition **n** 경기, 시합 / hold **v** 개최하다
authority **n** 권력 / urgent **a** 긴급한 / respect **v** 존경하다

Exercise

A. Complete the sentence.

1. Where were the _____ held in 1988?
   1988년에 올림픽이 어디서 개최되었지?

2. Isn't it too _____?
   너무 무겁지는 않니?

3. The little goats _____ around the house.
   새끼 염소들이 집안 여기저기로 숨는다.

4. You should respect your _____.
   너는 부모님을 공경해야 한다.

5. Riding a bicycle is my _____.
   자전거 타기는 내 취미이다.

6. It's an urgent _____.
   긴급한 명령이다.

7. Everybody cannot be a _____.
   누구나 다 영웅이 될 수 있는 것은 아니다.

8. She doesn't want to _____ her flute.
   그녀는 자신의 플루트를 잃고 싶지 않아.

9. It _____ three years ago.
   그것은 3년 전에 일어났다.

10. I want to buy a movie _____.
    영화 잡지를 하나 사고 싶어요.

11. Let me touch the _____ lamp only once.
    한번만 마법 램프를 만질 수 있게 해 주세요.

12. _____ I were you, I would apologize to her.
    만약 내가 너라면 그녀에게 사과할 텐데.

13. What's the _____ difference between the two offices?
    두 사무실 사이에 주요한 차이점이 뭔가요?

14. We are _____ sleeping bags.
    우리는 침낭을 꾸리고 있다.

15. You will _____ and have many children.
    당신은 결혼을 하고 많은 아이들을 갖게 될 거예요.

16. I have my _____ car.
    나에게는 내 차가 있다.

17. I got an excellent _____ on the last test.
    지난번 시험에서 훌륭한 점수를 받았다.

18. She puts on a new _____ of shoes.
    그녀는 새 신발 한 켤레를 신고 있습니다.

Hint

| if | main | hide | own | magic | hero | order | magazine | happen |
| pair | hobby | mark | heavy | parents | lose | marry | Olympic | pack |

Unit 3

Exercise

B. Fill in the word and meaning.

	Word	Meaning
01	hobby	
02	magazine	
03	own	
04	heavy	
05	if	
06	pair	
07	hide	
08	pack	
09	lose	
10	marry	
11	parents	
12	happen	
13	main	
14	Olympic	
15	mark	
16	order	
17	magic	
18	hero	

	Meaning	Word
01	일어나다	
02	무거운	
03	영웅	
04	숨다, 숨기다	
05	취미	
06	만약 ~라면	
07	잃다, 놓치다	
08	잡지	
09	마법	
10	주요한	
11	점수, 기호	
12	결혼하다	
13	올림픽	
14	명령, 순서	
15	자기 자신의	
16	싸다, 꾸리다	
17	한 쌍, 한 벌	
18	부모	

C. Listen, write the word and meaning. (Track 9)

	Word	Meaning
01		
02		
03		
04		
05		
06		
07		
08		
09		

	Word	Meaning
10		
11		
12		
13		
14		
15		
16		
17		
18		

Unit 4

🎧 Listen and repeat. (Track 10)

01 programmer
[próugræmər]
n 프로그래머   a person whose job is writing programs for computers
He is a computer **programmer**.
그는 컴퓨터 프로그래머야.

02 project
[prədʒékt]
n 계획, 과제   a planned piece of work
She decided to take direct control of the **project**.
그녀는 그 계획을 직접 지휘하기로 결심했다.

03 proud
[praud]
a 자랑으로 여기는   feeling pleased about something that you own
Koreans are very **proud** of their language.
한국인들은 그들의 언어를 매우 자랑스럽게 생각한다.

04 puzzle
[pʌ́zl]
n 퍼즐, 수수께끼   game that you have to think about answer
She showed me how to solve the **puzzle**.
그녀는 그 수수께끼 푸는 방법을 나에게 보여주었다.

05 quick
[kwik]
a 빠른, 즉석의   done with speed
Samba is a **quick** dance of Brazilian origin.
삼바는 브라질 고유의 빠른 춤이다.

06 race
[reis]
n 경주, 레이스   a competition between vehicles, etc.
Tom, Bill, and Mary are running a **race**.
Tom, Bill, Mary가 달리기 경주를 하고 있다.

07 shower
[ʃáuə:r]
n 샤워, 소나기   the act of washing yourself; a short period of rain
I'll watch TV after I take a **shower**.
나는 샤워를 한 다음에 TV를 볼 것이다.

08 site
[sait]
n 사이트, 장소   a place where a building is
It was the **site** of my house.
그 곳은 우리 집이 있던 자리야.

09 smart
[sma:rt]
a 영리한   clever; intelligent
Read many books to be a **smart** person.
똑똑한 사람이 되려면 책을 많이 읽으세요.

---

key words
direct a 직접의 / origin n 기원, 유래 / intelligent a 영리한

🎧 Listen and repeat. Track 11

10 snowy
[snóui]
a 눈의, 눈이 내리는   when a lot of snow falls
It's cold and **snowy** here.
여기는 춥고 눈이 내려.

11 solve
[salv]
v 풀다, 해결하다   to find a way of dealing with a problem
I can **solve** this problem in one minute.
나는 일분 안에 이 문제를 풀 수 있어.

12 sometimes
[sʌ́mtàimz]
ad 때때로   occasionally rather than all of the time
He **sometimes** takes a bus.
그는 때때로 버스를 타기도 한다.

13 through
[θruː]
prep ~을 통하여   from one side of something to the other
The sun is shining **through** the glass.
햇빛이 유리를 통해 반짝이고 있다.

14 title
[táitl]
n 제목   the name of a book, poem, etc.
Do you know the **title** of the book?
그 책의 제목을 아세요?

15 toothpaste
[túːθpèist]
n 치약   a substance that you use to clean teeth
I bought a tube of **toothpaste** yesterday.
나는 어제 치약을 샀다.

16 topic
[tápik]
n 화제   a subject that you discuss or write about
There are no more **topics** to write on.
글을 쓸 만한 주제들이 더 이상 없다.

17 touch
[tʌtʃ]
v 만지다   to put your hand on something in order to feel it
Don't **touch** my dog.
내 강아지를 만지지마.

18 tower
[táuər]
n 탑, 타워   a tall narrow part of a building
She knows Namsan **Tower** well.
그녀는 남산 타워에 대해 잘 알고 있다.

key words
deal **v** 처리하다 / occasionally **ad** 가끔 / narrow **a** 좁은

Unit 4

Exercise

A. Complete the sentence.

1. He _____ takes a bus.
   그는 때때로 버스를 타기도 한다.

2. She decided to take direct control of the _____.
   그녀는 그 계획을 직접 지휘하기로 결심했다.

3. She showed me how to solve the _____.
   그녀는 그 수수께끼 푸는 방법을 나에게 보여주었다.

4. Samba is a _____ dance of Brazilian origin.
   삼바는 브라질 고유의 빠른 춤이다.

5. Koreans are very _____ of their language.
   한국인들은 그들의 언어를 매우 자랑스럽게 생각한다.

6. I bought a tube of _____ yesterday.
   나는 어제 치약을 샀다.

7. Tom, Bill, and Mary are running a _____.
   Tom, Bill, Mary가 달리기 경주를 하고 있다.

8. I'll watch TV after I take a _____.
   나는 샤워를 한 다음에 TV를 볼 것이다.

9. It was the _____ of my house.
   그 곳은 우리 집이 있던 자리야.

10. He is a computer _____.
    그는 컴퓨터 프로그래머야.

11. She knows Namsan _____ well.
    그녀는 남산 타워에 대해 잘 알고 있다.

12. Read many books to be a _____ person.
    똑똑한 사람이 되려면 책을 많이 읽으세요.

13. Don't _____ my dog.
    내 강아지를 만지지마!

14. It's cold and _____ here.
    여기는 춥고 눈이 내려.

15. Do you know the _____ of the book?
    그 책의 제목을 아세요?

16. The sun is shining _____ the glass.
    햇빛이 유리를 통해 반짝이고 있다.

17. I can _____ this problem in one minute.
    나는 일분 안에 이 문제를 풀 수 있어.

18. There are no more _____ to write on.
    글을 쓸 만한 주제들이 더 이상 없다.

Hint

| smart | proud | title | race | programmer | snowy | topic | toothpaste | shower |
| project | solve | puzzle | tower | sometimes | quick | site | through | touch |

Exercise

B. Fill in the word and meaning.

	Word	Meaning
01	puzzle	
02	race	
03	site	
04	programmer	
05	solve	
06	quick	
07	sometimes	
08	proud	
09	toothpaste	
10	snowy	
11	through	
12	tower	
13	project	
14	touch	
15	smart	
16	topic	
17	title	
18	shower	

	Meaning	Word
01	프로그래머	
02	계획, 과제	
03	자랑으로 여기는	
04	퍼즐, 수수께끼	
05	빠른, 즉석의	
06	경주, 레이스	
07	샤워, 소나기	
08	사이트, 장소	
09	영리한	
10	눈의, 눈이 내리는	
11	풀다, 해결하다	
12	때때로	
13	~을 통하여	
14	제목	
15	치약	
16	화제	
17	만지다	
18	탑, 타워	

🎧 C. Listen, write the word and meaning. (Track 12)

	Word	Meaning		Word	Meaning
01			10		
02			11		
03			12		
04			13		
05			14		
06			15		
07			16		
08			17		
09			18		

Review 2

A. Read and fill in the word and meaning.

word	definition	meaning
	two things of the same type	
	the power to use supernatural forces	
	put clothes and other things into a bag	
	being the most important of its kind	
	to take place, especially without being planned	
	publication with a paper cover containing articles, photographs, etc	
	to indicate that something belongs to a person	
	weighing a lot; difficult to lift or move	
	a written or printed symbol	
	in authority to tell somebody to do something	
	your mother and father	
	to say that a thing will happen or can be true	
	to become the husband or wife of somebody	
	a man who is admired for doing something brave	
	a set of international sports competitions	
	an activity that you enjoy doing in your spare time	
	to be unable to find something / somebody	
	to put something in a place where they cannot be seen	

Hint

| if | hero | order | marry | magic | main | hide | happen | magazine |
| lose | hobby | mark | heavy | pack | pair | own | Olympic | parents |

B. Read and fill in the word and meaning.

word	definition	meaning
	when a lot of snow falls	
	a person whose job is writing programs for computers	
	to put your hand on something in order to feel it	
	a place where a building is	
	a tall narrow part of a building	
	clever; intelligent	
	a planned piece of work	
	the act of washing yourself; a short period of rain	
	a subject that you discuss or write about	
	done with speed	
	a competition between vehicles, etc.	
	to find a way of dealing with a problem	
	feeling pleased about something that you own	
	a substance that you use to clean teeth	
	occasionally rather than all of the time	
	from one side of something to the other	
	game that you have to think about answer	
	the name of a book, poem, etc.	

Hint

smart   proud   title   race   programmer   snowy   topic   toothpaste   shower
project   solve   puzzle   tower   sometimes   quick   site   through   touch

Unit 5

🎧 Listen and repeat. (Track 13)

01 adult [ədʌ́lt]
n 성인, 어른   a fully grown person
It costs **adults** ten thousand won.
어른용 입장권은 10,000원이다.

02 advice [ædváis]
n 충고, 조언   an opinion about what somebody should do
She gave me some good **advice**.
그녀는 내게 좋은 충고를 해 주었다.

03 afraid [əfréid]
a 두려워하는   feeling fear
They are **afraid** of the dragon.
그들은 용을 무서워한다.

04 agree [əgríː]
v 동의하다   to have the same opinion as somebody
I **agree** with him on that point.
나는 그 점에서 그 사람 의견에 동의해요.

05 ahead [əhéd]
ad 앞에, 전방에   further forward in space or time; in front
Go straight **ahead** and turn left at the traffic lights.
앞으로 곧장 가다가 신호등이 나오면 왼쪽으로 도세요.

06 aid [eid]
v 원조하다, 돕다   to help somebody / something
She **aided** me while I cooked.
그녀는 내가 요리하는 동안 나를 도왔다.

07 bake [beik]
v (빵 등을)굽다   to cook in an oven in dry heat
I could smell bread **baking** in the oven.
나는 오븐에서 구워지는 빵 냄새를 맡았다.

08 blond [bland]
a 금발의   pale gold in color
The woman began to cut off my long **blond** hair.
그 여자는 나의 긴 금발 머리를 자르기 시작했다.

09 blow [blou]
v (바람이) 불다   to be moving or to cause something to move through the air
The wind is **blowing** south.
바람이 남쪽으로 불고 있다.

---

key words
fully ad 충분히 / **opinion** n 의견 / **traffic** n 교통 / **pale** a 엷은

26 Unit 5

🎧 Listen and repeat. Track 14

10 borrow
[bɔ́(ː)rou]

v 빌리다   to take something that belongs to somebody else

Can I **borrow** your eraser for a minute?
네 지우개 좀 잠깐 빌려줄 수 있니?

11 brave
[breiv]

a 용감한   willing to do things which are difficult

The **brave** policeman caught the robber.
그 용감한 경찰이 강도를 잡았다.

12 brick
[brik]

n 벽돌   baked clay used for building walls

Bricks and dishes are made from various kinds of clay.
벽돌과 접시는 각종 진흙으로 만든다.

13 chat
[tʃæt]

n 잡담 / v 잡담하다   to talk in a friendly informal way to somebody

The couple is having a **chat** on the street corner.
커플이 길가 모퉁이에서 잡담을 하고 있다.

14 cheaply
[tʃíːpli]

ad 싸게, 값싸게   for a low price

She was so happy because she bought it **cheaply**.
그녀는 그것을 저렴하게 사서 정말 기뻤다.

15 check
[tʃek]

v 체크하다, 점검하다   to examine something to see if it is safe or correct

Check the train timetable at the station.
역에서 기차 시간표를 점검 하세요.

16 cheer
[tʃiər]

n 격려, 환호   a shout of joy

They gave a **cheer** when I appeared.
내가 나타났을 때 그들이 환호했다.

17 choice
[tʃɔis]

n 선택   an act of choosing between things or people

I approve your **choice**.
나는 네 선택에 찬성한다.

18 choose
[tʃuːz]

v 고르다, 선택하다   to decide which person or thing you want to have

You can **choose** what you want.
너는 네가 원하는 것을 선택 할 수 있다.

key words
robber n 강도 / various a 여러가지의 / clay n 점토 / examine v 검사하다, 조사하다
shout n 외침, 큰소리 / approve v 승인하다, 찬성하다

Exercise

A. Complete the sentence.

1. The wind is _____ south.
   바람이 남쪽으로 불고 있다.

2. You can _____ what you want.
   너는 네가 원하는 것을 선택 할 수 있다.

3. I approve your _____.
   나는 네 선택에 찬성한다.

4. She gave me some good _____.
   그녀는 내게 좋은 충고를 해 주었다.

5. I _____ with him on that point.
   나는 그 점에서 그 사람 의견에 동의해요.

6. Go straight _____ and turn left at the traffic lights.
   앞으로 곧장 가다가 신호등이 나오면 왼쪽으로 도세요.

7. They are _____ of the dragon.
   그들은 용을 무서워한다.

8. I could smell bread _____ in the oven.
   나는 오븐에서 구워지는 빵 냄새를 맡았다.

9. The woman began to cut off my long _____ hair.
   그 여자는 나의 긴 금발 머리를 자르기 시작했다.

10. It costs _____ ten thousand won.
    어른용 입장권은 10,000원이다.

11. _____ the train timetable at the station.
    역에서 기차 시간표를 점검 하세요.

12. Can I _____ your eraser for a minute?
    네 지우개 좀 잠깐 빌려줄 수 있니?

13. The _____ policeman caught the robber.
    그 용감한 경찰이 강도를 잡았다.

14. They gave a _____ when I appeared.
    내가 나타났을 때 그들이 환호했다.

15. _____ and dishes are made from various kinds of clay.
    벽돌과 접시는 각종 진흙으로 만든다.

16. The couple is having a _____ on the street corner.
    커플이 길가 모퉁이에서 잡담을 하고 있다.

17. She _____ me while I cooked.
    그녀는 내가 요리하는 동안 나를 도왔다.

18. She was so happy because she bought it _____.
    그녀는 그것을 저렴하게 사서 정말 기뻤다.

Hint

| agree | bake | cheaply | afraid | borrow | chat | aid | cheer | adult |
| check | brave | advice | choose | blond | ahead | choice | blow | brick |

Unit 5

Exercise

B. Fill in the word and meaning.

	Word	Meaning
01	ahead	
02	blond	
03	afraid	
04	chat	
05	bake	
06	cheer	
07	brave	
08	adult	
09	borrow	
10	cheaply	
11	aid	
12	choose	
13	agree	
14	brick	
15	choice	
16	blow	
17	check	
18	advice	

	Meaning	Word
01	성인, 어른	
02	충고, 조언	
03	두려워하는	
04	동의하다	
05	앞에, 전방에	
06	원조하다, 돕다	
07	(빵 등을)굽다	
08	금발의	
09	(바람이) 불다	
10	빌리다	
11	용감한	
12	벽돌	
13	잡담, 잡담하다	
14	싸게, 값싸게	
15	체크하다, 점검하다	
16	격려, 환호	
17	선택	
18	고르다, 선택하다	

🎧 **C. Listen, write the word and meaning.** (Track 15)

	Word	Meaning		Word	Meaning
01			10		
02			11		
03			12		
04			13		
05			14		
06			15		
07			16		
08			17		
09			18		

Unit 6

🎧 Listen and repeat. (Track 16)

01 delicious
[dilíʃəs]
a 맛있는   to have a very pleasant taste
Everything looks wonderful, and it smells **delicious**, too.
모든 것이 멋있어 보이고 맛있는 냄새도 나요.

02 dentist
[déntist]
n 치과의사   a person who is qualified to examine people's teeth
I have an appointment with the **dentist**.
치과 의사 선생님과 약속이 있어요.

03 department
[dipá:rtmənt]
n 부서, 부문   a section of a large organization
I work at the **department** of customer service.
나는 고객서비스부서에서 일해요.

04 destination
[dèstənéiʃən]
n 목적지   a place to which somebody is going
We will not reach our **destination**.
우리는 목적지에 도달할 수 없을 것이다.

05 diary
[dáiəri]
n 일기   a book in which you write down what happens each day
He keeps a **diary** in English.
그는 영어로 일기를 쓴다.

06 die
[dai]
v 죽다   to stop living
Why did your father **die**?
너희 아버지께서는 왜 돌아가셨니?

07 envelope
[énvəlòup]
n 봉투   a flat paper container used for sending letters in
You should write your address on the **envelope**.
너는 봉투에 네 주소를 써야 한다.

08 environment
[inváiərənmənt]
n 환경   the physical conditions that somebody exists in
I want a pleasant working **environment**.
나는 쾌적한 근무환경을 원합니다.

09 envy
[énvi]
v 부러워하다   to wish you had the same things
I **envy** your success and happiness.
나는 네 성공과 행복이 부러워.

key words
examine **v** 진찰하다 / appointment **n** 약속 / section **n** 부
reach **v** ~에 도달하다 / container **n** 용기 / condition **n** 상태, 상황

🎧 Listen and repeat. Track 17

10 erase
[iréis]
v 지우다   to remove something completely
The man is **erasing** the picture on the white board.
남자가 화이트보드의 그림을 지우고 있다.

11 escape
[iskéip]
v 달아나다   to succeed in getting away from a place
The boy struggled to **escape**.
소년은 달아나려고 몸부림쳤다.

12 even
[íːvən]
ad ~조차도   used to emphasize something unexpected
Computers can **even** cook food in the kitchen.
컴퓨터는 주방에서 음식을 요리하는 일조차 도와줄 수 있다.

13 focus
[fóukəs]
n 초점   the center of interest or attention
She found a **focus** on acting.
그녀는 연기 활동에만 초점을 맞췄다.

14 follow
[fálou]
v 따라가다   to go after or behind somebody / something
Follow the cookbook and try.
요리 책에 나온 대로 따라서 해 봐.

15 foolish
[fúːliʃ]
a 어리석은   not showing good sense or judgement
How **foolish** I was!
내가 얼마나 어리석었는지!

16 foreign
[fɔ́(ː)rin]
a 외국의   in a country that is not your own
It is fun to learn a **foreign** language.
외국어를 배우는 것은 재미있다.

17 forest
[fɔ́(ː)rist]
n 숲, 산림   a large area of land that is covered with trees
The hill has a pine **forest**.
그 언덕에는 소나무 숲이 있어요.

18 fuse
[fjuːz]
n 도화선   a device that is used to make a bomb, etc
The **fuse** of dynamite will explode soon.
다이너마이트의 도화선이 곧 폭발할거에요.

key words
remove v 지우다 / struggle v 버둥거리다, 노력하다 / emphasize v 강조하다
unexpected a 예기치 않은 / judgement n 판단 / device n 장치 / bomb n 폭탄 / explode v 폭발하다

Unit 6

Exercise

A. Complete the sentence.

1. Why did your father _____?
   너희 아버지께서는 왜 돌아가셨니?

2. Everything looks wonderful, and it smells _____, too.
   모든 것이 멋있어 보이고 맛있는 냄새도 나요.

3. He keeps a _____ in English.
   그는 영어로 일기를 쓴다.

4. She found a _____ on acting.
   그녀는 연기 활동에만 초점을 맞췄다.

5. I work at the _____ of customer service.
   나는 고객서비스부서에서 일해요.

6. It is fun to learn a _____ language.
   외국어를 배우는 것은 재미있다.

7. I have an appointment with the _____.
   치과 의사 선생님과 약속이 있어요.

8. You should write your address on the _____.
   너는 봉투에 네 주소를 써야 한다.

9. How _____ I was!
   내가 얼마나 어리석었는지!

10. I _____ your success and happiness.
    나는 네 성공과 행복이 부러워.

11. We will not reach our _____.
    우리는 목적지에 도달할 수 없을 것이다.

12. The hill has a pine _____.
    그 언덕에는 소나무 숲이 있어요.

13. The man is _____ the picture on the white board.
    남자가 화이트보드의 그림을 지우고 있다.

14. The boy struggled to _____.
    그 소년은 달아나려고 몸부림쳤다.

15. I want a pleasant working _____.
    나는 쾌적한 근무환경을 원합니다.

16. Computers can _____ cook food in the kitchen.
    컴퓨터는 주방에서 음식을 요리하는 일조차 도와줄 수 있다.

17. _____ the cookbook and try.
    요리 책에 나온 대로 따라서 해 봐.

18. The _____ of dynamite will explode soon.
    다이너마이트의 도화선이 곧 폭발할거예요.

Hint

| erase | fuse | department | even | focus | destination | delicious | foolish | envy |
| diary | die | envelope | foreign | dentist | environment | forest | escape | follow |

Unit 6

Exercise

B. Fill in the word and meaning.

	Word	Meaning
01	die	
02	envy	
03	delicious	
04	focus	
05	escape	
06	envelope	
07	foreign	
08	dentist	
09	foolish	
10	destination	
11	even	
12	forest	
13	department	
14	fuse	
15	environment	
16	follow	
17	erase	
18	diary	

	Meaning	Word
01	맛있는	
02	치과의사	
03	부서, 부문	
04	목적지	
05	일기	
06	죽다	
07	봉투	
08	환경	
09	부러워하다	
10	지우다	
11	달아나다	
12	~조차도	
13	초점	
14	따라가다	
15	어리석은	
16	외국의	
17	숲, 산림	
18	도화선	

🎧 C. Listen, write the word and meaning. (Track 18)

	Word	Meaning
01		
02		
03		
04		
05		
06		
07		
08		
09		

	Word	Meaning
10		
11		
12		
13		
14		
15		
16		
17		
18		

Review 3

A. Read and fill in the word and meaning.

word	definition	meaning
	baked clay used for building walls	
	to help somebody/something	
	to talk in a friendly informal way to somebody	
	to cook in an oven in dry heat	
	a fully grown person	
	for a low price	
	an opinion about what somebody should do	
	a shout of joy	
	pale gold in color	
	further forward in space or time; in front	
	willing to do things which are difficult	
	to examine something to see if it is safe or correct	
	to be moving or to cause something to move through the air	
	feeling fear	
	an act of choosing between things or people	
	to take something that belongs to somebody else	
	to decide which person or thing you want to have	
	to have the same opinion as somebody	

Hint

advice   choice   cheaply   agree   borrow   cheer   aid   adult   chat
check   ahead   afraid   blond   choose   brave   bake blow   brick

B. Read and fill in the word and meaning.

word	definition	meaning
focus	the center of interest or attention	
destination	a place to which somebody is going	
escape	to succeed in getting away from a place	
follow	to go after or behind somebody / something	
delicious	to have a very pleasant taste	
foolish	not showing good sense or judgement	
envy	to wish you had the same things	
foreign	in a country that is not your own	
erase	to remove something completely	
dentist	a person who is qualified to examine people's teeth	
forest	a large area of land that is covered with trees	
environment	the physical conditions that somebody exists in	
fuse	a device that is used to make a bomb, etc	
department	a section of a large organization	
envelope	a flat paper container used for sending letters in	
diary	a book in which you write down what happens each day	
even	used to emphasize something unexpected	
die	to stop living	

Hint

follow envy department even focus destination delicious foolish foreign
diary die forest fuse erase environment envelope escape dentist

Unit 7

🎧 Listen and repeat. (Track 19)

01 hockey
[háki]
n 하키   an outdoor game using long curved sticks
I played **hockey** yesterday with my cousin.
나는 어제 사촌과 함께 하키를 했어.

02 homeless
[hóumlis]
a 집없는   nowhere to live
These **homeless** children must be looked after.
이 집 없는 아이들은 보호를 필요로 한다.

03 hope
[houp]
v 바라다   to want something to be possible
I **hope** to see you soon.
빨리 너를 만나기를 바란다.

04 horn
[hɔːrn]
n 경적, 뿔   the hard pointed things that grow from animals' head
Rhinoceros means ' a **horn** on its nose .'
코뿔소라는 말은 '코에 난 뿔 '이란 뜻이야.

05 hunt
[hʌnt]
v 사냥하다   to chase something in order to catch them
Some animals **hunt** at night.
어떤 동물들은 밤에 사냥한다.

06 hurry
[hə́ːri]
v 서두르다 / n 매우 급함   the need or wish to do something quickly
She swims toward her child in a **hurry**.
그녀는 서둘러 아이에게 헤엄쳐 간다.

07 matter
[mǽtəːr]
n 문제, 일   a subject that you must consider or deal with
The **matter** was arranged privately.
그 일은 은밀히 준비되었다.

08 maybe
[méibi]
ad 아마   when you are not certain that something will happen
Maybe he doesn't even go to school.
아마 그는 학교에도 가지 않을 거야.

09 mean
[miːn]
v 의미하다   to express or show as a meaning
It **means** science fiction.
그것은 과학 소설이란 의미야.

key words
curved a 굽은 / rhinoceros n 코뿔소 / chase v 추적하다 / privately ad 은밀히, 개인적으로 / fiction n 소설

🎧 Listen and repeat. (Track 20)

10 medicine
[médəsən]
n 약, 약물   a substance that you drink to cure an illness
My doctor suggested changing the **medicine**.
나의 주치의는 그 약을 바꿀 것을 제안하였다.

11 memorial
[mimɔ́ːriəl]
a 기념의 / n 기념물(관)   a structure built to remind people of a famous person
Next stop will be the Jefferson **Memorial**.
다음 정류장은 제퍼슨 기념관이 되겠습니다.

12 moment
[móumənt]
n 순간, 잠깐   a very short period of time
Hold on for just a **moment**.
잠깐만 기다려주십시오.

13 pat
[pæt]
v 가볍게 치다   to touch somebody gently with your hand
Pat your face dry with a soft towel.
수건으로 가볍게 쳐서 얼굴을 말려.

14 pattern
[pǽtərn]
n 도안, 모형   the regular way in which something happens
It is just a basic sentence **pattern**.
이건 단지 기본적인 문장패턴일 뿐이야.

15 perfect
[pə́ːrfikt]
a 완전한   as good as something could possibly be
More **perfect** coloring cannot be imagined.
더 완전한 채색은 상상할 수도 없다.

16 pet
[pet]
n 애완동물   an animal that you have at home
I would like to have a **pet**.
나는 애완동물을 하나 갖고 싶어.

17 practice
[prǽktis]
v 연습하다 / n 연습   training regularly so that you can improve your skill
Practice makes perfect.
연습이 완벽을 만든다.

18 print
[print]
v 인쇄하다   to produce letters on paper using a machine
I need to **print** fifty copies.
나는 50장을 인쇄해야 해요.

---

key words
substance n 물질 / suggest v 제안하다 / remind v 생각나게 하다
gently ad 부드럽게 / train v 훈련하다 / improve v 향상시키다

Unit 7   37

Exercise

A. Complete the sentence.

1. These _____ children must be looked after.
   이 집 없는 아이들은 보호를 필요로 한다.

2. Rhinoceros means ' a _____ on its nose .'
   코뿔소라는 말은 '코에 난 뿔'이란 뜻이야.

3. It is just a basic sentence _____.
   이건 단지 기본적인 문장패턴일 뿐이야.

4. She swims toward her child in a _____.
   그녀는 서둘러 아이에게 헤엄쳐 간다.

5. _____ he doesn't even go to school.
   아마 그는 학교에도 가지 않을 거야.

6. I need to _____ fifty copies.
   나는 50장을 인쇄해야 해요.

7. It _____ science fiction.
   그것은 과학 소설이란 의미야.

8. I _____ to see you soon.
   빨리 너를 만나기를 바란다.

9. My doctor suggested changing the _____.
   나의 주치의는 그 약을 바꿀 것을 제안하였다.

10. I played _____ yesterday with my cousin.
    나는 어제 사촌과 함께 하키를 했어.

11. Next stop will be the Jefferson _____.
    다음 정류장은 제퍼슨 기념관이 되겠습니다.

12. Hold on for just a _____.
    잠깐만 기다려주십시오.

13. Some animals _____ at night.
    어떤 동물들은 밤에 사냥한다.

14. _____ your face dry with a soft towel.
    수건으로 가볍게 쳐서 얼굴을 말려.

15. More _____ coloring cannot be imagined.
    더 완전한 채색은 상상할 수도 없다.

16. The _____ was arranged privately.
    그 일은 은밀히 준비되었다.

17. I would like to have a _____.
    나는 애완동물을 하나 갖고 싶어.

18. _____ makes perfect.
    연습이 완벽을 만든다.

Hint

| horn | matter | print | hope | pat | memorial | perfect | hunt | maybe |
| pet | hockey | hurry | mean | medicine | homeless | practice | moment | pattern |

Exercise

B. Fill in the word and meaning.

	Word	Meaning
01	horn	
02	matter	
03	hurry	
04	memorial	
05	pat	
06	hockey	
07	moment	
08	pet	
09	maybe	
10	practice	
11	homeless	
12	medicine	
13	print	
14	hope	
15	perfect	
16	mean	
17	pattern	
18	hunt	

	Meaning	Word
01	하키	
02	집없는	
03	바라다	
04	경적, 뿔	
05	사냥하다	
06	서두르다, 매우 급함	
07	문제, 일	
08	아마	
09	의미하다	
10	약, 약물	
11	기념의, 기념물(관)	
12	순간, 잠깐	
13	가볍게 치다	
14	도안, 모형	
15	완전한	
16	애완동물	
17	연습하다, 연습	
18	인쇄하다	

C. Listen, write the word and meaning. (Track 21)

	Word	Meaning		Word	Meaning
01			10		
02			11		
03			12		
04			13		
05			14		
06			15		
07			16		
08			17		
09			18		

Unit 8

🎧 Listen and repeat. Track 22

01 really
[ríːəli]

ad 진짜로, 정말로   to say what is actually the truth

You **really** have a beautiful mind.
너는 정말로 아름다운 마음씨를 지녔구나.

02 refrigerator
[rifrídʒərèitəːr]

n 냉장고   a large electrical container to keep food cold and fresh

We need a **refrigerator** in this office.
사무실에 냉장고가 필요해요.

03 remember
[rimémbəːr]

v 기억하다   to have an image in your memory

Do you **remember** your school days?
너는 학창시절이 기억나니?

04 repeat
[ripíːt]

v 반복하다   to say or do something again or more than once

Don't **repeat** the same mistakes.
똑같은 실수를 반복하지 마세요.

05 report
[ripɔ́ːrt]

n 보고, 기사   a written or spoken account of an event

The **report** covers a period of five years.
그 보고서는 5년의 기간을 다루고 있다.

06 respond
[rispánd]

v 응답하다, 반응하다   to give spoken or written answer to somebody

I cannot **respond** to your request.
난 너희의 요구에 응답해 줄 수가 없다.

07 soon
[suːn]

ad 곧, 이내   in a short time from now

I hope you'll get better **soon**.
곧 회복하시기를 바랍니다.

08 sound
[saund]

n 소리, 음   something that you can hear

Everyone in the room is surprised to hear the noisy **sound**.
그 방에 있던 모든 사람이 그 시끄러운 소리에 깜짝 놀랐다.

09 sour
[sáuəːr]

a 신, 시큼한   having a bitter taste like the taste of a lemon

This kimchi has turned **sour**.
이 김치는 시었어요.

key words
actually ad 실제로 / electrical a 전기의 / noisy a 시끄러운 / bitter a 쓴

🎧 Listen and repeat. Track 23

10 space [speis]
n 공간　an amount of an area or a place
Keep some **space** between your car and the car ahead.
네 차와 앞 차 사이에 어느 정도의 공간을 유지해라.

11 spaghetti [spəgéti]
n 스파게티　a type of pasta which looks like long pieces of string
Are you going to eat chicken or **spaghetti**?
넌 닭고기를 먹을 거니, 아니면 스파게티를 먹을 거니?

12 special [spéʃəl]
a 특별한　different from what is normal
I heard it has some **special** food.
내가 듣기로는 특별한 음식이 있다던데요.

13 travel [trǽvəl]
v 여행하다　to go to another place especially over a long distance
My family has a plan to **travel** around the world.
우리 가족은 세계 여행을 할 계획입니다.

14 triangle [tráiæŋgəl]
n 삼각형　a shape with 3 straight sides and 3 angles
A **triangle** has three sides.
삼각형에는 세 개의 변이 있습니다.

15 trip [trip]
n (짧은) 여행　a journey to a place and back again for a short one
How was your **trip** to Europe?
유럽 여행은 어땠니?

16 type [taip]
n 형, 타입　particular qualities or features
This **type** of punishment is very terrible.
이런 형태의 체벌은 매우 끔찍하다.

17 unfair [ʌnfέər]
a 불공평한, 부당한　an action or situation is not right or fair
The umpire's judgment was **unfair**.
심판의 판단은 불공평했다.

18 unit [júːnit]
n 단위, 단원　one of the parts into which a series is divided
The family is the basic **unit** of society.
가정은 사회의 기본 단위이다.

key words
string n 줄, 끈 / straight a 곧은 / angle n 각 / feature n 특징 / punishment n 벌, 체벌 / umpire n 심판

Unit 8　41

Exercise

A. Complete the sentence.

1. How was your _____ to Europe?
   유럽 여행은 어땠니?

2. You _____ have a beautiful mind.
   너는 정말로 아름다운 마음씨를 지녔구나.

3. Don't _____ the same mistakes.
   똑같은 실수를 반복하지 마세요.

4. I cannot _____ to your request.
   난 너희의 요구에 응답해 줄 수가 없다.

5. The _____ covers a period of five years.
   그 보고서는 5년의 기간을 다루고 있다.

6. The umpire's judgment was _____.
   심판의 판단은 불공평했다.

7. We need a _____ in this office.
   사무실에 냉장고가 필요해요.

8. Everyone in the room is surprised to hear the noisy _____.
   그 방에 있던 모든 사람이 그 시끄러운 소리에 깜짝 놀랐다.

9. The family is the basic _____ of society.
   가정은 사회의 기본 단위이다.

10. This kimchi has turned _____.
    이 김치는 시었어요.

11. My family has a plan to _____ around the world.
    우리 가족은 세계 여행을 할 계획입니다.

12. Keep some _____ between your car and the car ahead.
    네 차와 앞 차 사이에 어느 정도의 공간을 유지해라.

13. I hope you'll get better _____.
    곧 회복하시기를 바랍니다.

14. Are you going to eat chicken or _____?
    넌 닭고기를 먹을 거니, 아니면 스파게티를 먹을 거니?

15. Do you _____ your school days?
    너는 학창시절이 기억나니?

16. I heard it has some _____ food.
    내가 듣기로는 특별한 음식이 있다던데요.

17. A _____ has three sides.
    삼각형에는 세 개의 변이 있습니다.

18. This _____ of punishment is very terrible.
    이런 형태의 체벌은 매우 끔찍하다.

Hint

| space | repeat | type | spaghetti | really | unit | soon | triangle | remember |
| trip | respond | sour | refrigerator | report | sound | unfair | travel | special |

Exercise

B. Fill in the word and meaning.

	Word	Meaning
01	soon	
02	travel	
03	refrigerator	
04	spaghetti	
05	trip	
06	space	
07	repeat	
08	unfair	
09	really	
10	sound	
11	unit	
12	report	
13	sour	
14	triangle	
15	remember	
16	special	
17	type	
18	respond	

	Meaning	Word
01	진짜로, 정말로	
02	냉장고	
03	기억하다	
04	반복하다	
05	보고, 기사	
06	응답하다, 반응하다	
07	곧, 이내	
08	소리, 음	
09	신, 시큼한	
10	공간	
11	스파게티	
12	특별한	
13	여행하다	
14	삼각형	
15	(짧은) 여행	
16	형, 타입	
17	불공평한, 부당한	
18	단위, 단원	

C. Listen, write the word and meaning. (Track 24)

	Word	Meaning		Word	Meaning
01			10		
02			11		
03			12		
04			13		
05			14		
06			15		
07			16		
08			17		
09			18		

Review 4

A. Read and fill in the word and meaning.

word	definition	meaning
	a subject that you must consider or deal with	
	to produce letters on paper using a machine	
	nowhere to live	
	training regularly so that you can improve your skill	
	the need or wish to do something quickly	
	when you are not certain that something will happen	
	an outdoor game using long curved sticks	
	an animal that you have at home	
	to express or show as a meaning	
	as good as something could possibly be	
	to want something to be possible	
	the regular way in which something happens	
	a substance that you drink to cure an illness	
	the hard pointed things that grow from animals' head	
	to touch somebody gently with your hand	
	a structure built to remind people of a famous person	
	to chase something in order to catch them	
	a very short period of time	

Hint

| horn | hunt | print | hope | pattern | memorial | perfect | matter | maybe |
| pet | pat | hurry | mean | medicine | practice | homeless | moment | hockey |

B. Read and fill in the word and meaning.

word	definition	meaning
	to go to another place especially over a long distance	
	to say what is actually the truth	
	a shape with 3 straight sides and 3 angles	
	different from what is normal	
	a large electrical container to keep food cold and fresh	
	a journey to a place and back again for a short one	
	a type of pasta which looks like long pieces of string	
	to have an image in your memory	
	particular qualities or features	
	an amount of an area or a place	
	to say or do something again or more than once	
	an action or situation is not right or fair	
	in a short time from now	
	a written or spoken account of an event	
	having a bitter taste like the taste of a lemon	
	one of the parts into which a series is divided	
	to give spoken or written answer to somebody	
	something that you can hear	

Hint

unit   repeat   type   respond   travel   space   spaghetti   soon   remember
trip   triangle sour   special   report   sound   unfair   really   refrigerator

Unit 9

🎧 Listen and repeat. Track 25

01 airport [έərpɔ̀:rt]
n 공항   a place where planes land and take off
The plane landed at the **airport**.
그 비행기는 공항에 착륙했어요.

02 aisle [ail]
n 복도, 통로   a passage between rows of seats in a building
Would you prefer a window or an **aisle** seat?
창가 쪽 좌석과 통로 쪽 좌석 중에 어느 것을 선호하나요?

03 alarm [əlá:rm]
n 자명종, 경보   a signal that warns people of a problem
Bring me the **alarm** clock.
그 자명종 시계를 갖다 주세요.

04 almost [ɔ́:lmoust]
ad 거의   very nearly; not quite
I go to the movies **almost** every Saturday.
전 거의 매주 토요일마다 영화를 보러 가요.

05 alone [əlóun]
ad 홀로, 단독으로   without any other people
When I was **alone**, I liked to paint.
홀로 있을 때에는 그림 그리기를 좋아했어요.

06 along [əlɔ́:ŋ]
prep ~을 따라   in a line that follows the side of something long
Go straight ahead **along** the river.
강을 따라 앞으로 곧장 가세요.

07 blank [blæŋk]
a 빈 / n 빈 곳   empty, with nothing written or recorded
They're filling in the **blanks**.
그들은 빈 칸을 채우고 있습니다.

08 bucket [bʌ́kit]
n 양동이   a round open container with a handle
The **bucket** hangs from the fence.
양동이가 울타리에 매달려 있다.

09 bug [bʌg]
n 벌레, 곤충   any small insect
Is there a **bug** going around?
주위에 벌레가 돌아다니나요?

key words
land v 착륙하다 / passage n 통로 / signal n 신호 / warn v 경고하다 / hang v 매달리다

🎧 Listen and repeat. Track 26

10 build
[bild]
v 짓다, 세우다   to make something, especially a building
We can **build** a very big apartment under the sea.
우리는 큰 아파트를 바다 밑에 건설할 수 있다.

11 business
[bíznis]
n 직업, 사업   the activity of something for money
My uncle's **business** is not successful.
제 삼촌의 사업이 잘 안 되고 있어요.

12 busy
[bízi]
a 바쁜   having a lot to do
He's always **busy** on business.
그는 항상 일에 바쁘잖아.

13 campus
[kǽmpəs]
n 교정, 학교 마당   the area of land where the main buildings of a college are
She suggested I show her the college **campus**.
그녀는 내가 대학 교정을 안내해줄 것을 제안했다.

14 classical
[klǽsikəl]
a 고전적인   traditional in style of idea
I'm very interested in **classical** music.
나는 고전음악에 아주 흥미가 있습니다.

15 clerk
[klə:rk]
n 점원, 사무원   a person whose job is to keep accounts in an office
The **clerk** ran out of the office at once.
그 사무원은 즉시 사무실에서 뛰어 나갔다.

16 click
[klik]
n 딸깍(하는 소리)   a short sharp sound
I heard the **click** of a latch.
나는 걸쇠가 딸깍하는 소리를 들었다.

17 clinic
[klínik]
n 전문병원, 진료소   a building where people go to receive medical treatment
It is the opening ceremony of a woman's health **clinic**.
여성들을 위한 건강 진료소의 개회식입니다.

18 closet
[klázit]
n 벽장   a piece of furniture with doors at the front and shelves inside
The shirts are hanging in the **closet**.
벽장 안에 셔츠들이 걸려 있다.

key words
traditional a 전통적인 / at once 당장, 즉시 / latch n 걸쇠 / treatment n 치료 / shelf n 선반

Exercise

A. Complete the sentence.

1. Would you prefer a window or an _____ seat?
   창가 쪽 좌석과 통로 쪽 좌석 중에 어느 것을 선호하나요?

2. When I was _____, I liked to paint.
   홀로 있을 때에는 그림 그리기를 좋아했어요.

3. The plane landed at the _____.
   그 비행기는 공항에 착륙했어요.

4. They're filling in the _____.
   그들은 빈 칸을 채우고 있습니다.

5. The _____ hangs from the fence.
   양동이가 울타리에 매달려 있다.

6. I go to the movies _____ every Saturday.
   전 거의 매주 토요일마다 영화를 보러 가요.

7. Is there a _____ going around?
   주위에 벌레가 돌아다니나요?

8. I heard the _____ of a latch.
   나는 걸쇠가 딸깍하는 소리를 들었다.

9. The shirts are hanging in the _____.
   벽장 안에 셔츠들이 걸려 있다.

10. We can _____ a very big apartment under the sea.
    우리는 큰 아파트를 바다 밑에 건설할 수 있다.

11. Bring me the _____ clock.
    그 자명종 시계를 갖다 주세요.

12. He's always _____ on business.
    그는 항상 일에 바쁘잖아.

13. She suggested I show her the college _____.
    그녀는 내가 대학 교정을 안내해줄 것을 제안했다.

14. Go straight ahead _____ the river.
    강을 따라 앞으로 곧장 가세요.

15. I'm very interested in _____ music.
    나는 고전음악에 아주 흥미가 있습니다.

16. The _____ ran out of the office at once.
    그 사무원은 즉시 사무실에서 뛰어 나갔다.

17. It is the opening ceremony of a woman's health _____.
    여성들을 위한 건강 진료소의 개회식입니다.

18. My uncle's _____ is not successful.
    제 삼촌의 사업이 잘 안 되고 있어요.

Hint

| blank | closet | along | classical | build | alarm | busy | clerk | airport |
| click | bucket | clinic | almost | aisle | bug | alone | business | campus |

Unit 9

Exercise

B. Fill in the word and meaning.

	Word	Meaning
01	alarm	
02	build	
03	campus	
04	airport	
05	clerk	
06	bucket	
07	clinic	
08	aisle	
09	busy	
10	alone	
11	bug	
12	closet	
13	almost	
14	click	
15	blank	
16	classical	
17	business	
18	along	

	Meaning	Word
01	공항	
02	복도, 통로	
03	자명종, 경보	
04	거의	
05	홀로, 단독으로	
06	~을 따라	
07	빈, 빈 곳	
08	양동이	
09	벌레, 곤충	
10	짓다, 세우다	
11	직업, 사업	
12	바쁜	
13	교정, 학교 마당	
14	고전적인	
15	점원, 사무원	
16	딸깍(하는 소리)	
17	전문병원, 진료소	
18	벽장	

🎧 C. Listen, write the word and meaning. (Track 27)

	Word	Meaning		Word	Meaning
01			10		
02			11		
03			12		
04			13		
05			14		
06			15		
07			16		
08			17		
09			18		

Unit 10

🎧 Listen and repeat. Track 28

01 diet
[dáiət]
n 다이어트, 규정식   the type of food that you regularly eat
The doctor instructed me to **diet**.
의사는 나에게 규정식이요법을 지시했다.

02 difference
[dífərəns]
n 다름, 차이   the way in which two things are unlike each other
There're some **differences** between the books.
그 두 책은 몇몇 다른 점이 있다.

03 difficult
[dífikʌ̀lt]
a 어려운   not easy; needing effort to do
It's **difficult** to finish the book.
그 책을 끝내는 것은 어렵다.

04 director
[diréktər]
n 감독, 지도자   a person who tells the actors, etc what to do in a film or play
The Best Director's Prize at the Venice Film Festival went to a Korean **director**.
베니스 영화제의 최우수 감독상이 한국 감독에게 돌아갔습니다.

05 discuss
[diskʌ́s]
v 토론하다, 의논하다   to talk about something with other people
We are going to **discuss** the sales report.
우리는 판매 보고서에 대해 의논할 것입니다.

06 district
[dístrikt]
n 지역, 지구   an official division of a town or country
Which is the largest **district** of Seoul?
서울에서 가장 넓은 지역은 어디입니까?

07 event
[ivént]
n 사건   a thing that happens
It was a very important historic **event**.
그건 정말 중요한 역사적 사건이었어.

08 exam
[igzǽm]
n 시험   a formal test, especially at school or college
The final **exam** is finally finished.
기말시험이 마침내 끝났다.

09 excellent
[éksələnt]
a 뛰어난   very good; of high quality
He is an **excellent** soccer player.
그 사람은 뛰어난 축구 선수에요.

---

key words
instruct v 지시하다, 가르치다 / play n 연극 / official a 공무상의
division n 구분, 구 / historic a 역사적인 / formal a 정규의, 정식의

🎧 Listen and repeat. (Track 29)

10 exchange [ikstʃéindʒ] — **v** 교환하다 — to replace something with a different thing
I'd like to **exchange** this one for another.
이것을 다른 물건으로 교환하고 싶습니다.

11 excite [iksáit] — **v** 흥분시키다 — to make somebody feel very pleased
The movie **excited** us.
그 영화는 우리를 흥분시켰다.

12 expensive [ikspénsiv] — **a** 값비싼 — costing a lot of money
He wears an **expensive** watch.
그 사람은 비싼 시계를 차고 있어요.

13 forget-me-not [fəːrgétminàt] — **n** 물망초 — a small wild plant with light blue flowers
The name of this flower is '**forget-me-not**.'
이 꽃의 이름은 물망초입니다.

14 form [fɔːrm] — **n** 형식, 모양 — an official document where you give answers
Would you fill out this **form**, please?
이 형식 좀 작성해 주십시오.

15 fresh [freʃ] — **a** 신선한, 새로운 — produced or made recently
I'm enjoying the blue sea and the **fresh** air.
나는 푸른 바다와 신선한 공기를 즐기고 있어.

16 function [fʌ́ŋkʃən] — **n** 기능, 구실 — a purpose or special duty of a person or thing
The **function** of education is to develop the mind.
교육의 기능은 정신을 계발하는 것이다.

17 funny [fʌ́ni] — **a** 우스운, 재미있는 — making you laugh; amusing
He told me a **funny** story.
그는 나에게 재미있는 이야기를 해 주었다.

18 fur [fəːr] — **n** 털, 모피 — the thick and soft hair that grows on the body of animals
His **fur** and tail are catching on fire.
그의 털과 꼬리에 불이 붙고 있어요.

---

key words
replace **v** 바꾸다 / document **n** 서류, 문서 / recently **ad** 최근에 / purpose **n** 목적, 용도

Unit 10 51

Exercise

A. Complete the sentence.

1. He wears an _____ watch.
   그 사람은 비싼 시계를 차고 있어요.

2. Which is the largest _____ of Seoul?
   서울에서 가장 넓은 지역은 어디입니까?

3. It was a very important historic _____.
   그건 정말 중요한 역사적 사건이었어.

4. It's _____ to finish the book.
   그 책을 끝내는 것은 어렵다.

5. The Best Director's Prize at the Venice Film Festival went to a Korean _____.
   베니스 영화제의 최우수 감독상이 한국 감독에게 돌아갔습니다.

6. His _____ and tail are catching on fire.
   그의 털과 꼬리에 불이 붙고 있어요.

7. We are going to _____ the sales report.
   우리는 판매 보고서에 대해 의논할 것입니다.

8. I'm enjoying the blue sea and the _____ air.
   나는 푸른 바다와 신선한 공기를 즐기고 있어.

9. The doctor instructed me to _____.
   의사는 나에게 규정식이요법을 지시했다.

10. The final _____ is finally finished.
    기말시험이 마침내 끝났다.

11. There're some _____ between the books.
    그 두 책은 몇몇 다른 점이 있다.

12. The movie _____ us.
    그 영화는 우리를 흥분시켰다.

13. The name of this flower is '_____.'
    이 꽃의 이름은 물망초입니다.

14. Would you fill out this _____, please?
    이 형식 좀 작성해 주십시오.

15. He is an _____ soccer player.
    그 사람은 뛰어난 축구 선수에요.

16. The _____ of education is to develop the mind.
    교육의 기능은 정신을 개발하는 것이다.

17. I'd like to _____ this one for another.
    이것을 다른 물건으로 교환하고 싶습니다.

18. He told me a _____ story.
    그는 나에게 재미있는 이야기를 해 주었다.

Hint

excite   function   diet   event   form   district   funny   excellent   difference
exchange discuss   fur   difficult   director fresh   exam   expensive   forget-me-not

Exercise

B. Fill in the word and meaning.

	Word	Meaning
01	director	
02	event	
03	fur	
04	difficult	
05	expensive	
06	diet	
07	function	
08	excellent	
09	forget-me-not	
10	difference	
11	excite	
12	funny	
13	discuss	
14	exchange	
15	form	
16	exam	
17	fresh	
18	district	

	Meaning	Word
01	다이어트, 규정식	
02	다름, 차이	
03	어려운	
04	감독, 지도자	
05	토론하다, 의논하다	
06	지역, 지구	
07	사건	
08	시험	
09	뛰어난	
10	교환하다	
11	흥분시키다	
12	값비싼	
13	물망초	
14	형식, 모양	
15	신선한, 새로운	
16	기능, 구실	
17	우스운, 재미있는	
18	털, 모피	

🎧 C. Listen, write the word and meaning. (Track 30)

	Word	Meaning		Word	Meaning
01			10		
02			11		
03			12		
04			13		
05			14		
06			15		
07			16		
08			17		
09			18		

Review 5

A. Read and fill in the word and meaning.

word	definition	meaning
	any small insect	
	a place where planes land and take off	
	a building where people go to receive medical treatment	
	a piece of furniture with doors at the front and shelves inside	
	a round open container with a handle	
	a short sharp sound	
	to make something, especially a building	
	a passage between rows of seats in a building	
	in a line that follows the side of something long	
	the activity of something for money	
	a signal that warns people of a problem	
	a person whose job is to keep accounts in an office	
	empty, with nothing written or recorded	
	very nearly; not quite	
	having a lot to do	
	traditional in style of idea	
	without any other people	
	the area of land where the main buildings of a college are	

Hint
blank   click   along   classical   build   aisle   busy   bucket   business
closet   alone   clinic   almost   alarm   bug   clerk   airport   campus

B. Read and fill in the word and meaning.

word	definition	meaning
difference	the way in which two things are unlike each other	
function	a purpose or special duty of a person or thing	
excite	to make somebody feel very pleased	
funny	making you laugh; amusing	
diet	the type of food that you regularly eat	
exchange	to replace something with a different thing	
fresh	produced or made recently	
excellent	very good; of high quality	
fur	the thick and soft hair that grows on the body of animals	
difficult	not easy; needing effort to do	
form	an official document where you give answers	
exam	a formal test, especially at school or college	
forget-me-not	a small wild plant with light blue flowers	
director	a person who tells the actors, etc what to do in a film or play	
event	a thing that happens	
discuss	to talk about something with other people	
expensive	costing a lot of money	
district	an official division of a town or country	

Hint

excite function diet event form district funny excellent difference
exchange discuss fur difficult director fresh exam expensive forget-me-not

Unit 11

🎧 Listen and repeat. Track 31

01 iguana [igwá:nə]
n 이구아나   a type of large lizard found in America
The **iguana** was ill and his owner was frantic.
이구아나가 아파서 주인이 안절부절 못했다.

02 imagine [imǽdʒin]
v 상상하다   to form a picture or idea in your mind
It wasn't what he had **imagined**.
그가 상상했던 것과는 달랐어요.

03 important [impɔ́:rtənt]
a 중요한   having great value or influence; very necessary
I have an **important** singing contest.
나는 중요한 노래 경연 대회가 있어.

04 interest [íntərist]
v 관심을 끌다   to become involved in something
I knew the book that **interested** her.
나는 그녀의 관심을 끈 책을 알고 있어.

05 Internet [íntərnèt]
n 인터넷   the computer network which allows to connect with computers all over the world
We can use the **Internet** easily through computer games.
컴퓨터 게임을 통해 인터넷을 쉽게 사용할 수 있다.

06 island [áilənd]
n 섬   a piece of land that is surrounded by water
Have you been to the **island**?
그 섬에 가본 적 있니?

07 meal [mi:l]
n 식사   the food that is eaten
Could you have a **meal** with me now?
지금 저랑 같이 식사하실래요?

08 metal [métl]
n 금속   a type of solid substance that is usually hard and shiny
The man is moving a large **metal** tank.
남자가 큰 금속 탱크를 옮기고 있다.

09 middle [mídl]
n 중앙, 한가운데   the part that is at the same distance from the two ends
Look at the first picture in the **middle**.
가운데에 있는 첫 번째 사진을 보세요.

key words
lizard n 도마뱀 / frantic a 미친 듯 날뛰는 / influence n 영향(력)
allow v 허락하다 / surround v 에워싸다 / shiny a 반짝이는 / distance n 거리

🎧 Listen and repeat. Track 32

10 mini
[míni]
a 소형의   very small
His hobby is to collect **mini** cars.
그의 취미는 소형 자동차를 모으는 것이다.

11 mix
[miks]
v 섞다, 혼합하다   combine two substance to be a single substance
Mix up the cornflakes with the milk.
콘플레이크를 우유와 잘 섞어라.

12 moon
[mu:n]
n 달   the object that shines in the sky at night
It's landing on the **moon** surface.
그것이 달 표면에 착륙하고 있는 중이다.

13 pass
[pæs]
v 지나다   to go past something without stopping
He stepped aside to let me **pass**.
그는 내가 지나가도록 옆으로 비켜섰다.

14 picnic
[píknik]
n 소풍, 피크닉   to eat outdoors usually in a field or forest
The **picnic** will be held, rain or shine.
비가 오든 화창하든 소풍을 갈 것이다.

15 picture
[píktʃər]
n 그림, 사진   a painting, drawing or photograph
There are many beautiful **pictures** of Australia.
아름다운 호주 사진들이 많이 있어요.

16 place
[pleis]
n 곳, 장소   a particular position or area
You cannot be in two **places** at the same time.
너는 동시에 두 장소에 있을 수 없다.

17 plant
[plænt]
n 식물, 풀   a living thing that grows in the ground
Plants take water from the soil.
식물은 땅에서 물을 얻는다.

18 playground
[pléigraund]
n 운동장, 놀이터   an area of land where children can play
A mother is looking for her child in the school **playground**.
한 엄마가 학교 운동장에서 아이를 찾고 있다.

key words
combine v 결합하다 / land v 착륙하다 / step v 걸음을 옮기다 / soil n 토양, 땅

Unit 11   57

Exercise

A. Complete the sentence.

1. I knew the book that _____ her.
   나는 그녀의 관심을 끈 책을 알고 있어.

2. The _____ was ill and his owner was frantic.
   이구아나가 아파서 주인이 안절부절 못했다.

3. There are many beautiful _____ of Australia.
   아름다운 호주 사진들이 많이 있어요.

4. I have an _____ singing contest.
   나는 중요한 노래 경연 대회가 있어.

5. We can use the _____ easily through computer games.
   컴퓨터 게임을 통해 인터넷을 쉽게 사용할 수 있다.

6. A mother is looking for her child in the school _____.
   한 엄마가 학교 운동장에서 아이를 찾고 있다.

7. Have you been to the _____?
   그 섬에 가본 적 있니?

8. Could you have a _____ with me now?
   지금 저랑 같이 식사하실래요?

9. His hobby is to collect _____ cars.
   그의 취미는 소형 자동차를 모으는 것이다.

10. _____ up the cornflakes with the milk.
    콘플레이크를 우유와 잘 섞어라.

11. It's landing on the _____ surface.
    그것이 달 표면에 착륙하고 있는 중이다.

12. The _____ will be held, rain or shine.
    비가 오든 화창하든 소풍을 갈 것이다.

13. The man is moving a large _____ tank.
    남자가 큰 금속 탱크를 옮기고 있다.

14. He stepped aside to let me _____.
    그는 내가 지나가도록 옆으로 비켜섰다.

15. Look at the first picture in the _____.
    가운데에 있는 첫 번째 사진을 보세요.

16. You cannot be in two _____ at the same time.
    너는 동시에 두 장소에 있을 수 없다.

17. It wasn't what he had _____.
    그가 상상했던 것과는 달랐어요.

18. _____ take water from the soil.
    식물은 땅에서 물을 얻는다.

Hint

| meal | imagine | place | mix | island | picnic | metal | interest | picture |
| middle | iguana | playground | important | mini | plant | Internet | moon | pass |

Exercise

B. Fill in the word and meaning.

	Word	Meaning
01	metal	
02	imagine	
03	mini	
04	moon	
05	island	
06	middle	
07	pass	
08	iguana	
09	picture	
10	playground	
11	important	
12	plant	
13	meal	
14	place	
15	Internet	
16	picnic	
17	mix	
18	interest	

	Meaning	Word
01	이구아나	
02	상상하다	
03	중요한	
04	관심을 끌다	
05	인터넷	
06	섬	
07	식사	
08	금속	
09	중앙, 한가운데	
10	소형의	
11	섞다, 혼합하다	
12	달	
13	지나다	
14	소풍, 피크닉	
15	그림, 사진	
16	곳, 장소	
17	식물, 풀	
18	운동장, 놀이터	

🎧 **C. Listen, write the word and meaning.** (Track 33)

	Word	Meaning		Word	Meaning
01			10		
02			11		
03			12		
04			13		
05			14		
06			15		
07			16		
08			17		
09			18		

Unit 12

🎧 Listen and repeat. Track 34

01 rock [rak]
n 바위   the hard, solid material that forms part of the earth
There are beautiful **rocks** all over the mountains.
산 여기저기에 아름다운 바위들이 있다.

02 round [raund]
a 둥근, 원형의   having the shape of a circle or a ball
It is a flat **round** piece of dough.
그것은 납작하고 둥근 밀가루 반죽이다.

03 row [rou]
n 열, 줄   a line of people or things or seats in a theater
The pots stood in a **row**.
화분들을 일렬로 세워 놓았습니다.

04 rush [rʌʃ]
v 돌진하다   to move or do with great speed, often too fast
The woman **rushed** into the bathroom.
여자가 욕실로 급히 들어갔다.

05 sale [seil]
n 판매   the action of selling or being sold
The car is on **sale**.
그 차는 판매 중이다.

06 situation [sitʃuéiʃən]
n 상황   the things that are happening in a particular place or time
In this **situation**, what would his mother say to him?
이 상황에서 그의 어머니가 그에게 뭐라고 말씀 하실까?

07 speed [spi:d]
n 속도, 속력   the rate at which somebody / something moves
He ran with constant **speed**.
그는 일정한 속도로 달렸다.

08 steak [steik]
n 스테이크   a thick flat piece of meat
Who ordered the **steak**?
누가 스테이크를 주문했죠?

09 stick [stik]
v 찌르다, 붙이다   to push a pointed object into something
Stick a fork into the meat to see if it's ready.
고기가 준비 되었는지 보려면 포크를 찔러 보세요.

key words
theater n 극장 / in a row 한 줄로 / sell v 판매하다 / rate n 비율 / constant a 일정한 / order v 주문하다

🎧 Listen and repeat. (Track 35)

10 still
[stil]
ad 아직도, 여전히 continuing until now or the time you are talking about
But the water is **still** cold.
하지만 물은 아직 차갑습니다.

11 storm
[stɔːrm]
n 폭풍 very bad weather, with a lot of rain, strong winds
A **storm** hit the country and killed a lot of people.
폭풍우가 그 나라를 강타해서 많은 사람들이 죽었어.

12 straight
[streit]
ad 곧장 / **a** 곧은 without stopping; with no bends or curves
Go **straight** two blocks and make a left turn at the corner.
곧장 두 블록을 가서 모퉁이에서 왼쪽으로 돌아가세요.

13 usual
[júːʒuəl]
a 보통의, 평소의 happening or used most often
I got on the bus as **usual**.
나는 평소처럼 버스를 탔다.

14 vacation
[veikéiʃən]
n 휴가, 방학 the periods of time when schools are closed; holiday
We are already on **vacation** here.
여기는 이미 방학 중이야.

15 view
[vjuː]
n 전망, 풍경 what you can see from beautiful natural scenery or place
The house interrupts the **view**.
그 집이 전망을 가로막고 있다.

16 village
[vílidʒ]
n 마을 a group of houses with other buildings
The **village** was destroyed by an earthquake.
그 마을은 지진으로 파괴되었다.

17 war
[wɔːr]
n 전쟁 a state of fighting between different countries
That was the end of the **war**.
그것이 전쟁의 끝이었다.

18 waste
[weist]
v 낭비하다 to use more of something than is useful
Don't **waste** your money.
돈을 낭비하지 마세요.

key words
curve **n** 곡선, 굴곡 / scenery **n** 풍경 / interrupt **v** 가로막다
destroy **v** 파괴하다 / earthquake **n** 지진 / useful **a** 쓸모 있는

Exercise

A. Complete the sentence.

1. There are beautiful _____ all over the mountains.
   산 여기저기에 아름다운 바위들이 있다.

2. Who ordered the _____?
   누가 스테이크를 주문했죠?

3. The pots stood in a _____.
   화분들을 일렬로 세워 놓았습니다.

4. The car is on _____.
   그 차는 판매 중이다.

5. In this _____, what would his mother say to him?
   이 상황에서 그의 어머니가 그에게 뭐라고 말씀 하실까?

6. He ran with constant _____.
   그는 일정한 속도로 달렸다.

7. The _____ was destroyed by an earthquake.
   그 마을은 지진으로 파괴되었다.

8. It is a flat _____ piece of dough.
   그것은 납작하고 둥근 밀가루 반죽이다.

9. A _____ hit the country and killed a lot of people.
   폭풍우가 그 나라를 강타해서 많은 사람들이 죽었어

10. That was the end of the _____.
    그것이 전쟁의 끝이었다.

11. Go _____ two blocks and make a left turn at the corner.
    곧장 두 블록을 가서 모퉁이에서 왼쪽으로 돌아가세요.

12. I got on the bus as _____.
    나는 평소처럼 버스를 탔다.

13. We are already on _____ here.
    여기는 이미 방학 중이야.

14. The woman _____ into the bathroom.
    여자가 욕실로 급히 들어갔다.

15. The house interrupts the _____.
    그 집이 전망을 가로막고 있다.

16. The old man is walking with a _____.
    그 노인은 지팡이를 짚고 걷고 있다.

17. Don't _____ your money.
    돈을 낭비하지 마세요.

18. But the water is _____ cold.
    하지만 물은 아직 차갑습니다.

Hint

| sale | rush | war | situation | usual | storm | row | village | steak |
| rock | speed | round | stick | still | view | waste | straight | vacation |

Exercise

B. Fill in the word and meaning.

	Word	Meaning
01	sale	
02	usual	
03	round	
04	steak	
05	row	
06	vacation	
07	situation	
08	village	
09	still	
10	rush	
11	storm	
12	waste	
13	speed	
14	war	
15	view	
16	straight	
17	rock	
18	stick	

	Meaning	Word
01	바위	
02	둥근, 원형의	
03	열, 줄	
04	돌진하다	
05	판매	
06	상황	
07	속도, 속력	
08	스테이크	
09	찌르다, 붙이다	
10	아직도, 여전히	
11	폭풍	
12	곧장, 곧은	
13	보통의, 평소의	
14	휴가, 방학	
15	전망, 풍경	
16	마을	
17	전쟁	
18	낭비하다	

C. Listen, write the word and meaning. (Track 36)

	Word	Meaning		Word	Meaning
01			10		
02			11		
03			12		
04			13		
05			14		
06			15		
07			16		
08			17		
09			18		

Review 6

A. Read and fill in the word and meaning.

word	definition	meaning
	very small	
	a type of large lizard found in America	
	a living thing that grows in the ground	
	the part that is at the same distance from the two ends	
	a particular position or area	
	combine two substance to be a single substance	
	to form a picture or idea in your mind	
	the object that shines in the sky at night	
	having great value or influence; very necessary	
	to go past something without stopping	
	a piece of land that is surrounded by water	
	a type of solid substance that is usually hard and shiny	
	to become involved in something	
	to eat outdoors usually in a field or forest	
	an area of land where children can play	
	the computer network which allows to connect with computers all over the world	
	the food that is eaten	
	a painting, drawing or photograph	

Hint

meal   imagine   place   mix   island   picnic   metal   interest   picture
middle iguana   playground   important   mini   plant   Internet   moon   pass

B. Read and fill in the word and meaning.

word	definition	meaning
	continuing until now or the time you are talking about	
	a state of fighting between different countries	
	to push a pointed object into something	
	a group of houses with other buildings	
	the hard, solid material that forms part of the earth	
	what you can see from beautiful natural scenery or place	
	a thick flat piece of meat	
	the periods of time when schools are closed; holiday	
	having the shape of a circle or a ball	
	without stopping; with no bends or curves	
	the rate at which somebody / something moves	
	happening or used most often	
	a line of people or things or seats in a theater	
	to use more of something than is useful	
	the things that are happening in a particular place or time	
	very bad weather, with a lot of rain, strong winds	
	to move or do with great speed, often too fast	
	the action of selling or being sold	

Hint
still   rush   speed   steak   usual   storm   row   village   situation
rock   war   round   stick   sale   view   waste   straight   vacation

Unit 13

🎧 Listen and repeat. Track 37

01 also
[ɔ́ːlsou]
ad 또한, 역시   in addition; too
They **also** make us depressed.
그것들은 또한 우리를 우울하게 한다.

02 altogether
[ɔ̀ːltəgéðər]
ad 아주, 전부   completely; including everything
I don't **altogether** agree with you.
내가 너에게 전부 동의하는 것은 아니다.

03 angel
[éindʒəl]
n 천사   a spirit who is believed to live in heaven with God
She is like an **angel** so I love her.
그녀는 천사 같아서 나는 그녀를 사랑한다.

04 angry
[ǽŋgri]
a 성난   feeling or showing anger
My mother was **angry** with me because I didn't clean my room.
내가 방 청소를 하지 않아서 엄마는 화가 나셨다.

05 another
[ənʌ́ðər]
a 또 하나의, 다른   one more person or thing of the same kind
I want to buy **another** computer game.
나는 다른 컴퓨터 게임을 사고 싶다.

06 base
[beis]
n 기초   the lowest part of something
My **base** study is so terrible.
나의 기초 학문은 너무 형편없다.

07 calendar
[kǽləndər]
n 달력   a list that shows the days, weeks and months
He is looking at the **calendar** on the desk.
그는 책상 위에 달력을 쳐다보고 있다.

08 cape
[keip]
n 망토   a piece of clothing with no sleeves
Her daughter wants to have this red **cape**.
그녀의 딸은 이 빨간 망토를 갖고 싶어해.

09 capital
[kǽpitl]
n 수도, 대문자   a city where the government is; a large form of alphabet
It's a problem about the **capital** of China.
그것은 중국의 수도에 관한 문제다.

key words
depressed a 우울한 / anger n 노염,성 / government n 정부

🎧 Listen and repeat. Track 38

10 captain [kǽptin]
n 선장, 장   the person who is in command of a ship or an aircraft
The man is the **captain** of the ship.
그 남자는 배의 선장이다.

11 care [kɛər]
n 돌봄, 주의, 걱정   looking after to have health and protection
The people of Australia take good **care** of koalas.
호주 사람들은 코알라를 잘 돌본다.

12 carve [ka:rv]
v 조각하다   to cut wood or stone to make an object or to put a writing
The statue is **carved** out of marble.
그 조각상은 대리석으로 조각한 것입니다.

13 collect [kəlékt]
v 모으다   to keep together many objects of a particular type as a hobby
Collect change in a jar for a whole month.
한 달 내내 단지에 동전을 모아봐.

14 comic [kámik]
n 만화 / a 희극의   a magazine that tells stories through pictures
Which of you has a **comic** book?
너희 중에 누가 만화책 갖고 있니?

15 concept [kánsept]
n 개념   an idea; a basic principle
It is difficult to understand the **concept** of the word.
그 단어의 개념을 이해하는 것은 어려워.

16 concert [kánsə(:)rt]
n 콘서트, 음악회   a performance of music
Would you like to go to the **concert** with me?
콘서트에 같이 갈래?

17 congratulation [kəngrætʃəléiʃən]
n 축하   used for telling that you are pleased about something
All of us offer **congratulations** on your success.
당신의 성공에 우리 모두 축하를 드려요.

18 connect [kənékt]
v 잇다, 연결하다   to join something to something else
He is **connecting** the stereo.
그는 스테레오를 연결하고 있다.

key words
command v 명령하다, 지배하다 / statue n 조각상 / marble n 대리석 / performance n 공연

Unit 13 67

Exercise

A. Complete the sentence.

1. He is _____ the stereo.
   그는 스테레오를 연결하고 있다.
2. My mother was _____ with me because I didn't clean my room.
   내가 방 청소를 하지 않아서 엄마는 화가 나셨다.
3. The people of Australia take good _____ of koalas.
   호주 사람들은 코알라를 잘 돌본다.
4. I want to buy _____ computer game.
   나는 다른 컴퓨터 게임을 사고 싶다.
5. My _____ study is so terrible.
   나의 기초 학문은 너무 형편없다.
6. Would you like to go to the _____ with me?
   콘서트에 같이 갈래?
7. He is looking at the _____ on the desk.
   그는 책상 위에 달력을 쳐다보고 있다.
8. Her daughter wants to have this red _____.
   그녀의 딸은 이 빨간 망토를 갖고 싶어해.
9. It's a problem about the _____ of China.
   그것은 중국의 수도에 관한 문제다.
10. They _____ make us depressed.
    그것들은 또한 우리를 우울하게 한다.
11. The man is the _____ of the ship.
    그 남자는 배의 선장이다.
12. I don't _____ agree with you.
    내가 너에게 전부 동의하는 것은 아니다.
13. The statue is _____ out of marble.
    그 조각상은 대리석으로 조각한 것입니다.
14. _____ change in a jar for a whole month.
    한 달 내내 단지에 동전을 모아봐.
15. Which of you has a _____ book?
    너희 중에 누가 만화책 갖고 있니?
16. It is difficult to understand the _____ of the word.
    그 단어의 개념을 이해하는 것은 어려워.
17. She is like an _____ so I love her.
    그녀는 천사 같아서 나는 그녀를 사랑한다.
18. All of us offer _____ on your success.
    당신의 성공에 우리 모두 축하를 드려요.

Hint

| also | angry | comic | cape | calendar | concert | captain | another | congratulation |
| carve | angel | care | connect | altogether | capital | base | collect | concept |

Exercise

B. Fill in the word and meaning.

	Word	Meaning
01	angel	
02	captain	
03	comic	
04	also	
05	collect	
06	concept	
07	altogether	
08	carve	
09	base	
10	connect	
11	calendar	
12	angry	
13	care	
14	concert	
15	cape	
16	congratulation	
17	another	
18	capital	

	Meaning	Word
01	또한, 역시	
02	아주, 전부	
03	천사	
04	성난	
05	또 하나의, 다른	
06	기초	
07	달력	
08	망토	
09	수도, 대문자	
10	선장, 장	
11	돌봄, 주의, 걱정	
12	조각하다	
13	모으다	
14	만화, 희극의	
15	개념	
16	콘서트, 음악회	
17	축하	
18	잇다, 연결하다	

🎧 C. Listen, write the word and meaning. (Track 39)

	Word	Meaning		Word	Meaning
01			10		
02			11		
03			12		
04			13		
05			14		
06			15		
07			16		
08			17		
09			18		

Unit 14

🎧 Listen and repeat. Track 40

01 different   a 다른, 상이한   not like somebody / something else
[dífərənt]
They are totally **different** from us in opinion.
그들의 견해는 우리의 견해와 전혀 다르다.

02 dot   n 점, 규정시각   a small, round mark; to mark with a dot
[dat]
It used twelve **dots** for the letters.
그것은 글자를 만들기 위해 12개의 점을 사용했다.

03 double   v 배로 늘다 / n 두 배   twice the number or amount
[dʌ́bəl]
She did **double** work yesterday.
그녀는 어제 2배의 일을 했다.

04 doughnut   n 도넛   a small cake in the shape of a ring
[dóunət]
The first **doughnuts** didn't have holes.
최초의 도넛에는 구멍이 없었다.

05 drama   n 극, 드라마   a play for the theater or television
[drá:mə]
He wants to go to **drama** school.
그는 연극학교에 가길 원한다.

06 drive   v 운전하다, 몰다   to control or operate a car, train, bus, etc
[draiv]
We are **driving** to the campground now.
우리는 지금 야영지로 차를 몰고 있다.

07 electric   a 전기의   connected with electricity
[iléktrik]
Electric organs are cheaper than pipe organs.
전기 오르간은 파이프 오르간보다 값이 싸다.

08 express   v 표현하다   to show something such as a feeling by words or actions
[iksprés]
Express your idea clearly.
네 생각을 명확하게 표현해라.

09 extend   v 연장하다   to make something longer or larger
[iksténd]
I need to **extend** my visa.
나는 비자 기한을 연장해야 돼.

---

key words
twice ad 두 배로 / operate v 작동하다 / campground n 야영지

🎧 Listen and repeat. (Track 41)

10 fall [fɔːl]
v 떨어지다, 넘어지다 to drop down towards the ground
The old man stumbled and **fell**.
그 노인은 비틀거리다 넘어졌다.

11 false [fɔːls]
a 거짓의, 틀린 not true; incorrect
It was a **false** report.
그것은 허위 보고서였다.

12 famous [féiməs]
a 유명한 well-known to many people
Who is the most **famous** artist?
가장 유명한 화가는 누구니?

13 gain [gein]
v 얻다, 획득하다 to obtain or win something that you want
He **gained** weight again in one week.
그는 일주일 만에 다시 몸무게가 늘었어.

14 genius [dʒíːnjəs]
n 천재 a person who has unusual ability
He has a **genius** for making money.
그는 돈 버는 데 천재다.

15 gentle [dʒéntl]
a 부드러운 not strong, violent or extreme
She speaks in a **gentle** tone.
그녀는 상냥한 어조로 말한다.

16 germ [dʒəːrm]
n 세균, 병원균 a very small living thing that causes disease
This drug kills **germs** but is harmless to people.
이 약은 세균은 죽이지만 인간에게는 무해하다.

17 ghost [goust]
n 유령 the spirit of a dead person that is seen or heard
On Halloween, American children dress up as **ghosts**.
할로윈에 미국 어린이들은 유령 분장을 한다.

18 gift [gift]
n 선물 something that you give to somebody
The man is about to open a **gift**.
남자가 막 선물 포장을 뜯으려고 한다.

---

key words
stumble v 비틀거리다 / violent a 격렬한 / extreme a 극단적인 / disease n 병 / harmless a 해가 없는

Unit 14 71

Exercise

A. Complete the sentence.

1. It used twelve _____ for the letters.
   그것은 글자를 만들기 위해 12개의 점을 사용했다.

2. She speaks in a _____ tone.
   그녀는 상냥한 어조로 말한다.

3. The first _____ didn't have holes.
   최초의 도넛에는 구멍이 없었다.

4. _____ organs are cheaper than pipe organs.
   전기 오르간은 파이프 오르간보다 값이 싸다.

5. She did _____ work yesterday.
   그녀는 어제 2배의 일을 했다.

6. This drug kills _____ but is harmless to people.
   이 약은 세균은 죽이지만 인간에게는 무해하다.

7. They are totally _____ from us in opinion.
   그들의 견해는 우리의 견해와 전혀 다르다.

8. The old man stumbled and _____.
   그 노인은 비틀거리다가 넘어졌다.

9. It was a _____ report.
   그것은 허위 보고서였다.

10. He _____ weight again in one week.
    그는 일주일 만에 다시 몸무게가 늘었어.

11. Who is the most _____ artist?
    가장 유명한 화가는 누구니?

12. He wants to go to _____ school.
    그는 연극학교에 가길 원한다.

13. He has a _____ for making money.
    그는 돈 버는 데 천재다.

14. The man is about to open a _____.
    남자가 막 선물 포장을 뜯으려고 한다.

15. _____ your idea clearly.
    네 생각을 명확하게 표현해라.

16. I need to _____ my visa.
    나는 비자 기한을 연장해야 돼.

17. On Halloween, American children dress up as _____.
    할로윈에 미국 어린이들은 유령 분장을 한다.

18. We are _____ to the campground now.
    우리는 지금 야영지로 차를 몰고 있다.

Hint

express	double	gain	different	genius	electric	fall	drive	gift
extend	doughnut	famous	germ	drama	ghost	dot	false	gentle

Exercise

B. Fill in the word and meaning.

	Word	Meaning
01	dot	
02	false	
03	electric	
04	gain	
05	different	
06	gentle	
07	doughnut	
08	ghost	
09	express	
10	gift	
11	germ	
12	drama	
13	genius	
14	extend	
15	famous	
16	drive	
17	fall	
18	double	

	Meaning	Word
01	다른, 상이한	
02	점, 규정시각	
03	배로 늘다, 두 배	
04	도넛	
05	극, 드라마	
06	운전하다, 몰다	
07	전기의	
08	표현하다	
09	연장하다	
10	떨어지다, 넘어지다	
11	거짓의, 틀린	
12	유명한	
13	얻다, 획득하다	
14	천재	
15	부드러운	
16	세균, 병원균	
17	유령	
18	선물	

🎧 **C. Listen, write the word and meaning.** (Track 42)

	Word	Meaning		Word	Meaning
01			10		
02			11		
03			12		
04			13		
05			14		
06			15		
07			16		
08			17		
09			18		

Unit 14

Review 7

A. Read and fill in the word and meaning.

word	definition	meaning
	a piece of clothing with no sleeves	
	to keep together many objects of a particular type as a hobby	
	one more person or thing of the same kind	
	the lowest part of something	
	a list that shows the days, weeks and months	
	to join something to something else	
	feeling or showing anger	
	a city where the government is; a large form of alphabet	
	an idea; a basic principle	
	a magazine that tells stories through pictures	
	the person who is in command of a shop or an aircraft	
	completely, including everything	
	a performance of music	
	to cut wood or stone to make an object or to put a writing	
	a spirit who is believed to live in heaven with God	
	looking after to have health and protection	
	used for telling that you are pleased about something	
	in addition; too	

Hint

also   angry   comic   cape   calendar   concert   captain   another   congratulation
carve   angel   care   connect altogether capital   base   collect   concept

B. Read and fill in the word and meaning.

word	definition	meaning
	to obtain or win something that you want	
	well-known to many people	
	a person who has unusual ability	
	not like somebody / something else	
	to drop down towards the ground	
	a small, round mark; to mark with a dot	
	not true; incorrect	
	to make something longer or larger	
	twice the number or amount	
	not strong, violent or extreme	
	something that you give to somebody	
	a play for the theater or television	
	connected with electricity	
	to control or operate a car, train, bus, etc	
	a very small living thing that causes disease	
	a small cake in the shape of a ring	
	to show something such as a feeling by words or actions	
	the spirit of a dead person that is seen or heard	

Hint
express double   gain   different   genius   electric   fall   drive   gift
extend   doughnut   famous   germ   drama   ghost   dot   false   gentle

Unit 15

🎧 Listen and repeat. Track 43

01 interesting
[íntəristiŋ]
a 흥미가 있는   enjoyable and entertaining
The book was **interesting** and instructive as well.
그 책은 흥미도 있거니와 또한 교훈적이었다.

02 introduce
[ìntrədjúːs]
v 소개하다   to bring in something new, take something for the first time
It was **introduced** in 1446.
그것은 1446년에 소개되었다.

03 invention
[invénʃən]
n 발명, 발명품   a machine, device, or system that has been invented by someone
Necessity is the mother of **invention**.
필요는 발명의 어머니이다.

04 jar
[dʒaːr]
n 항아리, 단지   a container with a lid used for keeping food, etc
I broke a large storage **jar** for flour.
나는 밀가루를 저장하는 커다란 항아리를 깨뜨렸다.

05 join
[dʒɔin]
v 가입하다, 결합하다   to become a member of a club or organization
I **joined** a tennis club activity this year.
나는 올해 클럽 활동으로 테니스 반에 가입했다.

06 judge
[dʒʌdʒ]
n 심판 / **v** 판단하다   to give an opinion based on the information you have
Don't **judge** a book by its cover.
표지를 보고 책을 판단하지 마라.

07 mathematics
[mæ̀θəmǽtiks]
n 수학   the science or study of numbers or quantities
We had a test in **mathematics** yesterday.
어제 수학 시험이 있었다.

08 more
[mɔːr]
a 더 많은, 여분의   something extra as well as that you have
Please tell me about it once **more**.
그것에 대해 내게 한 번 더 말해 주세요.

09 most
[moust]
a 대부분의   nearly all of a group of people or things
Most of the students are against keeping pets.
학생들 대부분은 애완동물을 키우는 것에 반대한다.

key words
entertain **v** 즐겁게 하다 / instructive **a** 교훈적인 / lid **n** 뚜껑 / nearly **ad** 거의

🎧 Listen and repeat. Track 44

10 mountain [máuntən]
n 산   a very high hill
What is the highest **mountain** in Korea?
한국에서 가장 높은 산이 무엇이니?

11 museum [mju:zí:əm]
n 박물관   a building where collections of valuable objects are shown
The class trip to the **museum** is next Wednesday.
학급의 박물관 견학은 다음 주 수요일이에요.

12 narrow [nǽrou]
a 폭이 좁은   having only a short distance from side to side
He took the straight and **narrow** street.
그는 곧게 뻗은 좁은 길을 택했다.

13 plate [pleit]
n 접시   a flat, usually round, dish for eating
The server is taking away a **plate**.
웨이터가 접시를 치우고 있습니다.

14 pleasure [pléʒər]
n 기쁨, 즐거움   the feeling of being happy or satisfied
It would be a **pleasure** to see you again.
너를 다시 만난다면 기쁠 것이다.

15 pole [poul]
n 막대기, 장대   a long, thin piece of wood or metal
It is a ten-foot **pole**.
그것은 10피트짜리 막대기이다.

16 police station [pəli:s steiʃən]
n 경찰서   the building for the official organization to prevent crime
As soon as I saw the **police station**, I began to run.
경찰서를 보자마자 나는 달리기 시작했다.

17 poll [poul]
n 여론조사, 투표   a survey in which people are asked their opinions about something
The people are taking a **poll**.
사람들이 투표하고 있다.

18 pollution [pəlú:ʃən]
n 오염   the action of making the air or water dirty
Air **pollution** in Seoul is serious.
서울의 대기 오염이 심각합니다.

key words
valuable a 귀중한 / satisfied a 만족한 / survey n 조사 / serious a 심각한, 중대한

Exercise

A. Complete the sentence.

1. We had a test in _____ yesterday.
   어제 수학 시험이 있었다.

2. It was _____ in 1446.
   그것은 1446년에 소개되었다.

3. It would be a _____ to see you again.
   너를 다시 만난다면 기쁠 것이다.

4. I broke a large storage _____ for flour.
   나는 밀가루를 저장하는 커다란 항아리를 깨뜨렸다.

5. As soon as I saw the _____, I began to run.
   경찰서를 보자마자 나는 달리기 시작했다.

6. Don't _____ a book by its cover.
   표지를 보고 책을 판단하지 마라.

7. _____ of the students are against keeping pets.
   학생들 대부분은 애완동물을 키우는 것에 반대한다.

8. The book was _____ and instructive as well.
   그 책은 흥미도 있거니와 또한 교훈적이었다.

9. What is the highest _____ in Korea?
   한국에서 가장 높은 산이 무엇이니?

10. He took the straight and _____ street.
    그는 곧게 뻗은 좁은 길을 택했다.

11. The server is taking away a _____.
    웨이터가 접시를 치우고 있습니다.

12. Please tell me about it once _____.
    그것에 대해 내게 한 번 더 말해 주세요.

13. It is a ten-foot _____.
    그것은 10피트짜리 막대기이다.

14. Air _____ in Seoul is serious.
    서울의 대기 오염이 심각합니다.

15. I _____ a tennis club activity this year.
    나는 올해 클럽 활동으로 테니스 반에 가입했다.

16. The class trip to the _____ is next Wednesday.
    학급의 박물관 견학은 다음 주 수요일이에요.

17. Necessity is the mother of _____.
    필요는 발명의 어머니이다.

18. The people are taking a _____.
    사람들이 투표하고 있다.

Hint

pollution   poll   jar   pleasure   more   join   narrow   mountain   police station
introduce   most   judge   interesting   museum   plate   pole   invention   mathematics

Exercise

B. Fill in the word and meaning.

	Word	Meaning
01	invention	
02	most	
03	pole	
04	interesting	
05	pleasure	
06	mathematics	
07	poll	
08	museum	
09	introduce	
10	plate	
11	jar	
12	narrow	
13	more	
14	pollution	
15	judge	
16	police station	
17	mountain	
18	join	

	Meaning	Word
01	흥미가 있는	
02	소개하다	
03	발명, 발명품	
04	항아리, 단지	
05	가입하다, 결합하다	
06	심판, 심판하다	
07	수학	
08	더 많은, 여분의	
09	대부분의	
10	산	
11	박물관	
12	폭이 좁은	
13	접시	
14	기쁨, 즐거움	
15	막대기, 장대	
16	경찰서	
17	여론조사, 투표	
18	오염	

C. Listen, write the word and meaning. (Track 45)

	Word	Meaning
01		
02		
03		
04		
05		
06		
07		
08		
09		

	Word	Meaning
10		
11		
12		
13		
14		
15		
16		
17		
18		

Unit 16

🎧 Listen and repeat. (Track 46)

01 save   v 구하다, 절약하다   to keep money instead of spending something
[seiv]
I'll buy those shoes after I **save** some money.
나는 돈을 절약한 후에, 저 구두를 살 것이다.

02 science   n 과학   the study of the physical world and natural laws
[sáiəns]
We get together and study math and **science** on Thursdays.
우리는 목요일마다 모여서 수학과 과학을 공부한다.

03 scissors   n 가위   a tool for cutting paper or fabric
[sízə:rz]
Be careful when you use the **scissors**.
가위를 사용할 때 조심해야 돼요.

04 season   n 계절   any of the four main periods of the year
[sí:zən]
What is the cycle of the **seasons**?
계절의 순환이란 무엇입니까?

05 second   a 둘째의   coming next after the first
[sékənd]
This is the **second** and last question.
이건 두 번째이자 마지막 질문입니다.

06 seed   n 씨앗   the small hard part produced by a plant
[si:d]
Did you plant the **seeds** in a garden?
정원에 씨앗을 심었니?

07 strange   a 이상한   unusual, especially in a way that is difficult to understand
[streindʒ]
My computer is doing some **strange** things.
내 컴퓨터가 좀 이상해요.

08 straw   n 짚   grain plants that have been cut and dried
[strɔ:]
My brothers made houses with **straw** and wood easily and quickly.
형들은 짚과 나무로 쉽고 빠르게 집을 지었다.

09 strike   v 치다, 때리다   to hit somebody / something hard
[straik]
Don't **strike** anyone smaller than yourself.
당신보다 작은 사람을 때리지 마세요.

key words
instead ad 그 대신에 / grain n 곡물

🎧 Listen and repeat. Track 47

10 thick [θik]
a 두꺼운   having a larger distance between opposite sides than normal
My sister has some **thick** books.
내 여동생은 두꺼운 책 몇 권을 갖고 있습니다.

11 thirsty [θə́ːrsti]
a 목마른   wanting to drink
I'm not **thirsty**, thanks.
감사하지만 목마르지 않아요.

12 thousand [θáuzənd]
n 천   number 1000
Two **thousand** people came to the concert.
2000명의 사람들이 연주회에 왔다.

13 usually [júːʒuəli]
ad 보통, 일반적으로   in the way that usual
What time do you **usually** finish school?
학교가 보통 몇 시에 끝나니?

14 weak [wiːk]
a 약한   not physically strong
He is a man of **weak** personality.
그는 개성이 약한 사람이다.

15 while [hwail]
conj ~하는 동안에   during the time that something is happening
He lost his wallet **while** he was asleep.
그는 잠이 든 동안에 자신의 지갑을 잃어버렸다.

16 whisper [hwíspəːr]
v 속삭이다   to speak very quietly
He **whispered** to me in the class.
그는 수업 중에 나에게 속삭였다.

17 will [wil]
aux ~할 것이다   used for predicting the future
My sister **will** make dolls during summer vacation.
내 여동생은 여름 방학 동안 인형들을 만들 것이다.

18 wise [waiz]
a 현명한, 신중한   having the knowledge or experience to make good decisions
It would be **wise** to wait for a few days.
며칠 더 기다려 보는 것이 현명할거야.

key words
opposite a 맞은 편의 / personality n 개성 / quietly ad 조용히 / predict v 예언하다

Unit 16 81

Exercise

A. Complete the sentence.

1. I'll buy those shoes after I _____ some money.
   나는 돈을 절약한 후에, 저 구두를 살 것이다.

2. What time do you _____ finish school?
   학교가 보통 몇 시에 끝나니?

3. I'm not _____, thanks.
   감사하지만 목마르지 않아요.

4. We get together and study math and _____ on Thursdays.
   우리는 목요일마다 모여서 수학과 과학을 공부한다.

5. What is the cycle of the _____?
   계절의 순환이란 무엇입니까?

6. He is a man of _____ personality.
   그는 개성이 약한 사람이다.

7. This is the _____ and last question.
   이건 두 번째이자 마지막 질문입니다.

8. He _____ to me in the class.
   그는 수업 중에 나에게 속삭였다.

9. My computer is doing some _____ things.
   내 컴퓨터가 좀 이상해요.

10. My brothers made houses with _____ and wood easily and quickly.
    형들은 짚과 나무로 쉽고 빠르게 집을 지었다.

11. It would be _____ to wait for a few days.
    며칠 더 기다려 보는 것이 현명할거야.

12. Don't _____ anyone smaller than yourself.
    당신보다 작은 사람을 때리지 마세요.

13. My sister has some _____ books.
    내 여동생은 두꺼운 책 몇 권을 갖고 있습니다.

14. Did you plant the _____ in a garden?
    정원에 씨앗을 심었니?

15. Two _____ people came to the concert.
    2000명의 사람들이 연주회에 왔다.

16. He lost his wallet _____ he was asleep.
    그는 잠이 든 동안에 자신의 지갑을 잃어버렸다.

17. Be careful when you use the _____.
    가위를 사용할 때 조심해야 돼요.

18. My sister _____ make dolls during summer vacation.
    내 여동생은 여름 방학 동안 인형들을 만들 것이다.

Hint

| strike | thirsty | season | whisper | save | while | seed | thick | second |
| usually | strange | will | science | weak | scissors | thousand | straw | wise |

Exercise

B. Fill in the word and meaning.

	Word	Meaning
01	straw	
02	season	
03	thick	
04	usually	
05	science	
06	weak	
07	strike	
08	save	
09	whisper	
10	will	
11	second	
12	wise	
13	while	
14	seed	
15	thirsty	
16	strange	
17	thousand	
18	scissors	

	Meaning	Word
01	구하다, 절약하다	
02	과학	
03	가위	
04	계절	
05	둘째의	
06	씨앗	
07	이상한	
08	짚	
09	치다, 때리다	
10	두꺼운	
11	목마른	
12	천	
13	보통, 일반적으로	
14	약한	
15	~하는 동안에	
16	속삭이다	
17	~할 것이다	
18	현명한, 신중한	

🎧 C. Listen, write the word and meaning. (Track 48)

	Word	Meaning		Word	Meaning
01			10		
02			11		
03			12		
04			13		
05			14		
06			15		
07			16		
08			17		
09			18		

Review 8

A. Read and fill in the word and meaning.

word	definition	meaning
	nearly all of a group of people or things	
	the action of making the air or water dirty	
	a very high hill	
	enjoyable and entertaining	
	something extra as well as that you have	
	a long, thin piece of wood or metal	
	to bring in something new, take something for the first time	
	a flat, usually round, dish for eating	
	the science or study of numbers or quantities	
	having only a short distance from side to side	
	a machine, device, or system that has been invented by someone	
	a building where collections of valuable objects are shown	
	to give an opinion based on the information you have	
	the feeling of being happy or satisfied	
	a container with a lid used for keeping food, etc	
	the building for the official organization to prevent crime	
	to become a member of a club or organization	
	a survey in which people are asked their opinions about something	

Hint
pollution   poll   jar   pleasure   more   join   narrow   mountain   police station
introduce   most   judge   interesting   museum   plate   pole   invention   mathematics

Review 8

B. Read and fill in the word and meaning.

word	definition	meaning
	not physically strong	
	the study of the physical world and natural laws	
	in the way that usual	
	a tool for cutting paper or fabric	
	number 1000	
	during the time that something is happening	
	to keep money instead of spending something	
	to speak very quietly	
	to hit somebody/something hard	
	used for predicting the future	
	wanting to drink	
	any of the four main periods of the year	
	having the knowledge or experience to make good decisions	
	the small hard part produced by a plant	
	grain plants that have been cut and dried	
	coming next after the first	
	having a larger distance between opposite sides than normal	
	unusual, especially in a way that is difficult to understand	

Hint

strike   thirsty   season   whisper   save   while   seed   thick   second
usually   strange   will   science   weak   scissors   thousand   straw   wise

Review 8

Unit 17

🎧 Listen and repeat. Track 49

01 advise [ædváiz]
v 충고하다, 조언하다   to tell somebody what you think they should do
I **advise** you not to smoke.
나는 담배 피지 말라는 충고를 할게.

02 artist [á:rtist]
n 미술가, 예술가   a person who creates works of art
Who is the most famous **artist**?
가장 유명한 예술가는 누구니?

03 attack [ətǽk]
n 공격 / v 공격하다   to use violence to try to hurt somebody
People fear that sharks will **attack** them.
사람들은 상어가 그들을 공격할까봐 두려워한다.

04 autumn [ɔ́:təm]
n 가을   the season of the year that comes between summer and winter
In **autumn** the leaves on the trees start to fall.
가을에는 나뭇잎들이 떨어지기 시작한다.

05 bat [bæt]
n 방망이, 박쥐   a piece of wood for hitting the ball in sports
She decided to buy a cricket **bat**.
그녀는 크리켓 방망이를 사려고 결심했다.

06 bathtub [bǽθtʌb]
n 욕조   a rectangular container which you fill with water
My mother is pouring water into a **bathtub**.
어머니께서 욕조에 물을 퍼붓고 계셔.

07 cart [ka:rt]
n 손수레, 카트   a light vehicle with wheels that you pull or push by hand
The shopping **cart** is near the gate.
쇼핑 카트가 입구 근처에 있다.

08 cartoon [ka:rtú:n]
n 만화   an amusing drawing in a newspaper or magazine
It was like a Warner Brothers **cartoon**.
그건 마치 워너 브라더스의 만화 같았어요.

09 cause [kɔ:z]
n 원인, 이유   the person or thing that makes something happen
The **cause** of the accident was engine failure.
그 사고의 원인은 엔진 고장이었다.

key words
violence n 폭력 / fear v 두려워하다 / pour v 쏟다, 퍼붓다 / amusing a 재미있는

🎧 Listen and repeat. (Track 50)

10 ceiling [síːliŋ] **n** 천장   the top inside surface of a room
His head touches the **ceiling**.
그의 머리는 천장에 닿는다.

11 century [séntʃuri] **n** 세기   a period of 100 years
It was built in the middle of the 8th **century**.
그것은 8세기 중반에 지어졌습니다.

12 channel [tʃǽnl] **n** 채널   a television station
In Korea, there are many television **channels**.
한국에는 많은 텔레비전 채널이 있다.

13 chop [tʃɑp] **v** 베다, 자르다   to cut something into pieces with knife, etc
Chop the onions up into small pieces.
양파를 작은 조각들로 자르세요.

14 cough [kɔ(ː)f] **n** 기침   to force air out of your throat with a sudden, harsh noise
This medicine will help your **cough**.
이 약을 먹으면 기침에 도움이 될 거예요.

15 couple [kʌ́pəl] **n** 한 쌍, 커플   two people or things
What will the **couple** do on the weekend?
커플이 주말에 하려는 것은 무엇인가?

16 coupon [kjúːpan] **n** 쿠폰, 우대권   a printed paper that you can exchange for something
I have a **coupon** for the movie.
나는 그 영화의 쿠폰을 갖고 있다.

17 course [kɔːrs] **n** 강의, 진로   a series of lessons
I plan to take a computer **course**.
나는 컴퓨터 강의를 수강할 계획이다.

18 crowd [kraud] **n** 군중   a large number of people gathered together in a public place
A **crowd** gathered around the winner.
군중이 승리자 주위로 모여들었다.

key words
harsh **a** 거친 / gather **v** 모이다

Exercise

A. Complete the sentence.

1. His head touches the _____.
   그의 머리는 천장에 닿는다.

2. Who is the most famous _____?
   가장 유명한 예술가는 누구니?

3. _____ the onions up into small pieces.
   양파를 작은 조각들로 자르세요.

4. In _____ the leaves on the trees start to fall.
   가을에는 나뭇잎들이 떨어지기 시작한다.

5. The shopping _____ is near the gate.
   쇼핑 카트가 입구 근처에 있다.

6. In Korea, there are many television _____.
   한국에는 많은 텔레비전 채널이 있다.

7. The _____ of the accident was engine failure.
   그 사고의 원인은 엔진 고장이었다.

8. A _____ gathered around the winner.
   군중이 승리자 주위로 모여들었다.

9. She decided to buy a cricket _____.
   그녀는 크리켓 방망이를 사려고 결심했다.

10. It was like a Warner Brothers _____.
    그건 마치 워너 브라더스의 만화 같았어요.

11. People fear that sharks will _____ them.
    사람들은 상어가 그들을 공격할까봐 두려워한다.

12. This medicine will help your _____.
    이 약을 먹으면 기침에 도움이 될 거예요.

13. It was built in the middle of the 8th _____.
    그것은 8세기 중반에 지어졌습니다.

14. What will the _____ do on the weekend?
    커플이 주말에 하려는 것은 무엇인가?

15. I have a _____ for the movie.
    나는 그 영화의 쿠폰을 갖고 있다.

16. I _____ you not to smoke.
    나는 담배 피우지 말라는 충고를 할게.

17. My mother is pouring water into a _____.
    어머니께서 욕조에 물을 퍼붓고 계셔.

18. I plan to take a computer _____.
    나는 컴퓨터 강의를 수강할 계획이다.

Hint

| cartoon | autumn | crowd | century | bat | ceiling | course | artist | cart |
| cause | chop | advise | couple | attack | coupon | bathtub | channel | cough |

Exercise

B. Fill in the word and meaning.

	Word	Meaning
01	bat	
02	advise	
03	century	
04	cart	
05	channel	
06	artist	
07	cough	
08	cartoon	
09	course	
10	chop	
11	crowd	
12	autumn	
13	coupon	
14	cause	
15	couple	
16	bathtub	
17	ceiling	
18	attack	

	Meaning	Word
01	충고하다, 조언하다	
02	미술가, 예술가	
03	공격, 공격하다	
04	가을	
05	방망이, 박쥐	
06	욕조	
07	손수레, 카트	
08	만화	
09	원인, 이유	
10	천장	
11	세기	
12	채널	
13	베다, 자르다	
14	기침	
15	한 쌍, 커플	
16	쿠폰, 우대권	
17	강의, 진로	
18	군중	

C. Listen, write the word and meaning. (Track 51)

	Word	Meaning		Word	Meaning
01			10		
02			11		
03			12		
04			13		
05			14		
06			15		
07			16		
08			17		
09			18		

Unit 18

🎧 Listen and repeat. Track 52

01 dull
[dʌl]
a 둔한, 무딘   slow in understanding
I always find Mrs. Smith **dull**.
스미스 부인은 언제 보아도 우둔하다.

02 during
[djúəriŋ]
prep ~동안에   all through a period of time
I have been following you **during** this camping trip.
난 이 캠핑 여행 동안에 너를 따라다녔다.

03 earth
[əːrθ]
n 지구   the planet that we live on
Which one is bigger, the sun or the **earth**?
태양과 지구 중에 어느 것이 더 클까?

04 either
[íːðər]
pron (둘 중) 어느 한쪽   one or the other of two
Either of you is right.
너희 둘 중 어느 한 쪽이 옳다.

05 electricity
[ilèktrísəti]
n 전기   a form of energy that is used for heating and lighting
This radio is run by **electricity**.
이 라디오는 전기로 작동된다.

06 expression
[ikspréʃən]
n 표현, 표정   the look on a person's face that shows a feeling
The facial **expression** can show a lot of things.
얼굴 표정은 많은 것을 말해준다.

07 fare
[fɛər]
n 운임, 통행료   the money that you pay to travel
The taxi driver is waiting for his **fare**.
택시 운전사가 요금을 받으려고 기다리고 있다.

08 fashion
[fǽʃən]
n 유행, 방식   a popular way of behaving
I don't know the latest **fashions**.
난 최근 유행에 대해선 잘 모른다.

09 fault
[fɔːlt]
n 과실, 잘못   a mistake in what someone is doing
No one is free from **fault**.
잘못이 없는 사람은 없다.

key words
run v 움직이다, 작동하다 / facial a 얼굴의 / latest a 최신의

🎧 Listen and repeat. Track 53

10 favorite [féivərit]
a 좋아하는   liked more than others of the same kind
Soccer is my **favorite** sport.
축구가 내가 가장 좋아하는 운동이야.

11 feed [fi:d]
v (음식을) 먹이다   to give food to a person or an animal
I **feed** them one loaf of bread.
난 그들에게 빵 한 덩어리를 먹여요.

12 fever [fí:vər]
n 열   a condition to have a temperature that is higher than normal
He has a high **fever**.
그는 고열이 있다.

13 glue [glu:]
n 접착제 / v 접착하다   a thick sticky liquid that is used for joining things
You can make **glue** from flour and water.
밀가루와 물로 접착제를 만들 수 있어요.

14 grade [greid]
n 학년, 등급   one of the levels in a school with children of similar age
She is in the third **grade** in our school.
그녀는 우리 학교에서 3학년이다.

15 grand [grænd]
a 웅대한, 당당한   impressive and large or important
They are **grand** and even beautiful.
그것들은 웅장하고 아름답기까지 하다.

16 greeting [grí:tiŋ]
n 인사, 인사말   the first words you say when you meet somebody
'Hello' and 'Hi' are informal **greetings**.
'핼로우'와 '하이'는 격식을 차리지 않는 인사말이다.

17 group [gru:p]
n 집단   a number of people or things that are connected in some way
People of many different social **groups** are coming together.
많은 다른 사회적 집단의 사람들이 함께 모이고 있다.

18 guess [ges]
v 추측하다   to find the right answer to a question
I can't **guess** his age.
나는 그의 나이를 추측할 수 없다.

key words
loaf n 덩어리 / condition n 상태 / sticky a 끈적한, 점착성의
flour n 밀가루, 분말 / impressive a 인상에 남는 / informal a 격식 차리지 않는

Unit 18

Exercise

A. Complete the sentence.

1. _____ of you is right.
   너희 둘 중 어느 한 쪽이 옳다.

2. You can make _____ from flour and water.
   밀가루와 물로 접착제를 만들 수 있어요.

3. I have been following you _____ this camping trip.
   난 이 캠핑 여행 동안에 너를 따라다녔다.

4. This radio is run by _____.
   이 라디오는 전기로 작동된다.

5. I always find Mrs. Smith _____.
   스미스 부인은 언제 보아도 우둔하다.

6. The taxi driver is waiting for his _____.
   택시 운전사가 요금을 받으려고 기다리고 있다.

7. 'Hello' and 'Hi' are informal _____.
   '헬로우'와 '하이'는 격식을 차리지 않는 인사말이다.

8. I don't know the latest _____.
   난 최근 유행에 대해선 잘 모른다.

9. People of many different social _____ are coming together.
   많은 다른 사회적 집단의 사람들이 함께 모이고 있다.

10. No one is free from _____.
    잘못이 없는 사람은 없다.

11. They are _____ and even beautiful.
    그것들은 웅장하고 아름답기까지 하다.

12. The facial _____ can show a lot of things.
    얼굴 표정은 많은 것을 말해준다.

13. Soccer is my _____ sport.
    축구가 내가 가장 좋아하는 운동이야.

14. I can't _____ his age.
    나는 그의 나이를 추측할 수 없다.

15. I _____ them one loaf of bread.
    난 그들에게 빵 한 덩어리를 먹여요.

16. Which one is bigger, the sun or the _____?
    태양과 지구 중에 어느 것이 더 클까?

17. He has a high _____.
    그는 고열이 있다.

18. She is in the third _____ in our school.
    그녀는 우리 학교에서 3학년이다.

Hint

| fashion | guess | fever | fare | during | fault | grade | expression | grand |
| glue | dull | group | feed | earth | either | favorite | electricity | greeting |

Exercise

B. Fill in the word and meaning.

	Word	Meaning
01	electricity	
02	fault	
03	glue	
04	during	
05	fever	
06	fare	
07	greeting	
08	dull	
09	favorite	
10	group	
11	earth	
12	feed	
13	guess	
14	expression	
15	grand	
16	fashion	
17	grade	
18	either	

	Meaning	Word
01	둔한, 무딘	
02	~ 동안에	
03	지구	
04	(둘 중) 어느 한쪽	
05	전기	
06	표현, 표정	
07	운임, 통행료	
08	유행, 방식	
09	과실, 잘못	
10	좋아하는	
11	(음식을) 먹이다	
12	열	
13	접착제, 접착하다	
14	학년, 등급	
15	웅대한, 당당한	
16	인사, 인사말	
17	집단	
18	추측하다	

🎧 C. Listen, write the word and meaning. (Track 54)

	Word	Meaning		Word	Meaning
01			10		
02			11		
03			12		
04			13		
05			14		
06			15		
07			16		
08			17		
09			18		

Unit 18

Review 9

A. Read and fill in the word and meaning.

word	definition	meaning
	to cut something into pieces with knife, etc	
	two people or things	
	a period of 100 years	
	to force air out of your throat with a sudden, harsh noise	
	a television station	
	to tell somebody what you think they should do	
	the top inside surface of a room	
	a large number of people gathered together in a public place	
	a printed paper that you can exchange for something	
	the person or thing that makes something happen	
	a rectangular container which you fill with water	
	a person who creates works of art	
	a light vehicle with wheels that you pull or push by hand	
	a series of lessons	
	to use violence to try to hurt somebody	
	an amusing drawing in a newspaper or magazine	
	a piece of wood for hitting the ball in sports	
	the season of the year between summer and winter	

Hint
cartoon   autumn   crowd   century   bat   ceiling   course   artist   cart
cause   chop   advise   couple   attack   coupon   bathtub   channel   cough

B. Read and fill in the word and meaning.

word	definition	meaning
feed	to give food to a person or an animal	
dull	slow in understanding	
fever	a condition to have a temperature that is higher than normal	
earth	the planet that we live on	
glue	a thick sticky liquid that is used for joining things	
during	all through a period of time	
grade	one of the levels in a school with children of similar age	
expression	the look on a person's face that shows a feeling	
fare	the money that you pay to travel	
group	a number of people or things that are connected in some way	
grand	impressive and large or important	
either	one or the other of two	
fashion	a popular way of behaving	
guess	to find the right answer to a question	
electricity	a form of energy that is used for heating and lighting	
fault	a mistake in what someone is doing	
favorite	liked more than others of the same kind	
greeting	the first words you say when you meet somebody	

Hint
fashion guess fever fare during fault grade expression grand
glue dull group feed earth either favorite electricity greeting

Unit 19

🎧 Listen and repeat. Track 55

01 leadership [líːdərʃip]
n 지도(력), 지휘   the qualities that a leader should have
She has got good **leadership**.
그녀는 뛰어난 지도 능력을 가지고 있어.

02 language [lǽŋgwidʒ]
n 언어   the system of communication in speech and writing
We express our thoughts through **language**.
우리는 사상을 언어로 표현한다.

03 lie [lai]
v 드러눕다   to be yourself in a flat position
I need to **lie** down for a few minutes.
잠깐 누워 있어야겠다.

04 lilac [láilək]
n 라일락   a small tree which has sweet-smelling purple or white flowers
The garden smells of **lilacs**.
정원에는 라일락 꽃 향기가 풍긴다.

05 loud [laud]
a 시끄러운   making a lot of noise
There were people who played **loud** music, and danced.
시끄러운 음악을 틀고 춤을 추는 사람들이 있었다.

06 luck [lʌk]
n 행운, 운   good things that happen to you by chance
The jealous man decided to try out his **luck**.
그 질투심 많은 사람은 자신의 운을 시험해 보기로 결심했다.

07 necklace [néklis]
n 목걸이   a jewellery consisting of a chain, string of beads, etc.
They gave 100 dollars for the **necklace**.
그들은 그 목걸이를 사는 데 100달러를 지불했다.

08 neighbor [néibər]
n 이웃사람   a person who lives near you
My **neighbors** are very friendly.
내 이웃들은 매우 호의적이다.

09 nobody [nóubàdi]
pron 아무도 ~않다   not a single person of a particular group
Nobody wants to be my friend.
아무도 나랑 친구 되기를 원하지 않아요.

---

key words
speech n 말 / jealous a 질투심이 많은 / consist v 이루어져 있다 / bead n 구슬

🎧 Listen and repeat. Track 56

10 noise
[nɔiz]
n 소리, 소음   a loud or unpleasant sound
Do not make **noise**.
시끄럽게 하지마라.

11 novel
[návəl]
n 소설   a long written story about imaginary people and events
The **novel** is about an evil king.
그 소설은 어떤 나쁜 왕에 관한 것이다.

12 office
[ɔ́(ː)fis]
n 사무실, 임무   a room where people work
The principal's **office** is on the second floor.
교장실은 2층에 있습니다.

13 pot
[pat]
n 그릇, 단지   a deep round container used for cooking
Put the honey into the **pot**.
꿀을 단지 속에 넣으세요.

14 powder
[páudər]
n 가루, 분말   a dry mass of very small fine pieces
Put two spoons of **powder** in warm water.
가루 두 스푼을 따뜻한 물에 넣으세요.

15 power
[páuər]
n 힘, 능력   the ability to do something
We are afraid of his **power**.
우리는 그의 힘을 두려워한다.

16 present
[prézənt]
n 선물   a thing that you give to somebody as a gift
The girl is wrapping a **present**.
소녀가 선물을 포장하고 있다.

17 president
[prézidənt]
n 대통령, 장   the leader of a republic
Did the first **president** live there?
초대 대통령이 그곳에 살았니?

18 price
[prais]
n 가격   the amount of money that you have to pay for something
The store raised the **price** of fruit.
그 가게는 과일값을 올렸다.

---

key words
imaginary **a** 상상의 / principal **n** 장, 교장 / wrap **v** 싸다, 포장하다 / leader **n** 선도자, 지도자

Exercise

A. Complete the sentence.

1. She has got good _____.
   그녀는 뛰어난 지도 능력을 가지고 있어.

2. My _____ are very friendly.
   내 이웃들은 매우 호의적이다.

3. The garden smells of _____.
   정원에는 라일락 꽃 향기가 풍긴다.

4. We are afraid of his _____.
   우리는 그의 힘을 두려워한다.

5. There were people who played _____ music, and danced.
   시끄러운 음악을 틀고 춤을 추는 사람들이 있었다.

6. Put two spoons of _____ in warm water.
   가루 두 스푼을 따뜻한 물에 넣으세요.

7. The jealous man decided to try out his _____.
   그 질투심 많은 사람은 자신의 운을 시험해 보기로 결심했다.

8. Did the first _____ live there?
   초대 대통령이 그곳에 살았니?

9. They gave 100 dollars for the _____.
   그들은 그 목걸이를 사는 데 100달러를 지불했다.

10. The girl is wrapping a _____.
    소녀가 선물을 포장하고 있다.

11. I need to _____ down for a few minutes.
    잠깐 누워 있어야겠다.

12. Do not make _____.
    시끄럽게 하지 마라.

13. The _____ is about an evil king.
    그 소설은 어떤 나쁜 왕에 관한 것이다.

14. The store raised the _____ of fruit.
    그 가게는 과일 값을 올렸다.

15. We express our thoughts through _____.
    우리는 사상을 언어로 표현한다.

16. The principal's _____ is on the second floor.
    교장실은 2층에 있습니다.

17. _____ wants to be my friend.
    아무도 나랑 친구 되기를 원하지 않아요.

18. Put the honey into the _____.
    꿀을 단지 속에 넣으세요.

Hint

| president | necklace | lie | office | nobody | loud | novel | power | leadership |
| language | powder | noise | luck | price | lilac | neighbor | pot | present |

Exercise

B. Fill in the word and meaning.

	Word	Meaning
01	necklace	
02	lie	
03	nobody	
04	office	
05	powder	
06	leadership	
07	power	
08	language	
09	price	
10	neighbor	
11	president	
12	lilac	
13	noise	
14	present	
15	luck	
16	pot	
17	novel	
18	loud	

	Meaning	Word
01	지도(력), 지휘	
02	언어	
03	드러눕다	
04	라일락	
05	시끄러운	
06	행운, 운	
07	목걸이	
08	이웃사람	
09	아무도 ~않다	
10	소리, 소음	
11	소설	
12	사무실, 임무	
13	그릇, 단지	
14	가루, 분말	
15	힘, 능력	
16	선물	
17	대통령, 장	
18	가격	

C. Listen, write the word and meaning. (Track 57)

	Word	Meaning
01		
02		
03		
04		
05		
06		
07		
08		
09		

	Word	Meaning
10		
11		
12		
13		
14		
15		
16		
17		
18		

Unit 20

🎧 Listen and repeat. Track 58

01 scientist [sáiəntist]
n 과학자 a person who studies the natural sciences
It was written by a famous computer **scientist**.
이 책은 유명한 컴퓨터 과학자가 썼어요.

02 series [síəri:z]
n 시리즈, 연속 several events of a similar kind
What is the theme of the **series**?
그 시리즈의 주제는 뭡니까?

03 shape [ʃeip]
n 모양, 형상 the form of the surfaces of something
In **shape** and size, the lion and the cat are very different.
모양과 크기 면에서, 사자와 고양이는 매우 다르다.

04 sharp [ʃa:rp]
a 날카로운 having a fine edge that can cut something
Don't touch **sharp** knives!
날카로운 칼에 손대지 마세요!

05 shock [ʃak]
v 깜짝 놀라게 하다 to surprise and upset somebody
His bad language **shocked** everyone there.
그의 못된 말은 거기 있던 모든 사람을 깜짝 놀라게 했다.

06 shout [ʃaut]
v 소리치다 to say something in a loud voice
She **shouted** to warn me.
그녀는 나에게 경고하려고 소리쳤다.

07 stupid [stjú:pid]
a 어리석은 showing a lack of thought
Ben is so **stupid** that he can't understand.
벤은 그것을 이해하지 못 할 만큼 어리석다.

08 sure [ʃuər]
a 확신하고 있는 confident that you know something
The policeman wasn't **sure** if he could catch a thief.
경찰은 도둑을 잡을 수 있을 지 확신할 수 없었다.

09 symbol [símbəl]
n 상징, 기호 a person or an object that represents a more general quality
The cross is the **symbol** of Christianity.
십자가는 그리스도교의 상징이다.

key words
warn v 경고하다 / lack n 부족 / confident a 확신하는 / represent v 표시하다 / Christianity n 기독교

🎧 Listen and repeat. Track 59

10 temple
[témpəl]
n 절, 신전   a building used for the worship of a god
What do you think the most typical Korean **temple** is?
가장 대표적인 한국의 절은 무엇이라고 생각하니?

11 terrible
[térəbəl]
a 심한, 지독한   used to show the degree of something bad
A girl had a **terrible** toothache.
한 소녀가 심한 치통을 앓았다.

12 text
[tekst]
n 본문, 원문   the written form of a speech, interview, etc
He printed the complete **text** of the interview.
그는 인터뷰의 전체 원문을 인쇄했다.

13 wish
[wiʃ]
v 바라다   to want something to happen
I **wish** I could meet more people.
나는 더 많은 사람들을 만나길 바랍니다.

14 wonder
[wʌ́ndəːr]
v 의아하게 여기다   to be very surprised by something
I **wondered** why he had done that.
그가 왜 그런 짓을 했는지 의아했다.

15 worry
[wə́ːri]
v 걱정하다   to keep thinking about problems that you have
A girl is **worrying** about her grandmother.
한 소녀가 할머니를 걱정하고 있습니다.

16 write
[rait]
v 쓰다   to make letters on a surface using a pen or pencil
It's a little difficult to read and **write**.
그건 읽고 쓰기가 좀 어려워요.

17 wrong
[rɔːŋ]
a 잘못된, 틀린   not right or correct
Something is **wrong** with the telephone.
전화기가 어딘지 이상해요.

18 yet
[jet]
ad 아직 ~않다   something that has not happened but you expect
The work is not **yet** finished.
일은 아직 끝나지 않았다.

key words
worship n 예배 / typical a 전형적인, 대표적인 / toothache n 치통

Unit 20 101

Exercise

A. Complete the sentence.

1. What is the theme of the _____?
   그 시리즈의 주제는 뭡니까?

2. The work is not _____ finished.
   일은 아직 끝나지 않았다.

3. In _____ and size, the lion and the cat are very different.
   모양과 크기 면에서, 사자와 고양이는 매우 다르다.

4. Don't touch _____ knives!
   날카로운 칼에 손대지 마세요!

5. I _____ I could meet more people.
   나는 더 많은 사람들을 만나길 바랍니다.

6. His bad language _____ everyone there.
   그의 못된 말은 거기 있던 모든 사람을 깜짝 놀라게 했다.

7. Something is _____ with the telephone.
   전화기가 어딘지 이상해요.

8. She _____ to warn me.
   그녀는 나에게 경고하려고 소리쳤다.

9. A girl is _____ about her grandmother.
   한 소녀가 할머니를 걱정하고 있습니다.

10. Ben is so _____ that he can't understand.
    벤은 그것을 이해하지 못 할 만큼 어리석다.

11. A girl had a _____ toothache.
    한 소녀가 심한 치통을 앓았다.

12. The policeman wasn't _____ if he could catch a thief.
    경찰은 도둑을 잡을 수 있을 지 확신할 수 없었다.

13. He printed the complete _____ of the interview.
    그는 인터뷰의 전체 원문을 인쇄했다.

14. The cross is the _____ of Christianity.
    십자가는 그리스도교의 상징이다.

15. What do you think the most typical Korean _____ is?
    가장 대표적인 한국의 절은 무엇이라고 생각하니?

16. I _____ why he had done that.
    그가 왜 그런 짓을 했는지 의아했다.

17. It was written by a famous computer _____.
    이 책은 유명한 컴퓨터 과학자가 썼어요.

18. It's a little difficult to read and _____.
    그건 읽고 쓰기가 좀 어려워요.

Hint

| sharp | yet | stupid | temple | wonder | scientist | shout | worry | terrible |
| shape | symbol | write | series | wrong | shock | text | sure | wish |

Exercise

B. Fill in the word and meaning.

	Word	Meaning
01	series	
02	temple	
03	wish	
04	shape	
05	wonder	
06	symbol	
07	wrong	
08	scientist	
09	text	
10	stupid	
11	yet	
12	sharp	
13	write	
14	sure	
15	worry	
16	shock	
17	terrible	
18	shout	

	Meaning	Word
01	과학자	
02	시리즈, 연속	
03	모양, 형상	
04	날카로운	
05	깜짝 놀라게 하다	
06	소리치다	
07	어리석은	
08	확신하고 있는	
09	상징, 기호	
10	절, 신전	
11	심한, 지독한	
12	본문, 원문	
13	바라다	
14	의아하게 여기다	
15	걱정하다	
16	쓰다	
17	잘못된, 틀린	
18	아직 ~않다	

C. Listen, write the word and meaning. (Track 60)

	Word	Meaning		Word	Meaning
01			10		
02			11		
03			12		
04			13		
05			14		
06			15		
07			16		
08			17		
09			18		

Review 10

A. Read and fill in the word and meaning.

word	definition	meaning
	a person who lives near you	
	good things that happen to you by chance	
	the amount of money that you have to pay for something	
	the qualities that a leader should have	
	a jewellery consisting of a chain, string of beads, etc.	
	the leader of a republic	
	not a single person of a particular group	
	a thing that you give to somebody as a gift	
	the system of communication in speech and writing	
	a loud or unpleasant sound	
	a deep round container used for cooking	
	the ability to do something	
	to be yourself in a flat position	
	a long written story about imaginary people and events	
	making a lot of noise	
	a room where people work	
	a small tree which has sweet-smelling purple or white flowers	
	a dry mass of very small fine pieces	

Hint
president necklace lie office nobody loud novel power leadership
language powder noise luck price lilac neighbor pot present

B. Read and fill in the word and meaning.

word	definition	meaning
	a person who studies the natural sciences	
	a person or an object that represents a more general quality	
	a building used for the worship of a god	
	to want something to happen	
	several events of a similar kind	
	used to show the degree of something bad	
	the form of the surfaces of something	
	confident that you know something	
	the written form of a speech, interview, etc	
	having a fine edge that can cut something	
	to be very surprised by something	
	showing a lack of thought	
	to surprise and upset somebody	
	something that has not happened but you expect	
	to keep thinking about problems that you have	
	not right or correct	
	to say something in a loud voice	
	to make letters on a surface using a pen or pencil	

Hint
sharp yet stupid temple wonder scientist shout worry terrible
shape symbol write series wrong shock text sure wish

Unit 21

🎧 Listen and repeat. (Track 61)

01 abroad
[əbrɔ́ːd]
ad 외국으로   to a foreign country
I'm reading an e-mail from **abroad**.
외국에서 온 이메일을 읽고 있어.

02 actor
[ǽktər]
n 배우   a man or woman whose job is to act in a play, film
Who is the most popular **actor** in this country?
이 나라에서 가장 인기 있는 배우는 누구입니까?

03 add
[æd]
v 더하다, 추가하다   to put something together with something else
You can **add** salt to it.
여러분은 여기에 소금을 추가 할 수 있다.

04 art
[aːrt]
n 예술, 미술   the imagination to express ideas or feeling
I'm interested in modern **art**.
나는 현대 미술에 관심 있다.

05 avoid
[əvɔ́id]
v 피하다, 막다   to keep away from somebody / something
I try to **avoid** junk food.
건강에 해로운 음식은 피하려고 노력하는 편입니다.

06 bend
[bend]
v 굽히다, 구부리다   to make something that was straight into a curved
Bend over and touch the floor.
몸을 구부려서 바닥을 만지세요.

07 best
[best]
a 최고의, 최상의   of the most excellent quality
Now I have the **best** garden in the world.
이제 내가 세상에서 제일 멋진 정원을 가지고 있다.

08 bit
[bit]
n 소량, 조금   a small amount of something
The ants ate up the cookie **bit** by **bit**.
개미는 그 과자를 조금씩 갉아 먹었다.

09 bite
[bait]
n 물린 상처 / **v** 물다   to use your teeth to cut into
The tiger **bit** off a piece of meat.
호랑이가 고기를 한 조각 물어뜯었다.

key words
imagination n 창작(품), 구상 / modern a 현대의 / junk n 쓰레기 / excellent a 우수한

🎧 Listen and repeat. Track 62

10 blind
[blaind]
a 눈 먼　not able to see
Helen Keller spent her life helping the **blind**.
Helen Keller는 한평생 맹인들을 돌보면서 지냈다.

11 bomb
[bam]
n 폭탄 / **v** 폭격하다　a device which explodes and damages or destroys a large area
He dropped **bombs** on a city.
그는 도시에 폭탄을 던졌다.

12 bow
[bau]
v 고개를 숙이다　to move your head forwards and downwards
Koreans **bow** to each other when they meet.
한국인은 만날 때 머리 숙여 인사한다.

13 cartoonist
[ka:rtú:nist]
n 만화가　a person who draws cartoons
My dream is to become a popular **cartoonist**.
나의 꿈은 인기 있는 만화가가 되는 거야.

14 chapter
[tʃǽptər]
n (책, 논문의) 장　one of the parts into which a book is divided
Please read **Chapter** 2 of the book for homework.
숙제로 책의 2장을 읽어오세요.

15 chew
[tʃu:]
v 씹다　to use your teeth to break food up in your mouth
Tender meat is easy to **chew**.
연한 고기는 씹기 쉽다.

16 chief
[tʃi:f]
a 주요한　most important; main
His **chief** merit is kindness.
그의 주요한 장점은 친절이다.

17 chimney
[tʃímni]
n 굴뚝　a pipe through which smoke goes up into the air
Smoke is rising from a **chimney**.
굴뚝에서 연기가 나고 있어.

18 chip
[tʃip]
n 토막, 얇은 조각　a small piece which has been broken off something
Wood **chips** covered the floor of the workshop.
작업장의 바닥은 부서진 나무 조각들로 덮여 있었다.

key words
device **n** 장치 / destroy **v** 파괴하다 / popular **a** 인기 있는
tender **a** 부드러운 / merit **n** 장점 / workshop **n** 작업장

Exercise

A. Complete the sentence.

1. Helen Keller spent her life helping the _____.
   Helen Keller는 한평생 맹인들을 돌보면서 지냈다.

2. Who is the most popular _____ in this country?
   이 나라에서 가장 인기 있는 배우는 누구입니까?

3. The tiger _____ off a piece of meat.
   호랑이가 고기를 한 조각 물어뜯었다.

4. Smoke is rising from a _____.
   굴뚝에서 연기가 나고 있어.

5. I'm interested in modern _____.
   나는 현대 미술에 관심 있다.

6. Please read _____ 2 of the book for homework.
   숙제로 책의 2장을 읽어오세요.

7. I try to _____ junk food.
   건강에 해로운 음식은 피하려고 노력하는 편입니다.

8. _____ over and touch the floor.
   몸을 구부려서 바닥을 만지세요.

9. My dream is to become a popular _____.
   나의 꿈은 인기 있는 만화가가 되는 거야.

10. The ants ate up the cookie _____ by _____.
    개미는 그 과자를 조금씩 갉아 먹었다.

11. His _____ merit is kindness.
    그의 주요한 장점은 친절이다.

12. He dropped _____ on a city.
    그는 도시에 폭탄을 던졌다.

13. I'm reading an e-mail from _____.
    외국에서 온 이메일을 읽고 있어.

14. Koreans _____ to each other when they meet.
    한국인은 만날 때 머리 숙여 인사한다.

15. You can _____ salt to it.
    여러분은 여기에 소금을 추가 할 수 있다.

16. Tender meat is easy to _____.
    연한 고기는 씹기 쉽다.

17. Now I have the _____ garden in the world.
    이제 내가 세상에서 제일 멋진 정원을 가지고 있다.

18. Wood _____ covered the floor of the workshop.
    작업장의 바닥은 부서진 나무 조각들로 덮여 있었다.

Hint

| cartoonist | bend | art | bite | bow | actor | chimney | blind | avoid |
| chapter | bit | abroad | chip | add | chief | best | chew | bomb |

Exercise

B. Fill in the word and meaning.

	Word	Meaning
01	bend	
02	chimney	
03	bite	
04	abroad	
05	best	
06	chapter	
07	actor	
08	bit	
09	chew	
10	chip	
11	add	
12	blind	
13	chief	
14	bomb	
15	cartoonist	
16	avoid	
17	bow	
18	art	

	Meaning	Word
01	외국으로	
02	배우	
03	더하다, 추가하다	
04	예술, 미술	
05	피하다, 막다	
06	굽히다, 구부리다	
07	최고의, 최상의	
08	소량, 조금	
09	물린 상처, 물다	
10	눈 먼	
11	폭탄, 폭격하다	
12	고개를 숙이다	
13	만화가	
14	(책, 논문의) 장	
15	씹다	
16	주요한	
17	굴뚝	
18	토막, 얇은 조각	

🎧 C. Listen, write the word and meaning. (Track 63)

	Word	Meaning		Word	Meaning
01			10		
02			11		
03			12		
04			13		
05			14		
06			15		
07			16		
08			17		
09			18		

Unit 21

Unit 22

🎧 Listen and repeat. Track 64

01 couch
[kautʃ]
n 침상, 소파   a comfortable seat for the people to sit on
They're using a car to move a **couch**.
그들은 차를 사용하여 소파를 옮기고 있다.

02 couple
[kʌ́pəl]
n 한 쌍, 둘   two people or things
The **couple** is cooking hamburgers.
그 커플은 햄버거를 요리하고 있다.

03 courageous
[kəréidʒəs]
a 용기 있는, 용감한   having the ability to control fear in a dangerous situation
She was **courageous** in spite of her long illness.
그녀는 오랫동안 앓은 병에도 불구하고 용기 있었다.

04 court
[kɔːrt]
n 법정, 안뜰   a place where legal matters are decided by a judge
The powers of the **courts** are defined by law.
법원의 권한은 법으로 규정되어 있다.

05 crab
[kræb]
n 게   a sea creature with a hard shell, eight legs and two pincers
I want to eat a king **crab**, right now.
난 지금 당장 대게가 먹고 싶어.

06 crocodile
[krákədàil]
n 악어   a large reptile with a long body and strong jaws
Are there many **crocodiles** around here?
이 근처에 악어가 많습니까?

07 download
[dáunlòud]
v 다운로드하다   to move data to a smaller computer from a larger one
You can **download** programs.
프로그램을 다운로드 받을 수 있다.

08 drain
[drein]
n 배수, 배수관   a pipe that carries away dirty water
The **drain** is completely stopped up.
그 배수관은 아주 꽉 막혔어.

09 duty
[djúːti]
n 의무   something that you feel you have to do
Every citizen has civil rights and **duties**.
모든 시민은 시민의 권리와 의무를 갖고 있다.

key words
in spite of ~에도 불구하고 / legal **a** 법률의 / judge **n** 재판관
define **v** 규정짓다 / pincers **n** 집게발 / reptile **n** 파충류 / civil **a** 시민의

🎧 Listen and repeat. Track 65

10 dye [dai]
v 염색하다   to change the color of something
My grandmother is **dyeing** her hair black.
할머니께서는 검게 머리 염색을 하고 계세요.

11 eager [íːgər]
a 간절히 바라는   full of desire or interest
She was very **eager** to meet me.
그녀는 나를 간절히 만나고 싶어 했다.

12 edge [edʒ]
n 가장자리, 모서리   the outside limit of an object
The man is taping the **edge** of a piece of glass.
남자가 유리의 가장자리를 테이프로 붙이고 있다.

13 fume [fjuːm]
v 노발대발하다 / n 증기   to be very angry about something
I sometimes **fume** at waiters.
나는 가끔 웨이터들에게 심하게 화를 낸다.

14 furniture [fə́ːrnitʃəːr]
n 가구   the things that can be moved in a room, house or office
She likes to buy antique **furniture**.
그녀는 고풍스러운 가구를 사는 것을 좋아해.

15 gain [gein]
v 얻다, 늘리다   to obtain something that you want
He **gained** everlasting fame.
그는 불후의 명성을 얻었다.

16 gallery [gǽləri]
n 화랑, 미술관   a room for showing works of art
I have wanted to visit the **gallery** for a long time.
나는 오랫동안 그 미술관을 방문하기를 원해 왔다.

17 garage [gərάːʒ]
n 차고   a building for keeping cars
The car I rented is parked in the hotel **garage**.
제가 빌린 차는 지금 호텔 주차장에 있습니다.

18 include [inklúːd]
v 포함하다   to have as one part; to contain
The package **includes** a book of instructions.
그 꾸러미는 설명서를 포함하고 있다.

key words
everlasting a 불후의 / fame n 명성 / rent v 빌리다 / park v 주차하다 / contain v 가지다, 포함하다

Exercise

A. Complete the sentence.

1. She was very _____ to meet me.
   그녀는 나를 간절히 만나고 싶어 했다.
2. They're using a car to move a _____.
   그들은 차를 사용하여 소파를 옮기고 있다.
3. He _____ everlasting fame.
   그는 불후의 명성을 얻었다.
4. She was _____ in spite of her long illness.
   그녀는 오랫동안 앓은 병에도 불구하고 용기 있었다.
5. You can _____ programs.
   프로그램을 다운로드 받을 수 있다.
6. Are there many _____ around here?
   이 근처에 악어가 많습니까?
7. The _____ is completely stopped up.
   그 배수관은 아주 꽉 막혔어.
8. I sometimes _____ at waiters.
   나는 가끔 웨이터들에게 심하게 화를 낸다.
9. I want to eat a king _____, right now.
   난 지금 당장 대게가 먹고 싶어.
10. The man is taping the _____ of a piece of glass.
    남자가 유리의 가장자리를 테이프로 붙이고 있다.
11. The powers of the _____ are defined by law.
    법원의 권한은 법으로 규정되어 있다.
12. She likes to buy antique _____.
    그녀는 고풍스러운 가구를 사는 것을 좋아해.
13. The _____ is cooking hamburgers.
    그 커플은 햄버거를 요리하고 있다.
14. My grandmother is _____ her hair black.
    할머니께서는 검게 머리 염색을 하고 계세요.
15. I have wanted to visit the _____ for a long time.
    나는 오랫동안 그 미술관을 방문하기를 원해 왔다.
16. Every citizen has civil rights and _____.
    모든 시민은 시민의 권리와 의무를 갖고 있다.
17. The car I rented is parked in the hotel _____.
    제가 빌린 차는 지금 호텔 주차장에 있습니다.
18. The package _____ a book of instructions.
    그 꾸러미는 설명서를 포함하고 있다.

Hint

| crocodile | gallery | couple | fume | dye | crab | include | edge | courageous |
| download | eager | garage | duty | couch | furniture | court | drain | gain |

Exercise

B. Fill in the word and meaning.

	Word	Meaning
01	download	
02	furniture	
03	couple	
04	drain	
05	gain	
06	courageous	
07	include	
08	garage	
09	court	
10	duty	
11	eager	
12	crab	
13	dye	
14	gallery	
15	crocodile	
16	edge	
17	fume	
18	couch	

	Meaning	Word
01	침상, 소파	
02	한 쌍, 둘	
03	용기 있는, 용감한	
04	법정, 안뜰	
05	게	
06	악어	
07	다운로드하다	
08	배수, 배수관	
09	의무	
10	염색하다	
11	간절히 바라는	
12	가장자리, 모서리	
13	노발대발하다, 증기	
14	가구	
15	얻다, 늘리다	
16	화랑, 미술관	
17	차고	
18	포함하다	

C. Listen, write the word and meaning. (Track 66)

	Word	Meaning		Word	Meaning
01			10		
02			11		
03			12		
04			13		
05			14		
06			15		
07			16		
08			17		
09			18		

Unit 22

Review 11

A. Read and fill in the word and meaning.

word	definition	meaning
	a person who draws cartoons	
	to make something that was straight into a curved	
	one of the parts into which a book is divided	
	to keep away from somebody/something	
	to use your teeth to cut into	
	the imagination to express ideas or feeling	
	of the most excellent quality	
	to move your head forwards and downwards	
	to a foreign country	
	to use your teeth to break food up in your mouth	
	a small amount of something	
	a pipe through which smoke goes up into the air	
	a man or woman whose job is to act in a play, film	
	not able to see	
	most important; main	
	to put something together with something else	
	a small piece which has been broken off something	
	a device which explodes and damages or destroys a large area	

Hint

cartoonist   bend   art   bite   bow   actor   chimney   blind   avoid
chapter   bit   abroad   chip   add   chief   best   chew   bomb

 Review 11

B. Read and fill in the word and meaning.

word	definition	meaning
garage	a building for keeping cars	
couch	a comfortable seat for the people to sit on	
gain	to obtain something that you want	
furniture	the things that can be moved in a room, house or office	
gallery	a room for showing works of art	
couple	two people or things	
include	to have as one part; to contain	
courageous	having the ability to control fear in a dangerous situation	
duty	something that you feel you have to do	
eager	full of desire or interest	
court	a place where legal matters are decided by a judge	
dye	to change the color of something	
download	to move data to a smaller computer from a larger one	
edge	the outside limit of an object	
crab	a sea creature with a hard shell, eight legs and two pincers	
fume	to be very angry about something	
drain	a pipe that carries away dirty water	
crocodile	a large reptile with a long body and strong jaws	

Hint

crocodile gallery couple fume dye crab include edge courageous
download eager garage duty couch furniture court drain gain

Unit 23

🎧 Listen and repeat. (Track 67)

01 information
[ìnfərméiʃən]

n 정보   facts or details about somebody / something

They sometimes lose important **information**.
그들은 때때로 중요한 정보를 잃어버린다.

02 insect
[ínsekt]

n 곤충   a small creature with six legs and three parts of a body

Butterflies are the most beautiful **insects** in the animal kingdom.
나비는 동물 세계에서 가장 아름다운 곤충이다.

03 instead
[instéd]

ad 대신에   in the place of somebody / something

I chose to buy the flower vase **instead** of the ancient tea table.
나는 오래된 티 테이블 대신에 꽃병을 사기로 했다.

04 interested
[íntəristid]

a 관심이 있는   giving your attention to something

The children are **interested** in the different kinds of fish.
아이들은 여러 종류의 물고기들에 관심이 있어요.

05 link
[líŋk]

v 잇다, 관련 짓다   to make a connection between one thing and another

He tried to **link** the human heart to nature.
그는 인간의 마음과 자연을 연결하려고 애썼다.

06 loan
[lóun]

v 빌려주다   to lend something to somebody

Books in the library can be **loaned** out to anybody.
도서관의 책은 누구에게나 빌려줄 수 있다.

07 monster
[mάnstər]

n 괴물   an imaginary creature that is very large

He defeats a **monster**, and then dances with a princess.
그는 괴물을 물리치고 나서 공주와 춤을 춰요.

08 mood
[mú:d]

n 기분, 분위기   the way you are feeling at a particular time

Her **moods** change very quickly.
그녀의 기분은 변덕이 심하다.

09 mule
[mjú:l]

n 노새   an animal that is used for carrying heavy loads

He loaded a big package on a **mule**.
그는 큰 꾸러미를 노새에 실었다.

---

key words
detail **n** 세목 / animal kingdom **n** 동물계 / vase **n** 꽃병 / ancient **a** 오래된
attention **n** 주의 / imaginary **a** 상상의 / defeat **v** 쳐부수다

🎧 Listen and repeat. `Track 68`

10 muscle
[mʌ́səl]
n 근육, 힘줄   a piece of tissue inside body which connects two bones
Physical exercise develops **muscle**.
운동을 하면 근육이 발달된다.

11 neat
[ni:t]
a 깔끔한, 단정한   looking tidy or doing things in a tidy way
He is always **neat** in his appearance.
그는 외모가 항상 단정한 사람이다.

12 plum
[plʌm]
n 서양자두   a soft round fruit with red or purple skin
A **plum** has a lot of vitamins.
서양자두는 비타민을 많이 함유하고 있다.

13 poem
[póuim]
n 시, 운문   a writing arranged in short lines for beauty and sound
There are **poems** on the walls of the classrooms.
교실 벽에는 시들이 써져 있습니다.

14 poison
[pɔ́izən]
n 독   a substance that kills or harms you
He was killed by **poison** gas.
그는 독가스로 살해 당했다.

15 popular
[pápjələr]
a 인기 있는, 대중적인   liked by a large number of people
Soccer is one of the most **popular** sports.
축구는 가장 인기 있는 운동 중 하나이다.

16 possible
[pásəbəl]
a 가능한   that can be done or achieved
I want to see the car if it is **possible**.
가능하면 그 차를 보고 싶은데요.

17 proverb
[právə:rb]
n 속담   a sentence that gives advice that is generally true
A **proverb** says that time is money.
시간은 금이라는 속담이 있다.

18 rate
[reit]
n 비율, 요금   a measurement of the number of times something happens
Why is the return **rate** so high?
반품률이 왜 그렇게 높은 거예요?

key words
tissue **n** 조직 / tidy **a** 단정한, 말쑥한 / arrange **v** 배열하다 / achieve **v** 이루다
measurement **n** 측정 / return **n** 반품

Exercise

A. Complete the sentence.

1. He was killed by _____ gas.
   그는 독가스로 살해 당했다.
2. Butterflies are the most beautiful _____ in the animal kingdom.
   나비는 동물 세계에서 가장 아름다운 곤충이다.
3. He tried to _____ the human heart to nature.
   그는 인간의 마음과 자연을 연결하려고 애썼다.
4. There are _____ on the walls of the classrooms.
   교실 벽에는 시들이 쓰여 있습니다.
5. I chose to buy the flower vase _____ of the ancient tea table.
   나는 오래된 티 테이블 대신에 꽃병을 사기로 했다.
6. The children are _____ in the different kinds of fish.
   아이들은 여러 종류의 물고기들에 관심이 있어요.
7. Books in the library can be _____ out to anybody.
   도서관의 책은 누구에게나 빌려줄 수 있다.
8. I want to see the car if it is _____.
   가능하면 그 차를 보고 싶은데요.
9. He defeats a _____, and then dances with a princess.
   그는 괴물을 물리치고 나서 공주와 춤을 춰요.
10. A _____ says that time is money.
    시간은 금이라는 속담이 있다.
11. Her _____ change very quickly.
    그녀의 기분은 변덕이 심하다.
12. Physical exercise develops _____.
    운동을 하면 근육이 발달된다.
13. He is always _____ in his appearance.
    그는 외모가 항상 단정한 사람이다.
14. They sometimes lose important _____.
    그들은 때때로 중요한 정보를 잃어버린다.
15. A _____ has a lot of vitamins.
    서양자두는 비타민을 많이 함유하고 있다.
16. Soccer is one of the most _____ sports.
    축구는 가장 인기 있는 운동 중 하나이다.
17. He loaded a big package on a _____.
    그는 큰 꾸러미를 노새에 실었다.
18. Why is the return _____ so high?
    반품률이 왜 그렇게 높은 거예요?

Hint

| plum | mood | neat | possible | monster | loan | poem | instead | proverb |
| link | popular | muscle | information | interested | rate | insect | mule | poison |

Unit 23

Exercise

B. Fill in the word and meaning.

	Word	Meaning
01	interested	
02	monster	
03	insect	
04	neat	
05	plum	
06	instead	
07	popular	
08	mule	
09	possible	
10	loan	
11	rate	
12	poison	
13	proverb	
14	information	
15	muscle	
16	poem	
17	link	
18	mood	

	Meaning	Word
01	정보	
02	곤충	
03	대신에	
04	관심이 있는	
05	잇다, 관련 짓다	
06	빌려주다	
07	괴물	
08	기분, 분위기	
09	노새	
10	근육, 힘줄	
11	깔끔한, 단정한	
12	서양자두	
13	시, 운문	
14	독	
15	인기 있는, 대중적인	
16	가능한	
17	속담	
18	비율, 요금	

🎧 C. Listen, write the word and meaning. (Track 69)

	Word	Meaning		Word	Meaning
01			10		
02			11		
03			12		
04			13		
05			14		
06			15		
07			16		
08			17		
09			18		

Unit 24

🎧 Listen and repeat. (Track 70)

01 rub [rʌb]
v 비비다, 문지르다 — to move something backwards and forwards over it
Don't **rub** your eyes or nose.
눈이나 코를 비비지 마세요.

02 rubber [rʌ́bəːr]
n 고무, 고무줄 — a elastic substance made from the juice of a tropical tree
The **rubber** band stretches.
고무줄은 늘어난다.

03 rude [ruːd]
a 버릇없는, 무례한 — having a lack of respect
That guy is no good, and **rude**.
저 남자는 약하고 무례하다.

04 rug [rʌg]
n 깔개, 융단 — a piece of thick material that covers a small part of a floor
She spilt a cup of coffee over a new **rug**.
그녀는 새 깔개 위에 커피를 쏟았다.

05 safety [séifti]
n 안전, 무사 — the state of being protected from danger
Safety is important to everyone.
안전은 모두에게 중요하다.

06 smooth [smuːð]
a 매끄러운 — completely flat
Her skin is as **smooth** as silk.
그녀의 피부는 비단처럼 매끄럽다.

07 soil [sɔil]
n 흙, 토양 — the substance on the surface of the earth
Plants take water from the **soil**.
식물은 토양에서 물을 얻는다.

08 solution [səlúːʃən]
n 해결, 용해 — a way of dealing with a problem
The detective found a **solution** to the mystery.
그 탐정은 미스터리의 해결책을 알아냈다.

09 sort [sɔːrt]
n 종류 — a type of people or things
It's a **sort** of chemical weapons.
그것은 화학 무기의 한 종류이다.

---

key words
elastic a 탄력 있는 / stretch v 늘이다 / detective n 탐정 / weapon n 무기

🎧 Listen and repeat. Track 71

10 sparkle
[spá:rkəl]
n 불꽃, 번쩍임   shining with many small points of light
Did you see the **sparkle** over the mountain?
산 너머에서 번쩍이는 것을 봤니?

11 speech
[spi:tʃ]
n 연설, 말   a talk that a person gives to an audience
His **speech** heightened the crowd's excitement.
그의 연설은 군중들의 흥분을 고조시켰다.

12 survey
[sə:rvéi]
v 조사하다   to look carefully at the whole of something
He **surveyed** me from head to foot.
그는 머리부터 발끝까지 나를 조사했다.

13 tomb
[tu:m]
n 무덤, 묘   a large grave that is above ground
The Pyramids were built as **tombs** of the kings of ancient Egypt.
피라미드는 고대 이집트 왕의 무덤으로 만들어졌다.

14 tool
[tu:l]
n 도구, 연장   an instrument that you hold in your hand
You don't need any special **tools**.
너는 특별한 도구가 전혀 필요하지 않아.

15 trade
[treid]
v 거래하다 / **n** 무역   to buy and sell things
A **trade** mission was sent to Africa.
무역 사절단이 아프리카에 파견되었다.

16 traffic
[træfik]
n 교통   the vehicles that are on a road at a particular time
The police are stopping **traffic**.
경찰이 교통을 차단하고 있다.

17 trash
[træʃ]
n 쓰레기   the waste material such as used paper or bottles
The **trash** can is between the refrigerator and the oven.
쓰레기통이 냉장고와 오븐 사이에 있다.

18 treat
[tri:t]
v 다루다, 대우하다   to consider something in a particular way
I **treat** this car like my best friend.
나는 이 차를 소중한 친구처럼 다룬답니다.

key words
audience **n** 청중 / heighten **v** 높이다, 증가시키다 / excitement **n** 흥분
instrument **n** 기구, 도구 / mission **n** 사절단

Exercise

A. Complete the sentence.

1. It's a _____ of chemical weapons.
   그것은 화학 무기의 한 종류이다.

2. The _____ band stretches.
   고무줄은 늘어난다.

3. He _____ me from head to foot.
   그는 머리부터 발끝까지 나를 조사했다.

4. She spilt a cup of coffee over a new _____.
   그녀는 새 깔개 위에 커피를 쏟았다.

5. _____ is important to everyone.
   안전은 모두에게 중요하다.

6. Plants take water from the _____.
   식물은 토양에서 물을 얻는다.

7. I _____ this car like my best friend.
   나는 이 차를 소중한 친구처럼 다룬답니다.

8. His _____ heightened the crowd's excitement.
   그의 연설은 군중들의 흥분을 고조시켰다.

9. That guy is no good, and _____.
   저 남자는 악하고 무례하다.

10. The Pyramids were built as _____ of the kings of ancient Egypt.
    피라미드는 고대 이집트 왕의 무덤으로 만들어졌다.

11. You don't need any special _____.
    너는 특별한 도구가 전혀 필요하지 않아.

12. Don't _____ your eyes or nose.
    눈이나 코를 비비지 마세요.

13. Her skin is as _____ as silk.
    그녀의 피부는 비단처럼 매끄럽다.

14. A _____ mission was sent to Africa.
    무역 사절단이 아프리카에 파견되었다.

15. The detective found a _____ to the mystery.
    그 탐정은 미스터리의 해결책을 알아냈다.

16. The police are stopping _____.
    경찰이 교통을 차단하고 있다.

17. Did you see the _____ over the mountain?
    산 너머에서 번쩍이는 것을 봤니?

18. The _____ can is between the refrigerator and the oven.
    쓰레기통이 냉장고와 오븐 사이에 있다.

Hint

| sparkle | traffic | smooth | rubber | treat | tool | solution | rub | soil |
| rude | trade | speech | rug | safety | sort | survey | tomb | trash |

Exercise

B. Fill in the word and meaning.

	Word	Meaning
01	smooth	
02	sparkle	
03	rub	
04	survey	
05	rubber	
06	speech	
07	trade	
08	rude	
09	traffic	
10	soil	
11	trash	
12	rug	
13	treat	
14	solution	
15	tool	
16	sort	
17	tomb	
18	safety	

	Meaning	Word
01	비비다, 문지르다	
02	고무, 고무줄	
03	버릇없는, 무례한	
04	깔개, 융단	
05	안전, 무사	
06	매끄러운	
07	흙, 토양	
08	해결, 용해	
09	종류	
10	불꽃, 번쩍임	
11	연설, 말	
12	조사하다	
13	무덤, 묘	
14	도구, 연장	
15	거래하다, 무역	
16	교통	
17	쓰레기	
18	다루다, 대우하다	

C. Listen, write the word and meaning. (Track 72)

	Word	Meaning		Word	Meaning
01			10		
02			11		
03			12		
04			13		
05			14		
06			15		
07			16		
08			17		
09			18		

Review 12

A. Read and fill in the word and meaning.

word	definition	meaning
	facts or details about somebody/something	
	a piece of tissue inside body which connects two bones	
	looking tidy or doing things in a tidy way	
	an animal that is used for carrying heavy loads	
	a soft round fruit with red or purple skin	
	a small creature with six legs and three parts of a body	
	a writing arranged in short lines for beauty and sound	
	a measurement of the number of times something happens	
	a substance that kills or harms you	
	in the place of somebody/something	
	liked by a large number of people	
	the way you are feeling at a particular time	
	giving your attention to something	
	an imaginary creature that is very large	
	that can be done or achieved	
	to lend something to somebody	
	a sentence that gives advice that is generally true	
	to make a connection between one thing and another	

Hint

plum   mood   neat   possible   monster   loan   poem   instead   proverb
link   popular   muscle   information   interested   rate   insect   mule   poison

B. Read and fill in the word and meaning.

word	definition	meaning
	the state of being protected from danger	
	a large grave that is above ground	
	a piece of thick material that covers a small part of a floor	
	to look carefully at the whole of something	
	an instrument that you hold in your hand	
	completely flat	
	a elastic substance made from the juice of a tropical tree	
	to buy and sell things	
	the substance on the surface of the earth	
	the vehicles that are on a road at a particular time	
	a way of dealing with a problem	
	to move something backwards and forwards over it	
	the waste material such as used paper or bottles	
	shining with many small points of light	
	to consider something in a particular way	
	a type of people or things	
	having a lack of respect	
	a talk that a person gives to an audience	

Hint

sparkle traffic smooth rubber treat tool solution rub soil
rude trade speech rug safety sort survey tomb trash

Unit 25

🎧 Listen and repeat. Track 73

01 accident [ǽksidənt]
n 사고, 재난   an unpleasant event that causes injury or damage
I was surprised to hear about your **accident**.
너의 사고 소식을 듣고 놀랐어.

02 agreement [əgríːmənt]
n 동의, 협정   the state of agreeing with somebody / something
She nodded her head in **agreement**.
그녀는 동의의 뜻으로 고개를 끄덕였다.

03 alcohol [ǽlkəhɔ(ː)l]
n 알코올, 술   drinks such as beer, whisky, wine, etc
He was addicted to **alcohol**.
그는 술에 중독되어 있었다.

04 alike [əláik]
a 똑같은   very similar
No two men think **alike**.
두 사람의 생각이 같은 경우는 전혀 없다.

05 allow [əláu]
v 허락하다   to let somebody / something do something
Most supervisors **allow** two weeks at a time.
대부분의 관리자들은 한번에 2주까지만 허락하고 있어요.

06 already [ɔːlrédi]
ad 이미, 벌써   before a particular time in the past
The players are **already** on the field except one.
한 사람을 제외하고 선수들은 이미 경기장에 나와 있다.

07 boil [bɔil]
v 끓다, 끓이다   to be heated to the point something turns to steam
Turn on the gas to **boil** the rice.
가스를 켜서 쌀을 끓여라.

08 bone [boun]
n 뼈   the skeleton of the body of a human or an animal
Leave some **bones** for the dog.
개에게 뼈를 좀 남겨 주어라.

09 border [bɔ́ːrdər]
n 국경, 경계   the line that divides two areas
Her husband will cross the **border** into the country.
그녀의 남편은 국경을 넘어 타국으로 갈 것입니다.

key words
injury **n** 상해 / nod **v** 끄덕이다 / addict **v** 중독되다 / supervisor **n** 관리자 / skeleton **n** 골격

🎧 Listen and repeat. Track 74

10 bored [bɔːrd]
a 지루한, 싫증나는   feeling tired because you have nothing to do
We yawn when sleepy or **bored**.
우리는 졸리거나 따분할 때 하품을 한다.

11 bottom [bátəm]
n 바닥, 밑바닥   the lowest part of something
These fish live at the **bottom** of the ocean.
이런 물고기들은 바다의 밑바닥에 산다.

12 brain [brein]
n 뇌, 두뇌   the organ inside the head
My father has been **brain** dead since the traffic accident.
아버지는 교통사고 후 줄곧 뇌사 상태에 있다.

13 choice [tʃɔis]
n 선택   an act of choosing
He made his **choice**, although later he regretted it.
비록 나중에 후회하긴 했지만 그가 선택을 한 것이었다.

14 cigarette [sìɡərét]
n 담배   a thin tube of paper filled with tobacco
Please don't litter with your **cigarette** butts.
담배꽁초를 함부로 버리지 마세요.

15 clap [klæp]
v (손뼉을)치다   to hit your open hands together
The excited crowd **clapped** loudly.
흥분한 관중은 크게 박수를 쳤다.

16 clay [klei]
n 찰흙, 점토   a kind of earth that is soft and sticky when it is wet
The sculptor is working with **clay**.
조각가가 점토로 작업을 하고 있다.

17 clown [klaun]
n 어릿광대   an entertainer who wears funny clothes
The man is dressed like a **clown**.
남자는 어릿광대 차림을 하고 있다.

18 coach [koutʃ]
n 지도자   somebody who trains a person or team
The **coach** doesn't say very much at half time, does he?
그 코치는 중간 휴식시간에 별로 말씀이 없으시죠?

key words
yawn v 하품하다 / organ n 기관 / regret v 후회하다 / litter v (물건을)흩뜨리다
butt n 담배꽁초 / sculptor n 조각가 / entertainer n 연예인

Exercise

A. Complete the sentence.

1. The man is dressed like a _____.
   남자는 어릿광대 차림을 하고 있다.

2. Most supervisors _____ two weeks at a time.
   대부분의 관리자들은 한번에 2주까지만 허락하고 있어요.

3. These fish live at the _____ of the ocean.
   이런 물고기들은 바다의 밑바닥에 산다.

4. The players are _____ on the field except one.
   한 사람을 제외하고 선수들은 이미 경기장에 나와 있다.

5. The sculptor is working with _____.
   조각가가 점토로 작업을 하고 있다.

6. Turn on the gas to _____ the rice.
   가스를 켜서 쌀을 끓여라.

7. I was surprised to hear about your _____.
   너의 사고 소식을 듣고 놀랐어.

8. Her husband will cross the _____ into the country.
   그녀의 남편은 국경을 넘어 타국으로 갈 것입니다.

9. The excited crowd _____ loudly.
   흥분한 관중은 크게 박수를 쳤다.

10. No two men think _____.
    두 사람의 생각이 같은 경우는 전혀 없다.

11. My father has been _____ dead since the traffic accident.
    아버지는 교통사고 후 줄곧 뇌사 상태에 있다.

12. She nodded her head in _____.
    그녀는 동의의 뜻으로 고개를 끄덕였다.

13. He made his _____, although later he regretted it.
    비록 나중에 후회하긴 했지만 그가 선택을 한 것이었다.

14. Please don't litter with your _____ butts.
    담배꽁초를 함부로 버리지 마세요.

15. Leave some _____ for the dog.
    개에게 뼈를 좀 남겨 주어라.

16. He was addicted to _____.
    그는 술에 중독되어 있었다.

17. The _____ doesn't say very much at half time, does he?
    그 코치는 중간 휴식시간에 별로 말씀이 없으시죠?

18. We yawn when sleepy or _____.
    우리는 졸리거나 따분할 때 하품을 한다.

Hint

| boil | clap | alike | bone | cigarette | already | choice | bottom | agreement |
| coach | bored | accident | alcohol | border | clay | allow | brain | clown |

Unit 25

Exercise

B. Fill in the word and meaning.

	Word	Meaning
01	agreement	
02	bone	
03	clown	
04	bottom	
05	allow	
06	brain	
07	alcohol	
08	cigarette	
09	boil	
10	clay	
11	alike	
12	clap	
13	coach	
14	already	
15	choice	
16	bored	
17	accident	
18	border	

	Meaning	Word
01	사고, 재난	
02	동의, 협정	
03	알코올, 술	
04	똑같은	
05	허락하다	
06	이미, 벌써	
07	끓다, 끓이다	
08	뼈	
09	국경, 경계	
10	지루한, 싫증나는	
11	바닥, 밑바닥	
12	뇌, 두뇌	
13	선택	
14	담배	
15	(손뼉을)치다	
16	찰흙, 점토	
17	어릿광대	
18	지도자	

🎧 C. Listen, write the word and meaning. (Track 75)

	Word	Meaning		Word	Meaning
01			10		
02			11		
03			12		
04			13		
05			14		
06			15		
07			16		
08			17		
09			18		

Unit 26

🎧 Listen and repeat. Track 76

01 crop [krɑp]
n 수확, 농작물   a plant that is grown in large quantities
The main **crops** of this country are coffee and rice.
이 나라의 주요 농작물은 커피와 쌀이다.

02 crown [kraun]
n 왕관   a circular ornament that a king or queen wears
Among them, a gold **crown** was his favorite.
그 중에도 금관이 가장 그의 마음에 드는 것이었다.

03 cube [kju:b]
n 입방체, 정육면체   a solid shape that has six equal square sides
The shape of dice is a **cube**.
주사위의 모양은 정육면체이다.

04 cure [kjuər]
n 치료 / v 치료하다   to make an illness go away
It'll **cure** any disease of the eyes.
그것은 어떠한 눈병도 치료할 수 있어요.

05 curly [kə́:rli]
a 곱슬머리의   having a lot of curls
He's short and heavy, and he has **curly** hair.
그는 키가 작고 뚱뚱하며 곱슬머리입니다.

06 curve [kə:rv]
n 곡선, 커브   a line that bends gradually
The truck is going around a **curve**.
트럭이 커브 길을 돌고 있다.

07 elegance [éligəns]
n 우아함, 고상   a good or attractive style
Elegance is important to her.
우아함은 그녀에게 중요하다.

08 equal [í:kwəl]
a 같은, 동등한   the same in size, amount, value, number, etc
This animal is **equal** in weight to a small car.
이 동물은 작은 자동차의 무게와 같다.

09 error [érər]
n 잘못, 실수   a mistake
The telephone bill was too high due to a computer **error**.
컴퓨터 상의 실수로 전화요금이 너무 많이 나왔어요.

key words
ornament n 장식품 / dice n 주사위 / gradually ad 점차로

🎧 Listen and repeat. Track 77

10 escalator
[éskəlèitər]
n 에스컬레이터   a moving staircase that carries people
People are going up and down the **escalator**.
사람들이 에스컬레이터를 오르내리고 있다.

11 escape
[iskéip]
v 달아나다   to get away from a place
She wants to **escape** from the same routine.
그녀는 똑같은 일상사에서 벗어나고 싶어 한다.

12 especially
[ispéʃəli]
ad 특히, 특별히   for a particular purpose, person, etc.
I **especially** love to cook Mexican food.
나는 특히 멕시코 요리하는 것을 좋아한다.

13 general
[dʒénərəl]
n 일반 / a 일반의   normal; usual
In **general**, every achievement requires trial and error.
일반적으로 모든 업적은 시행착오를 거치게 된다.

14 giant
[dʒáiənt]
n 거인 / a 거대한   very large
There are **giant** companies on this street.
이 거리에는 거대한 회사들이 있습니다.

15 goal
[goul]
n 목적   something that you hope to achieve
An athlete's **goal** is to win the first prize in a competition.
운동선수의 목표는 경기에서 1등을 하는 것이다.

16 goose
[gu:s]
n 거위   a bird like a large duck with a long neck
Can you see the **goose** in the pond?
연못에 있는 거위가 보이나요?

17 greenhouse
[grí:nhàus]
n 온실   a building with glass sides for growing plants in
Was there a big **greenhouse**?
큰 온실이 있었습니까?

18 guard
[ga:rd]
v 지키다, 경계하다   to protect property or people from attack or danger
The men came to **guard** the playground.
남자들이 운동장을 지키러 왔다.

---

key words
staircase n 계단 / routine n 일상의 일 / property n 재산

Unit 26 **131**

Exercise

A. Complete the sentence.

1. Among them, a gold _____ was his favorite.
   그 중에도 금관이 가장 그의 마음에 드는 것이었다.

2. There are _____ companies on this street.
   이 거리에는 거대한 회사들이 있습니다.

3. He's short and heavy, and he has _____ hair.
   그는 키가 작고 뚱뚱하며 곱슬머리입니다.

4. The men came to _____ the playground.
   남자들이 운동장을 지키러 왔다.

5. This animal is _____ in weight to a small car.
   이 동물은 작은 자동차의 무게와 같다.

6. The truck is going around a _____.
   트럭이 커브 길을 돌고 있다.

7. Was there a big _____?
   큰 온실이 있었습니까?

8. The shape of dice is a _____.
   주사위의 모양은 정육면체이다.

9. It'll _____ any disease of the eyes.
   그것은 어떠한 눈병도 치료할 수 있어요.

10. Can you see the _____ in the pond?
    연못에 있는 거위가 보이나요?

11. The main _____ of this country are coffee and rice.
    이 나라의 주요 농작물은 커피와 쌀이다.

12. _____ is important to her.
    우아함은 그녀에게 중요하다.

13. The telephone bill was too high due to a computer _____.
    컴퓨터 상의 실수로 전화요금이 너무 많이 나왔어요.

14. She wants to _____ from the same routine.
    그녀는 똑같은 일상사에서 벗어나고 싶어 한다.

15. I _____ love to cook Mexican food.
    나는 특히 멕시코 요리하는 것을 좋아한다.

16. In _____, every achievement requires trial and error.
    일반적으로 모든 업적은 시행착오를 거치게 된다.

17. People are going up and down the _____.
    사람들이 에스컬레이터를 오르내리고 있다.

18. An athlete's _____ is to win the first prize in a competition.
    운동선수의 목표는 경기에서 1등을 하는 것이다.

Hint

| cure | escalator | crown | goose | equal | curly | crop | cube | elegance |
| giant | especially | escape | error | greenhouse | guard | goal | general | curve |

Unit 26

Exercise

B. Fill in the word and meaning.

	Word	Meaning
01	cube	
02	elegance	
03	curve	
04	escalator	
05	crop	
06	giant	
07	error	
08	greenhouse	
09	guard	
10	crown	
11	especially	
12	goose	
13	goal	
14	escape	
15	curly	
16	equal	
17	general	
18	cure	

	Meaning	Word
01	수확, 농작물	
02	왕관	
03	입방체, 정육면체	
04	치료, 치료하다	
05	곱슬머리의	
06	곡선, 커브	
07	우아함, 고상	
08	같은, 동등한	
09	잘못, 실수	
10	에스컬레이터	
11	달아나다	
12	특히, 특별히	
13	일반, 일반의	
14	거인, 거대한	
15	목적	
16	거위	
17	온실	
18	지키다, 경계하다	

C. Listen, write the word and meaning. (Track 78)

	Word	Meaning		Word	Meaning
01			10		
02			11		
03			12		
04			13		
05			14		
06			15		
07			16		
08			17		
09			18		

Review 13

A. Read and fill in the word and meaning.

word	definition	meaning
	very similar	
	feeling tired because you have nothing to do	
	somebody who trains a person or team	
	drinks such as beer, whisky, wine, etc	
	an entertainer who wears funny clothes	
	the line that divides two areas	
	an unpleasant event that causes injury or damage	
	a kind of earth that is soft and sticky when it is wet	
	an act of choosing	
	the lowest part of something	
	a thin tube of paper filled with tobacco	
	the skeleton of the body of a human or an animal	
	the state of agreeing with somebody / something	
	to hit your open hands together	
	the organ inside the head	
	before a particular time in the past	
	to be heated to the point something turns to steam	
	to let somebody/something do something	

Hint
boil   clap   alike   bone   cigarette   already   choice   bottom   agreement
coach   bored   accident   alcohol   border   clay   allow   brain   clown

B. Read and fill in the word and meaning.

word	definition	meaning
	a mistake	
	a circular ornament that a king or queen wears	
	to get away from a place	
	a plant that is grown in large quantities	
	a moving staircase that carries people	
	to make an illness go away	
	very large	
	the same in size, amount, value, number, etc	
	a solid shape that has six equal square sides	
	normal; usual	
	a line that bends gradually	
	for a particular purpose, person, etc.	
	something that you hope to achieve	
	a good or attractive style	
	a building with glass sides for growing plants in	
	having a lot of curls	
	a bird like a large duck with a long neck	
	to protect property or people from attack or danger	

Hint

cure   escalator   crown   goose   equal   curly   crop   cube   elegance
giant especially escape error   greenhouse guard   goal   general   curve

Unit 27

🎧 Listen and repeat. Track 79

01 interview [íntərvjùː]
n 면접   a meeting at which somebody is asked questions for a job, etc
I would like to have an **interview** with you this Friday.
이번 주 금요일에 당신과 면접하고 싶습니다.

02 invent [invént]
v 발명하다   to produce something that has not existed
The microscope was **invented** in Holland in 1570.
현미경은 1570년 네덜란드에서 발명되었다.

03 iron [áiərn]
n 철, 철제   a hard strong metal that is used to make steel
The man is making an **iron** sculpture.
남자가 철제 조각상을 만들고 있다.

04 item [áitəm]
n 품목, 조항   one single thing on a list of things
She is moving around the store, choosing the **items**.
그녀는 가게를 돌아다니면서 품목들을 고르고 있어.

05 jewel [dʒúːəl]
n 보석   a precious stone such as a diamond, ruby, etc.
There are precious **jewels** here.
여기에 귀중한 보석들이 있다.

06 jog [dʒag]
v 조깅하다   to run slowly and steadily for a long time
I **jog** every morning before breakfast.
나는 매일 아침식사 전에 조깅한다.

07 needle [níːdl]
n 바늘   a small thin piece of steel
She ran the **needle** into her left hand.
그녀는 왼손을 바늘에 찔렸다.

08 nod [nad]
n 끄덕임 / v 끄덕이다   to move head up and down
He **nodded** his head in greeting.
그는 인사로 머리를 끄덕였다.

09 noisy [nɔ́izi]
a 시끄러운   making a lot of noise
The park was so **noisy** that I couldn't rest.
공원이 너무 시끄러워서 나는 쉬지를 못했다.

key words
microscope n 현미경 / sculpture n 조각상 / precious a 비싼, 귀중한 / steadily ad 꾸준하게

🎧 Listen and repeat. Track 80

10 nonstop
[nánstáp]
a 직행의   without any stops
Our **nonstop** service to Incheon will take two hours and 10 minutes.
이 직행 여객기는 인천까지 2시간 10분이 걸릴 예정입니다.

11 noodle
[núːdl]
n 국수   a long thin strip of pasta
She eats rice as well as **noodles**.
그녀는 국수뿐만 아니라 밥도 먹는다.

12 ostrich
[ɔ́(ː)stritʃ]
n 타조   a very large African bird with a long neck and legs
They are painting an **ostrich** on the wall.
그들은 벽에 타조 그림을 그리고 있어.

13 portable
[pɔ́ːrtəbəl]
a 휴대용의   that is easy to carry or to move
I'm looking for a **portable** printer for a laptop computer.
랩톱 컴퓨터에 사용할 휴대용 프린터를 찾고 있어요.

14 pour
[pɔ́ːr]
v 쏟다, 따르다   to make a liquid flow steadily out of a container
The man is **pouring** water from one bucket into another.
남자가 물을 한 양동이에서 다른 양동이에 따르고 있다.

15 powerful
[páuərfəl]
a 강한, 강력한   having great strength or force
Every man hopes to have a **powerful** engine in his car.
모든 남자는 강력한 엔진을 가진 차를 갖고 싶어한다.

16 present
[prézənt]
a 출석한   being in a particular place
I was entirely ignorant that he was **present**.
나는 그가 출석했다는 것을 전혀 몰랐다.

17 pride
[praid]
n 자랑, 자만심   the feeling that you are better than other people
He is the **pride** of our nation.
그는 우리나라의 자랑이다.

18 prison
[prízn]
n 감옥, 교도소   a building where criminals are kept as punishment
He left **prison** quite a changed man.
그가 감옥을 나올 때는 사람이 아주 변해 있었다.

key words
strip **n** 길고 가느다란 조각 / entirely **ad** 아주, 완전히 / ignorant **a** 모르는, 무지한 / punishment **n** 벌

Unit 27 137

Exercise

A. Complete the sentence.

1. He is the _____ of our nation.
   그는 우리나라의 자랑이다.

2. She eats rice as well as _____.
   그녀는 국수뿐만 아니라 밥도 먹는다.

3. The microscope was _____ in Holland in 1570.
   현미경은 1570년 네덜란드에서 발명되었다.

4. She is moving around the store, choosing the _____.
   그녀는 가게를 돌아다니면서 품목들을 고르고 있어.

5. There are precious _____ here.
   여기에 귀중한 보석들이 있다.

6. I would like to have an _____ with you this Friday.
   이번 주 금요일에 당신과 면접하고 싶습니다.

7. He _____ his head in greeting.
   그는 인사로 머리를 끄덕였다.

8. He left _____ quite a changed man.
   그가 감옥을 나올 때는 사람이 아주 변해 있었다.

9. Our _____ service to Incheon will take two hours and 10 minutes.
   이 직행 여객기는 인천까지 2시간 10분이 걸릴 예정입니다.

10. They are painting an _____ on the wall.
    그들은 벽에 타조 그림을 그리고 있어.

11. I'm looking for a _____ printer for a laptop computer.
    랩톱 컴퓨터에 사용할 휴대용 프린터를 찾고 있어요.

12. The man is making an _____ sculpture.
    남자가 철제 조각상을 만들고 있다.

13. She ran the _____ into her left hand.
    그녀는 왼손을 바늘에 찔렸다.

14. The man is _____ water from one bucket into another.
    남자가 물을 한 양동이에서 다른 양동이에 따르고 있다.

15. Every man hopes to have a _____ engine in his car.
    모든 남자는 강력한 엔진을 가진 차를 갖고 싶어한다.

16. The park was so _____ that I couldn't rest.
    공원이 너무 시끄러워서 나는 쉬지를 못했다.

17. I _____ every morning before breakfast.
    나는 매일 아침식사 전에 조깅한다.

18. I was entirely ignorant that he was _____.
    나는 그가 출석했다는 것을 전혀 몰랐다.

Hint

| item | pride | noisy | powerful | iron | present | nonstop | portable | prison |
| ostrich | jewel | nod | interview | needle | invent | jog | noodle | pour |

Exercise

B. Fill in the word and meaning.

	Word	Meaning
01	jog	
02	invent	
03	portable	
04	nod	
05	iron	
06	powerful	
07	nonstop	
08	item	
09	prison	
10	noisy	
11	present	
12	jewel	
13	ostrich	
14	pride	
15	needle	
16	pour	
17	noodle	
18	interview	

	Meaning	Word
01	면접	
02	발명하다	
03	철, 철제	
04	품목, 조항	
05	보석	
06	조깅하다	
07	바늘	
08	끄덕임, 끄덕이다	
09	시끄러운	
10	직행의	
11	국수	
12	타조	
13	휴대용의	
14	쏟다, 따르다	
15	강한, 강력한	
16	출석한	
17	자랑, 자만심	
18	감옥, 교도서	

C. Listen, write the word and meaning. (Track 81)

	Word	Meaning		Word	Meaning
01			10		
02			11		
03			12		
04			13		
05			14		
06			15		
07			16		
08			17		
09			18		

Unit 28

🎧 Listen and repeat. Track 82

01 salmon [sǽmən]
n 연어   a large fish with silver skin and pink meat that we eat
My parents like to have smoked **salmons** at dinner.
부모님은 저녁 식사 때 훈제 연어를 드시는 것을 좋아하세요.

02 salty [sɔ́:lti]
a 짠, 소금기가 있는   tasting of salt
It's good, but a little too **salty**.
좋아요, 그런데 좀 짜군요.

03 scene [si:n]
n 장면, 현장   one part of a book, film, etc in which the events happen
I remember the **scene** well.
난 그 장면을 잘 기억한다.

04 seashore [sí:ʃɔ́:r]
n 해변, 바닷가   the land along the edge of the sea
The man who is sitting at the **seashore** has a problem.
해변에 앉아 있는 그 남자는 문제가 있다.

05 second [sékənd]
n (몇) 초   one of the 60 parts into which a minute is divided
It takes fifty **seconds** to find the book.
그 책을 찾는데 50초가 걸려.

06 seek [si:k]
v 찾다, 추구하다   to look for something / somebody
Seek the positive rather than the negative.
부정적인 것보다 긍정적인 것을 찾아라.

07 spider [spáidər]
n 거미   a small creature with eight thin legs
Why are you so terrified of **spiders**?
넌 왜 그렇게 거미를 무서워 하니?

08 spin [spin]
v 실을 내다, 잣다   to produce thread from a mass of wool or cotton
Everyone knows that a spider **spins** a web.
거미가 거미줄을 친다는 사실은 모두 알고 있어.

09 stadium [stéidiəm]
n 경기장   a large sports ground
The **stadium** was filled for the big game.
그 큰 시합 때문에 경기장이 만원이 되었다.

key words
smoke **v** 훈제로 만들다 / taste **v** 맛을 느끼다 / thread **n** 실

🎧 Listen and repeat. Track 83

10 stomach [stʌ́mək]
n 위, 배   the organ in your body where food goes after you have eaten it
He went to the doctor with **stomach** pains.
그는 위가 아파서 의사에게 갔다.

11 stranger [stréindʒəːr]
n 낯선 사람   a person that you do not know
I had to ask a **stranger** to help me.
나는 낯선 사람에게 나를 도와달라고 요청해야만 했다.

12 stream [striːm]
n 시내, 개울   a small narrow river
A large brook is called a **stream**.
큰 개천은 개울이라 불린다.

13 tray [trei]
n 쟁반   a flat piece of metal or plastic for holding things
He carried a breakfast **tray**.
그는 아침 식사가 담긴 쟁반을 가져왔다.

14 treasure [tréʒəːr]
n 보물   a collection of valuable things such as jewellery
The man is excavating a **treasure**.
그 남자가 보물을 발굴하고 있다.

15 trouble [trʌ́bəl]
n 고생, 근심   a situation causing a problem or worry
Adults forget the **troubles** of their youth.
어른들은 젊었을 때의 고생을 잊어버린다.

16 trousers [tráuzəːrz]
n 바지   a piece of clothing that covers the whole of both your legs
What size **trousers** do you wear?
당신 바지의 치수는 얼마입니까?

17 union [júːnjən]
n 결합, 단결   the act of joining two or more things together
Love is a **union** made in heaven.
사랑이란 하늘이 맺어 준 결합이다.

18 university [jùːnəvə́ːrsəti]
n 대학교   an institution at the highest level of education
He graduated from Harvard **university**.
그는 하버드 대학을 졸업했다.

key words
brook n 시내 / excavate v 발굴하다 / institution n 기관, 시설 / education n 교육 / graduate v 졸업하다

Exercise

A. Complete the sentence.

1. My parents like to have smoked _____ at dinner.
   부모님은 저녁 식사 때 훈제 연어를 드시는 것을 좋아하세요.
2. The man who is sitting at the _____ has a problem.
   해변에 앉아 있는 그 남자는 문제가 있다.
3. Everyone knows that a spider _____ a web.
   거미가 거미줄을 친다는 사실은 모두 알고 있어.
4. He graduated from Harvard _____.
   그는 하버드 대학을 졸업했다.
5. Why are you so terrified of _____?
   넌 왜 그렇게 거미를 무서워 하니?
6. The _____ was filled for the big game.
   그 큰 시합 때문에 경기장이 만원이 되었다.
7. He went to the doctor with _____ pains.
   그는 위가 아파서 의사에게 갔다.
8. Love is a _____ made in heaven.
   사랑이란 하늘이 맺어 준 결합이다.
9. I had to ask a _____ to help me.
   나는 낯선 사람에게 나를 도와달라고 요청해야만 했다.
10. He carried a breakfast _____.
    그는 아침 식사가 담긴 쟁반을 가져왔다.
11. It's good, but a little too _____.
    좋아요. 그런데 좀 짜군요.
12. The man is excavating a _____.
    그 남자가 보물을 발굴하고 있다.
13. It takes fifty _____ to find the book.
    그 책을 찾는데 50 초가 걸려.
14. Adults forget the _____ of their youth.
    어른들은 젊었을 때의 고생을 잊어버린다.
15. _____ the positive rather than the negative.
    부정적인 것보다 긍정적인 것을 찾아라.
16. What size _____ do you wear?
    당신 바지의 치수는 얼마입니까?
17. A large brook is called a _____.
    큰 개천은 개울이라 불린다.
18. I remember the _____ well.
    난 그 장면을 잘 기억한다.

Hint

| seashore | salmon | tray | seek | salty | stranger | treasure | scene | trouble |
| second | spider | union | spin | stadium | university | stomach | trousers | stream |

Exercise

B. Fill in the word and meaning.

	Word	Meaning
01	stomach	
02	salmon	
03	tray	
04	scene	
05	university	
06	second	
07	union	
08	salty	
09	stream	
10	spin	
11	stranger	
12	trousers	
13	seashore	
14	stadium	
15	trouble	
16	seek	
17	treasure	
18	spider	

	Meaning	Word
01	연어	
02	짠, 소금기가 있는	
03	장면, 현장	
04	해변, 바닷가	
05	(몇) 초	
06	찾다, 추구하다	
07	거미	
08	실을 내다, 잣다	
09	경기장	
10	위, 배	
11	낯선 사람	
12	시내, 개울	
13	쟁반	
14	보물	
15	고생, 근심	
16	바지	
17	결합, 단결	
18	대학교	

🎧 C. Listen, write the word and meaning. (Track 84)

	Word	Meaning		Word	Meaning
01			10		
02			11		
03			12		
04			13		
05			14		
06			15		
07			16		
08			17		
09			18		

Review 14

A. Read and fill in the word and meaning.

word	definition	meaning
	a very large African bird with a long neck and legs	
	without any stops	
	that is easy to carry or to move	
	a meeting at which somebody is asked questions for a job, etc	
	to make a liquid flow steadily out of a container	
	making a lot of noise	
	to produce something that has not existed	
	a long thin strip of pasta	
	a building where criminals are kept as punishment	
	a hard strong metal that is used to make steel	
	a precious stone such as a diamond, ruby, etc.	
	one single thing on a list of things	
	a small thin piece of steel	
	having great strength or force	
	to run slowly and steadily for a long time	
	being in a particular place	
	to move head up and down	
	the feeling that you are better than other people	

Hint

item   pride   noisy   powerful   iron   present   nonstop   portable   prison
ostrich   jewel   nod   interview   needle   invent   jog   noodle   pour

B. Read and fill in the word and meaning.

word	definition	meaning
salmon	a large fish with silver skin and pink meat that we eat	
trousers	a piece of clothing that covers the whole of both your legs	
stadium	a large sports ground	
trouble	a situation causing a problem or worry	
salty	tasting of salt	
stomach	the organ in your body where food goes after you have eaten it	
union	the act of joining two or more things togethe	
seek	to look for something/somebody	
university	an institution at the highest level of education	
spider	a small creature with eight thin legs	
scene	one part of a book, film, etc in which the events happen	
treasure	a collection of valuable things such as jewellery	
spin	to produce thread from a mass of wool or cotton	
seashore	the land along the edge of the sea	
tray	a flat piece of metal or plastic for holding things	
second	one of the 60 parts into which a minute is divided	
stranger	a person that you do not know	
stream	a small narrow river	

Hint

seashore salmon tray seek salty stranger treasure scene trouble
second spider union spin stadium university stomach trousers stream

Unit 29

🎧 Listen and repeat. Track 85

01 affair [əfɛ́ər]
n 일, 사건   all event or situation
The whole **affair** has been extremely unpleasant.
모든 사건이 끔찍하게도 불쾌하다.

02 anxious [ǽŋkʃəs]
a 걱정스러운   feeling worried or nervous
I began to get **anxious** about my exam.
나는 시험에 대해서 걱정되기 시작했다.

03 apart [əpáːrt]
ad 떨어져서   separated by a distance
Two buildings were set up 2 miles **apart**.
두 건물은 2 마일 떨어져서 건립되었다.

04 appearance [əpíərəns]
n 외관, 출현   the coming of somebody / something
His **appearance** surprised me.
그의 출현에 나는 놀랐다.

05 area [ɛ́əriə]
n 구역, 지역   part of a place, town, etc.
He provided health care for the people in that **area**.
그는 그 지역 사람들의 건강을 돌보아 주었다.

06 argue [áːrgjuː]
v 논하다, 논쟁하다   to speak angrily to somebody
I **argue** with my brother all the time.
나는 항상 형과 논쟁을 한다.

07 bar [baːr]
n 술집, 막대기   a place where you can drink alcohol
The man is choosing a whiskey at the **bar**.
남자가 술집에서 위스키를 선택하고 있다.

08 behave [bihéiv]
v 행동하다   to act in a particular way
I think you **behaved** very badly towards your father.
나는 네가 네 아버지께 매우 무례하게 행동했다고 생각해.

09 broadcast [brɔ́ːdkæst]
v 방송하다   to send out programs on television or radio
The concert was **broadcasted** by relay.
그 음악회는 중계 방송되었다.

---

key words
nervous a 불안한, 신경질적인 / alcohol n 술, 알코올 음료 / relay n 중계 통신

🎧 Listen and repeat. Track 86

10 bubble [bʌ́bəl]
n 거품　a ball of air or gas, in liquid or floating in the air
We knew where there were fish because of the **bubbles** on the surface of the water.
우리는 물의 표면에 뜬 거품으로 어디에 물고기가 있는지 알 수 있다.

11 bullet [búlit]
n 탄알　a small metal object that is fired from a gun
The **bullet** could not penetrate the wall.
총알은 벽을 관통하지 못했다.

12 butterfly [bʌ́tərflài]
n 나비　an insect with large colorful wings and a thin body
Moths have less brightly colored wings than **butterflies**.
나방은 나비보다 날개 색깔이 덜 밝다.

13 buzz [bʌz]
n (윙윙)울리는 소리　the sound that a bee, etc makes when flying
I'm nervous because of the **buzz** of insects.
나는 곤충들의 윙윙거리는 소리 때문에 짜증이 나.

14 cabbage [kǽbidʒ]
n 양배추　a round vegetable with white, green or purple leaves
The **cabbage** has a large head.
양배추 통이 크다.

15 coal [koul]
n 석탄　a hard black mineral that is found below the ground
They substituted **coal** for oil.
그들은 석유 대신에 석탄을 사용했다.

16 coast [koust]
n 해안, 연안　the area of land that is close to the sea or ocean
I'd like to see the beaches on the West **Coast**.
서해안의 바닷가를 보고 싶어.

17 code [koud]
n 규범, 암호　a system of words, numbers, etc that are used to make a message secret
They wrote letters to each other in **code**.
그들은 서로에게 암호로 편지를 썼다.

18 college [kálidʒ]
n 단과대학　one of the main divisions of some large universities
I would like to study at an art **college** in Parsons university.
나는 파슨스 대학교의 예술단과대학에서 공부하고 싶다.

key words
penetrate v 관통하다 / moth n 나방 / mineral n 광물 / substitute v ~을 대신하다

Exercise

A. Complete the sentence.

1. I began to get _____ about my exam.
   나는 시험에 대해서 걱정되기 시작했다.

2. They wrote letters to each other in _____.
   그들은 서로에게 암호로 편지를 썼다.

3. His _____ surprised me.
   그의 출현에 나는 놀랐다.

4. The _____ could not penetrate the wall.
   총알은 벽을 관통하지 못했다.

5. He provided health care for the people in that _____.
   그는 그 지역 사람들의 건강을 돌보아 주었다.

6. I think you _____ very badly towards your father.
   나는 네가 네 아버지께 매우 무례하게 행동했다고 생각해.

7. The concert was _____ by relay.
   그 음악회는 중계 방송되었다.

8. We knew where there were fish because of the _____ on the surface of the water.
   우리는 물의 표면에 뜬 거품으로 어디에 물고기가 있는지 알 수 있다.

9. I'd like to see the beaches on the West _____.
   서해안의 바닷가를 보고 싶어.

10. The whole _____ has been extremely unpleasant.
    모든 사건이 끔찍하게도 불쾌하다.

11. Moths have less brightly colored wings than _____.
    나방은 나비보다 날개 색깔이 덜 밝다.

12. I'm nervous because of the _____ of insects.
    나는 곤충들의 윙윙거리는 소리 때문에 짜증이 나.

13. The _____ has a large head.
    양배추 통이 크다.

14. Two buildings were set up 2 miles _____.
    두 건물은 2 마일 떨어져서 건립되었다.

15. The man is choosing a whiskey at the _____.
    남자가 술집에서 위스키를 선택하고 있다.

16. They substituted _____ for oil.
    그들은 석유 대신에 석탄을 사용했다.

17. I _____ with my brother all the time.
    나는 항상 형과 논쟁을 한다.

18. I would like to study at an art _____ in Parsons university.
    나는 파슨스 대학교의 예술단과대학에서 공부하고 싶다.

Hint

| butterfly | apart | coal | broadcast | bar | cabbage | bubble | bullet | college |
| behave | anxious | code | affair | area | appearance | argue | buzz | coast |

Exercise

B. Fill in the word and meaning.

	Word	Meaning
01	apart	
02	bar	
03	cabbage	
04	anxious	
05	coast	
06	broadcast	
07	buzz	
08	appearance	
09	bubble	
10	code	
11	behave	
12	affair	
13	college	
14	butterfly	
15	argue	
16	coal	
17	bullet	
18	area	

	Meaning	Word
01	일, 사건	
02	걱정스러운	
03	떨어져서	
04	외관, 출현	
05	구역, 지역	
06	논하다, 논쟁하다	
07	술집, 막대기	
08	행동하다	
09	방송하다	
10	거품	
11	탄알	
12	나비	
13	(윙윙)울리는 소리	
14	양배추	
15	석탄	
16	해안, 연안	
17	규범, 암호	
18	단과대학	

C. Listen, write the word and meaning. (Track 87)

	Word	Meaning		Word	Meaning
01			10		
02			11		
03			12		
04			13		
05			14		
06			15		
07			16		
08			17		
09			18		

Unit 30

🎧 Listen and repeat. Track 88

01 colored [kʌ́lərd]
a 채색된, ~색의   having a particular color
He is wearing red **colored** glasses.
그는 빨갛게 채색된 안경을 쓰고 있어.

02 comedy [kámədi]
n 희극, 코미디   a play that is intended to be funny
Don't forget that Sunday night is **comedy** night!
일요일 밤은 코미디의 밤이라는 것을 기억해 주십시오!

03 creature [kríːtʃər]
n 피조물, 생물   a living thing such as an animal
It is my pleasure to look at the sea **creatures**.
바다 생물들을 관찰하는 것이 나의 즐거움이다.

04 decide [disáid]
v 결정하다, 결심하다   to think carefully about the different possibilities
We **decide** what we must do and must not.
우리는 우리가 무엇을 해야 할 것이고 하지 말아야 할 것을 결정한다.

05 desert [dézərt]
n 사막   a large area of land that is covered by sand
Camels are useful in the **desert**.
낙타는 사막에서는 쓸모가 있다.

06 excited [iksáitid]
a 흥분한   nervous or upset and unable to relax
The children become more and more **excited**.
아이들이 점점 더 흥분하고 있다.

07 express [iksprés]
v 표현하다, 나타내다   to show a feeling by looks or actions
Express your idea clearly.
네 생각을 명확하게 표현해라.

08 extra [ékstrə]
a 여분의, 임시의   more than is usual or than exists already
Your physical activity will use **extra** calories.
당신의 신체활동은 여분의 칼로리를 소모할 것이다.

09 factory [fǽktəri]
n 공장   a building where goods are made
Factories produce less pollution than before.
공장들은 이전보다 오염을 덜 만든다.

---

key words
intend v 의도하다 / camel n 낙타 / relax v 긴장을 풀다

🎧 Listen and repeat. Track 89

10 fail
[feil]
v 실패하다, 떨어지다   not to be successful in achieving something
Though I **fail**, I will try again.
비록 실패할지라도 나는 다시 시도하겠다.

11 fairy
[fέəri]
n 요정   a creature like a small person, who has magic powers
A **fairy** is flying to my sister.
한 요정이 내 여동생에게로 날아가고 있어요.

12 handkerchief
[hǽŋkərtʃif]
n 손수건   a small piece of fabric using for blowing your nose
I've always wanted this kind of **handkerchief**.
늘 이런 종류의 손수건을 갖고 싶었어.

13 hang
[hæŋ]
v 걸다, 매달다   to be attached high place or position
Hang up your jacket on the hanger.
네 재킷을 옷걸이에 걸어라.

14 healthy
[hélθi]
a 건강한   having good health
The key to **healthy** weight is regular physical activity.
건강한 체중의 열쇠는 규칙적인 신체 활동이다.

15 herb
[həːrb]
n 약용식물, 풀잎   a plant whose leaves are used in medicines
I went to pick **herbs** in the mountains yesterday.
나는 어제 산으로 약용식물 뜯으러 갔다.

16 history
[hístəri]
n 역사   all the events of the past
He will go down in **history** as a hero.
그는 영웅으로서 역사에 남을 것이다.

17 host
[houst]
n 주인   a person who invites guests to a meal, a party, etc.
We thanked our **hosts** for the lovely party.
우리는 멋진 파티에 대해 주인에게 감사했다.

18 knowledge
[nάlidʒ]
n 지식   the information that you gain through education
He has a good **knowledge** of history.
그의 역사 지식은 상당히 깊다.

key words
attach v 달다, 붙이다 / past n 과거 / invite v 초대하다

Exercise

A. Complete the sentence.

1. He will go down in _____ as a hero.
   그는 영웅으로서 역사에 남을 것이다.

2. Camels are useful in the _____.
   낙타는 사막에서는 쓸모가 있다.

3. Don't forget that Sunday night is _____ night!
   일요일 밤은 코미디의 밤이라는 것을 기억해 주십시오!

4. _____ up your jacket on the hanger.
   네 재킷을 옷걸이에 걸어라.

5. It is my pleasure to look at the sea _____.
   바다 생물들을 관찰하는 것이 나의 즐거움이다.

6. We _____ what we must do and must not.
   우리는 우리가 무엇을 해야 할 것이고 하지 말아야 할 것을 결정한다.

7. The children become more and more _____.
   아이들이 점점 더 흥분하고 있다.

8. He is wearing red _____ glasses.
   그는 빨갛게 채색된 안경을 쓰고 있어.

9. I went to pick _____ in the mountains yesterday.
   나는 어제 산으로 약용식물 뜯으러 갔다.

10. _____ your idea clearly.
    네 생각을 명확하게 표현해라.

11. I've always wanted this kind of _____.
    늘 이런 종류의 손수건을 갖고 싶었어.

12. Your physical activity will use _____ calories.
    당신의 신체활동은 여분의 칼로리를 소모할 것이다.

13. _____ produce less pollution than before.
    공장들은 이전보다 오염을 덜 만든다.

14. He has a good _____ of history.
    그의 역사 지식은 상당히 깊다.

15. Though I _____, I will try again.
    비록 실패할지라도 나는 다시 시도하겠다.

16. A _____ is flying to my sister.
    한 요정이 내 여동생에게 날아가고 있어요.

17. The key to _____ weight is regular physical activity.
    건강한 체중의 열쇠는 규칙적인 신체 활동이다.

18. We thanked our _____ for the lovely party.
    우리는 멋진 파티에 대해 주인에게 감사했다.

Hint

| extra | hang | decide | colored | host | fail | handkerchief | excited | comedy |
| creature | herb | express | factory | desert | history | knowledge | fairy | healthy |

Exercise

B. Fill in the word and meaning.

	Word	Meaning
01	creature	
02	express	
03	factory	
04	colored	
05	hang	
06	comedy	
07	fairy	
08	handkerchief	
09	extra	
10	herb	
11	knowledge	
12	decide	
13	history	
14	excited	
15	host	
16	healthy	
17	fail	
18	desert	

	Meaning	Word
01	채색된, ~색의	
02	희극, 코미디	
03	피조물, 생물	
04	결정하다, 결심하다	
05	사막	
06	흥분한	
07	표현하다, 나타내다	
08	여분의, 임시의	
09	공장	
10	실패하다, 떨어지다	
11	요정	
12	손수건	
13	걸다, 매달다	
14	건강한	
15	약용식물, 풀잎	
16	역사	
17	주인	
18	지식	

C. Listen, write the word and meaning. (Track 90)

	Word	Meaning
01		
02		
03		
04		
05		
06		
07		
08		
09		

	Word	Meaning
10		
11		
12		
13		
14		
15		
16		
17		
18		

Review 15

A. Read and fill in the word and meaning.

word	definition	meaning
	a small metal object that is fired from a gun	
	all event or situation	
	one of the main divisions of some large universities	
	to send out programs on television or radio	
	feeling worried or nervous	
	a ball of air or gas, in liquid or floating in the air	
	a round vegetable with white, green or purple leaves	
	a system of words, numbers, etc that are used to make a message secret	
	to act in a particular way	
	the coming of somebody / something	
	an insect with large colorful wings and a thin body	
	to speak angrily to somebody	
	the sound that a bee, etc makes when flying	
	separated by a distance	
	a hard black mineral that is found below the ground	
	the area of land that is close to the sea or ocean	
	a place where you can drink alcohol	
	part of a place, town, etc.	

Hint

butterfly   apart   coal   broadcast   bar   cabbage   bubble   bullet   college
behave   anxious   code   affair   area   appearance   argue   buzz   coast

B. Read and fill in the word and meaning.

word	definition	meaning
	a person who invites guests to a meal, a party, etc.	
	a large area of land that is covered by sand	
	nervous or upset and unable to relax	
	all the events of the past	
	having a particular color	
	to think carefully about the different possibilities	
	to show a feeling by looks or actions	
	a plant whose leaves are used in medicines	
	a play that is intended to be funny	
	the information that you gain through education	
	not to be successful in achieving something	
	a living thing such as an animal	
	a small piece of fabric using for blowing your nose	
	having good health	
	a building where goods are made	
	more than is usual or than exists already	
	a creature like a small person, who has magic powers	
	to be attached high place or position	

Hint
extra   hang   decide   colored   host   fail   handkerchief   excited   comedy
creature   herb   express   factory   desert   history   knowledge   fairy   healthy

Unit 31

🎧 Listen and repeat. (Track 91)

01 keyboard
[kí:bɔ̀:rd]
n 자판   the set of keys on a computer
I asked my parents to buy a new **keyboard**.
나는 부모님께 새 자판을 사달라고 부탁했다.

02 kick
[kik]
v 차다   to hit something with your foot
The king is very angry so he **kicks** the pot.
왕은 화가 나서 냄비를 발로 찬다.

03 kindergarten
[kíndərgà:rtn]
n 유치원   a class to prepare children aged five for school
I take my child to and from the **kindergarten** everyday.
나는 매일 아이를 유치원에 데려가고 데려와.

04 ladder
[lǽdə:r]
n 사다리   an equipment for climbing up and down a wall
The firemen are coming down the **ladder**.
소방수들이 사다리를 내려오고 있다.

05 least
[li:st]
n 최소, 최저   the smallest in size, amount, etc
I usually walk for at **least** 30 minutes.
나는 보통 최소한 30분을 걸어.

06 level
[lévəl]
n 수준   a particular standard or quality
Each color indicates the **level** or degree of the practitioner's skills in this martial art.
각각의 색깔은 이 무술 수련자의 기술 수준 또는 정도를 나타낸다.

07 most
[moust]
a 대부분의   almost all of somebody / something
Most people visited the island from the United States.
미국에서 온 대부분의 사람들은 그 섬을 방문했다.

08 nut
[nʌt]
n 견과   a small hard fruit with a very hard shell
The **nut** is very hard to crack.
그 견과는 잘 깨지지 않는다.

09 ocean
[óuʃən]
n 대양, 바다   the mass of salt water that covers most of the earth
It was to sail across the **ocean** to New York city.
바다를 건너 뉴욕시로 갈 예정이었습니다.

key words
practitioner n 개업자, 전문가 / martial art n 무술 / crack v ~을 금가게 하다

🎧 Listen and repeat. (Track 92)

10 officer
[ɔ́(ː)fisər]
n 장교, 공무원　who is in a position of authority in the army or government
He is an **officer** pretty well-known for being intrepid.
그는 용맹하기로 꽤 유명한 장교다.

11 oneself
[wʌnsélf]
pron 스스로, 자기 자신을　used when the person who does an action is also affected by it
One can teach **oneself** to play the piano but it is easier to have lessons.
사람은 스스로 피아노를 치는 것 보다 남에게 배우는 것이 더 쉽다.

12 operate
[άpərèit]
v 작동하다, 움직이다　to be used or working
The lamp can be **operated** with a wall switch.
램프는 벽의 스위치로 작동될 수 있다.

13 opinion
[əpínjən]
n 의견, 견해　your thoughts about something
My **opinion** is not different from yours.
내 의견은 당신과 다르지 않다.

14 quarter
[kwɔ́ːrtər]
n 4분의 1　one of four equal parts of something
He asked me to cut all the apples into **quarters**.
그는 나에게 모든 사과들을 4분의 1 조각으로 잘라달라고 부탁했다.

15 quite
[kwait]
ad 아주, 완전히　completely; very
The operation of this machine is **quite** simple.
이 기계의 조작은 아주 간단하다.

16 raw
[rɔː]
a 생것의, 날것의　not cooked
Don't eat **raw** eggs.
생달걀은 먹지 마세요.

17 reason
[ríːzən]
n 이유, 까닭　a cause for something that has happened
A gas leak is very dangerous for two main **reasons**.
가스 누출은 두 가지 주된 이유 때문에 매우 위험하다.

18 receive
[risíːv]
v 받다, 맞이하다　to get something that is given to you
I'm very thankful to **receive** this reward.
이 상을 받게 된 것을 매우 감사하게 생각합니다.

key words
authority n 권위, 권력 / intrepidity n 용맹 / reward n 보수, 포상

Exercise

A. Complete the sentence.

1. I usually walk for at _____ 30 minutes.
   나는 보통 최소한 30분은 걸어.

2. It was to sail across the _____ to New York city.
   바다를 건너 뉴욕시로 갈 예정이었습니다.

3. _____ people visited the island from the United States.
   미국에서 온 대부분의 사람들은 그 섬을 방문했다.

4. I take my child to and from the _____ everyday.
   나는 매일 아이를 유치원에 데려가고 데려와.

5. Don't eat _____ eggs.
   생달걀은 먹지 마세요.

6. Each color indicates the _____ or degree of the practitioner's skills in this martial art.
   각각의 색깔은 이 무술 수련자의 기술 수준 또는 정도를 나타낸다.

7. The _____ is very hard to crack.
   그 견과는 잘 깨지지 않는다.

8. One can teach _____ to play the piano but it is easier to have lessons.
   사람은 스스로 피아노를 치는 것 보다 남에게 배우는 것이 더 쉽다.

9. I asked my parents to buy a new _____.
   나는 부모님께 새 자판을 사달라고 부탁했다.

10. The firemen are coming down the _____.
    소방수들이 사다리를 내려오고 있다.

11. The lamp can be _____ with a wall switch.
    램프는 벽의 스위치로 작동될 수 있다.

12. He asked me to cut all apples into _____.
    그는 나에게 모든 사과들을 4분의 1 조각으로 잘라달라고 부탁했다.

13. My _____ is not different from yours.
    내 의견은 당신과 다르지 않다.

14. The operation of this machine is _____ simple.
    이 기계의 조작은 아주 간단하다.

15. A gas leak is very dangerous for two main _____.
    가스 누출은 두 가지 주된 이유 때문에 매우 위험하다.

16. He is an _____ pretty well-known for being intrepid.
    그는 용맹하기로 꽤 유명한 장교다.

17. The king is very angry so he _____ the pot.
    왕은 화가 나서 냄비를 발로 찬다.

18. I'm very thankful to _____ this reward.
    이 상을 받게 된 것을 매우 감사하게 생각합니다.

Hint

quarter	least	kick	ocean	keyboard	reason	oneself	ladder	opinion
most	nut	receive	officer	kindergarten	raw	level	operate	quite

Exercise

B. Fill in the word and meaning.

	Word	Meaning
01	ladder	
02	nut	
03	oneself	
04	keyboard	
05	opinion	
06	level	
07	quite	
08	ocean	
09	raw	
10	kindergarten	
11	reason	
12	officer	
13	receive	
14	least	
15	quarter	
16	most	
17	operate	
18	kick	

	Meaning	Word
01	자판	
02	차다	
03	유치원	
04	사다리	
05	최소, 최저	
06	수준	
07	대부분의	
08	견과	
09	대양, 바다	
10	장교, 공무원	
11	스스로, 자기 자신을	
12	작동하다, 움직이다	
13	의견, 견해	
14	4분의 1	
15	아주, 완전히	
16	생것의, 날것의	
17	이유, 까닭	
18	받다, 맞이하다	

🎧 C. Listen, write the word and meaning. (Track 93)

	Word	Meaning		Word	Meaning
01			10		
02			11		
03			12		
04			13		
05			14		
06			15		
07			16		
08			17		
09			18		

Unit 31

Unit 32

🎧 Listen and repeat. Track 94

01 seminar
[sémənàːr]
n 세미나   a meeting for discussion
What did the man say about the **seminar**?
남자가 세미나에 대해 뭐라고 말했나요?

02 senior
[síːnjər]
a 연상의, 선배의   who is older or of a high position
Senior students are usually allowed certain privileges.
선배학생들에게는 보통 어떤 특권이 부여된다.

03 sense
[sens]
n 감각, 직감   the ability to think in a reasonable or sensible way
I have a good **sense** about people.
나는 사람을 보는 좋은 감각이 있다.

04 sentence
[séntəns]
n 문장   a set of words expressing a statement
The meaning of that **sentence** is clear.
그 문장의 뜻은 분명하다.

05 serve
[səːrv]
v (음식을) 차려내다, 봉사하다   to give somebody food or drink
What dishes do you **serve** for breakfast?
아침으로 어떤 음식을 차리는가?

06 shake
[ʃeik]
v 흔들다   to move something quickly up and down
Shake hard for five minutes.
5분간 세게 흔드세요.

07 stress
[stres]
n 압박, 스트레스   pressure or worry caused by the problem
The **stress** of everyday living can really get you down.
매일 겪는 스트레스는 당신을 우울하게 만들 수 있습니다.

08 stuff
[stʌf]
v 채우다, 메우다   to fill something with something
I **stuff** feathers into my pillow.
나는 베개에 깃털을 채운다.

09 success
[səksés]
n 성공   the fact that you have achieved something that you want
His latest novel was a **success**.
그의 가장 최근 소설은 성공적이었다.

key words
allow v 인정하다, 허용하다 / privilege n 특권, 특전 / reasonable a 분별 있는
sensible a 느낄 수 있는 / statement n 진술

🎧 Listen and repeat. (Track 95)

10 suit
[suːt]

v 어울리다 / n 한 벌   a set of clothes made of the same fabric
The man is putting on a **suit**.
남자가 옷 한 벌을 입고 있다.

11 surprise
[sərpráiz]

n 놀람 / v 놀라게 하다   cause to feel wonder or astonishment
I am going to **surprise** my friends!
친구들을 깜짝 놀라게 해 줘야지!

12 sweep
[swiːp]

v 청소하다, 쓸다   to clean a room, surface, etc.
He helps his wife **sweep** the floor.
그는 그의 부인이 바닥 청소하는 것을 도와 줍니다.

13 trace
[treis]

n 자취, 흔적, 발자국   a mark or a sign that shows that somebody / something existed
We could not see any **traces**.
우리는 아무 흔적도 볼 수 없었다.

14 valley
[vǽli]

n 계곡, 골짜기   an area of low land between mountains
The people living in the **valley** feared a deluge.
그 계곡에 사는 사람들은 홍수를 두려워했다.

15 value
[vǽljuː]

n 가치, 가격   how much something is worth in money or other goods
The **value** of the dollar is falling.
달러의 가치가 하락하고 있다.

16 vet
[vet]

n 수의사   a person whose job is to treat animals
The **vet** gives our dogs shots twice a year.
그 수의사는 우리 개들에게 일 년에 두 번 주사를 놓아준다.

17 voice
[vɔis]

n 목소리, 음성   sounds produced through the mouth by a person speaking
A well-known **voice** reached me.
귀에 익은 목소리가 들려왔다.

18 vote
[vout]

n 투표 / v 투표하다   to show formally a choice by marking a piece of paper.
Only 40 percent of people **voted**.
40%의 사람들만 투표를 했다.

key words
astonishment n 놀람 / mark n 자국 / deluge n 큰 홍수 / shot n (주사)한 대, 발포
well-known a 유명한, 잘 알고 있는 / formally ad 공식적으로

Unit 32 **161**

Exercise

A. Complete the sentence.

1. The meaning of that _____ is clear.
   그 문장의 뜻은 분명하다.

2. _____ students are usually allowed certain privileges.
   선배학생들에게는 보통 어떤 특권이 부여된다.

3. The _____ of the dollar is falling.
   달러의 가치가 하락하고 있다.

4. I have a good _____ about people.
   나는 사람을 보는 좋은 감각이 있다.

5. A well-known _____ reached me.
   귀에 익은 목소리가 들려왔다.

6. What dishes do you _____ for breakfast?
   아침으로 어떤 음식을 차리는가?

7. He helps his wife _____ the floor.
   그는 그의 부인이 바닥 청소하는 것을 도와 줍니다.

8. We could not see any _____.
   우리는 아무 흔적도 볼 수 없었다.

9. _____ hard for five minutes.
   5분간 세게 흔드세요.

10. The _____ of everyday living can really get you down.
    매일 겪는 스트레스는 당신을 우울하게 만들 수 있습니다.

11. I _____ feathers into my pillow.
    나는 베개에 깃털을 채운다.

12. The people living in the _____ feared a deluge.
    계곡에 사는 사람들은 홍수를 두려워했다.

13. Only 40 percent of people _____.
    40%의 사람들만 투표를 했다.

14. The man is putting on a _____.
    남자가 옷 한 벌을 입고 있다.

15. I am going to _____ my friends!
    친구들을 깜짝 놀라게 해 줘야지!

16. What did the man say about the _____?
    남자가 세미나에 대해 뭐라고 말했나요?

17. His latest novel was a _____.
    그의 가장 최근 소설은 성공적이었다.

18. The _____ gives our dogs shots twice a year.
    그 수의사는 우리 개들에게 일 년에 두 번 주사를 놓아준다.

Hint

| stuff | vet | stress | trace | sense | sweep | vote | success | seminar |
| value | senior | suit | shake | voice | serve | sentence | valley | surprise |

Unit 32

Exercise

B. Fill in the word and meaning.

	Word	Meaning
01	success	
02	senior	
03	trace	
04	shake	
05	suit	
06	valley	
07	seminar	
08	sweep	
09	voice	
10	stress	
11	vote	
12	sense	
13	vet	
14	stuff	
15	value	
16	serve	
17	surprise	
18	sentence	

	Meaning	Word
01	세미나	
02	연상의, 선배의	
03	감각, 직감	
04	문장	
05	(음식을)차려내다, 봉사하다	
06	흔들다	
07	압박, 스트레스	
08	채우다, 메우다	
09	성공	
10	어울리다, 한 벌	
11	놀람, 놀라게 하다	
12	청소하다, 쓸다	
13	자취, 흔적, 발자국	
14	계곡, 골짜기	
15	가치, 가격	
16	수의사	
17	목소리, 음성	
18	투표, 투표하다	

C. Listen, write the word and meaning. (Track 96)

	Word	Meaning		Word	Meaning
01			10		
02			11		
03			12		
04			13		
05			14		
06			15		
07			16		
08			17		
09			18		

Review 16

A. Read and fill in the word and meaning.

word	definition	meaning
	a cause for something that has happened	
	to get something that is given to you	
	the set of keys on a computer	
	the mass of salt water that covers most of the earth	
	not cooked	
	to hit something with your foot	
	completely; very	
	who is in a position of authority in the army or government	
	a class to prepare children aged five for school	
	a small hard fruit with a very hard shell	
	used when the person who does an action is also affected by it	
	an equipment for climbing up and down a wall	
	to be used or working	
	a particular standard or quality	
	one of four equal parts of something	
	the smallest in size, amount, etc	
	your thoughts about something	
	almost all of somebody / something	

Hint

quarter least kick ocean keyboard reason oneself ladder opinion
most nut receive officer kindergarten raw level operate quite

B. Read and fill in the word and meaning.

word	definition	meaning
	to clean a room, surface, etc.	
	the ability to think in a reasonable or sensible way	
	the fact that you have achieved something that you want	
	a mark or a sign that shows that somebody / something existed	
	a meeting for discussion	
	cause to feel wonder or astonishment	
	an area of low land between mountains	
	who is older or of a high position	
	how much something is worth in money or other goods	
	a set of clothes made of the same fabric	
	a set of words expressing a statement	
	to fill something with something	
	a person whose job is to treat animals	
	to give somebody food or drink	
	pressure or worry caused by the problem	
	sounds produced through the mouth by a person speaking	
	to move something quickly up and down	
	to show formally a choice by marking a piece of paper	

Hint

stuff   vet   stress   trace   sense   sweep   vote   success   seminar
value   senior suit   shake   voice   serve   sentence valley   surprise

Unit 33

🎧 Listen and repeat. Track 97

01 arrow
[ǽrou]

n 화살   a long thin weapon which is sharp and pointed at one end

Everything depended on my final **arrow**.
모든 것은 나의 마지막 화살에 달려 있었다.

02 ash
[æʃ]

n 재, 화산재   the grey or black powder that is left after something is burnt

The **ash** was so hot that people couldn't get out of their houses.
재가 너무 뜨거워서, 사람들은 집 밖으로 나올 수 없었다.

03 assistant
[əsístənt]

n 보조자   a person who supports somebody

I think we'll need at least two more **assistants**.
제 생각엔 보조자가 최소한 2명은 더 있어야 할 것 같아요.

04 attention
[əténʃən]

n 주의, 돌봄   thinking about something / somebody carefully

He shows **attention** to everything.
그는 모든 것에 주의를 기울인다.

05 bacteria
[bæktíəriə]

n 세균, 박테리아   very small organisms that can cause disease

Our bodies have the natural ability to fight off **bacteria** and diseases.
우리 몸은 박테리아나 질병을 스스로 퇴치하는 능력이 있다.

06 bakery
[béikəri]

n 제과점   a place where bread are made and sold

Is there a French **bakery** in this neighborhood?
이 근처에 프랑스 제과점이 있습니까?

07 calm
[ka:m]

a 고요한, 잔잔한   not excited, nervous or upset

He stared at the **calm** sea for a long time.
그는 잔잔한 바다를 오랫동안 응시했다.

08 camp
[kæmp]

v 야영하다   to stay in a tent and live in it

They had never **camped** there before.
그들은 지금까지 야영 한 적이 없습니다.

09 campaign
[kæmpéin]

n 캠페인, 선거운동   a planned set of activities over a period of time to achieve their aim

The **campaign** had made quite an impact on young people.
그 캠페인은 젊은이들에게 꽤 영향을 주었다.

key words
support v 지지하다, 원조하다 / organism n 유기체 / stay v 머무르다 / impact n 영향, 충격

🎧 Listen and repeat. (Track 98)

10 cane [kein]
n 지팡이   a piece of a thin rod, used to help somebody to walk
The older woman is walking with a **cane**.
할머니가 지팡이를 짚고 걷고 있다.

11 cash [kæʃ]
n 현금, 현찰   money in the form of coins or bills
Can you convert this traveler's check into **cash**?
이 여행자 수표를 현금으로 바꿔주시겠어요?

12 castle [kǽsl]
n 성, 성곽   a large building with thick, high walls that were built by kings
The **castle** was enclosed by tall mountains.
그 성은 높은 산들로 둘러싸여 있었다.

13 common [kámən]
a 평범한, 보통의   ordinary; not unusual
In fact, this is one of the most **common** causes about accidents.
사실, 이것은 사고를 야기하는 가장 평범한 형태 중 하나이다.

14 community [kəmjúːnəti]
n 지역사회   all the people who live in a particular area
He worked for the good of the **community**.
그는 지역 사회의 유익을 위해 일했다.

15 company [kámpəni]
n 회사, 교제   a business organization that makes money
The **company** is expecting a large sale of the new models.
그 회사는 신 모델의 대량 판매를 기대하고 있다.

16 compass [kámpəs]
n 나침반, 컴퍼스   an instrument for finding direction
The **compass** points to thirty degrees.
나침반이 방위 30도를 가리키고 있다.

17 connect [kənékt]
v 잇다, 연결하다   to be joined together
He is **connecting** a cable to the computer.
남자가 전선을 컴퓨터에 연결하고 있다.

18 contain [kəntéin]
v 포함하다   to have something inside or as part of itself
This book **contains** many interesting stories.
이 책은 재미있는 이야기를 많이 포함한다.

key words
rod **n** 막대 / convert **v** 전환하다, 교환하다 / check **n** 수표 / enclose **v** 둘러싸다 / ordinary **a** 보통의

Unit 33

Exercise

A. Complete the sentence.

1. In fact, this is one of the most _____ causes about accidents.
   사실, 이것은 사고를 야기하는 가장 평범한 형태 중 하나이다.

2. Is there a French _____ in this neighborhood?
   이 근처에 프랑스 제과점이 있습니까?

3. Everything depended on my final _____.
   모든 것은 나의 마지막 화살에 달려 있었다.

4. This book _____ many interesting stories.
   이 책은 재미있는 이야기를 많이 포함한다.

5. The _____ points to thirty degrees.
   나침반이 방위 30도를 가리키고 있다.

6. I think we'll need at least two more _____.
   제 생각엔 보조자가 최소한 2명은 더 있어야 할 것 같아요.

7. The _____ was enclosed by tall mountains.
   그 성은 높은 산들로 둘러싸여 있었다.

8. He shows _____ to everything.
   그는 모든 것에 주의를 기울인다.

9. He worked for the good of the _____.
   그는 지역 사회의 유익을 위해 일했다.

10. Our bodies have the natural ability to fight off _____ and diseases.
    우리 몸은 박테리아나 질병을 스스로 퇴치하는 능력이 있다.

11. He stared at the _____ sea for a long time.
    그는 잔잔한 바다를 오랫동안 응시했다.

12. They had never _____ there before.
    그들은 지금까지 야영 한 적이 없습니다.

13. The _____ had made quite an impact on young people.
    그 캠페인은 젊은이들에게 꽤 영향을 주었다.

14. The _____ was so hot that people couldn't get out of their houses.
    재가 너무 뜨거워서, 사람들은 집 밖으로 나올 수 없었다.

15. The older woman is walking with a _____.
    할머니가 지팡이를 짚고 걷고 있다.

16. Can you convert this traveler's check into _____?
    이 여행자 수표를 현금으로 바꿔주시겠어요?

17. The _____ is expecting a large sale of the new models.
    그 회사는 신 모델의 대량 판매를 기대하고 있다.

18. He is _____ a cable to the computer.
    남자가 전선을 컴퓨터에 연결하고 있다.

Hint

| campaign | bacteria | contain | cane | assistant | common | arrow | cash | bakery |
| community | connect | ash | calm | compass | attention | castle | camp | company |

Exercise

B. Fill in the word and meaning.

	Word	Meaning
01	bacteria	
02	arrow	
03	cane	
04	bakery	
05	cash	
06	community	
07	connect	
08	assistant	
09	contain	
10	compass	
11	company	
12	attention	
13	common	
14	camp	
15	campaign	
16	castle	
17	calm	
18	ash	

	Meaning	Word
01	화살	
02	재, 화산재	
03	보조자	
04	주의, 돌봄	
05	세균, 박테리아	
06	제과점	
07	고요한, 잔잔한	
08	야영하다	
09	캠페인, 선거운동	
10	지팡이	
11	현금, 현찰	
12	성, 성곽	
13	평범한, 보통의	
14	지역사회	
15	회사, 교제	
16	나침반, 컴퍼스	
17	잇다, 연결하다	
18	포함하다	

🎧 **C. Listen, write the word and meaning.** (Track 99)

	Word	Meaning		Word	Meaning
01			10		
02			11		
03			12		
04			13		
05			14		
06			15		
07			16		
08			17		
09			18		

Unit 34

🎧 Listen and repeat. (Track 100)

01 destination [dèstənéiʃən]
n 목적, 목적지   a place to which somebody / something is going
I finally reached my **destination** two hours late.
나는 마침내 두 시간이나 늦게 목적지에 도착했다.

02 detail [díːteil]
n 상세, 세부   the small facts or features of something
The **details** were sent by fax.
세부적인 내용은 팩스로 보내졌다.

03 dew [djuː]
n 이슬   the very small drops of water that form on the ground
If the sun shines, **dew** goes away.
태양이 빛나면 이슬은 사라진다.

04 dice [dais]
n 주사위   a small square object with a different number of spots on each side
Throw the **dice** to see who goes first.
주사위를 던져서 누가 첫 번째인지 알아보자.

05 dig [dig]
v 파다   to make a hole in the ground
The worker uses a machine to **dig** the hole.
인부가 기계로 구멍을 파고 있다.

06 direct [dirékt]
v 길을 가리키다   to show somebody how to get to somewhere
Could you **direct** me to the Shilla Hotel?
신라호텔까지 가는 길 좀 가르쳐주실래요?

07 fan [fæn]
n 팬   a person who admires somebody
The **fans** are leaving the stadium.
팬들이 경기장을 떠나고 있다.

08 feather [féðər]
n 깃털   one of the light, soft things that grow in a bird's skin
He is plucking **feathers** from a chicken.
그는 닭의 깃털을 뽑고 있어요.

09 festival [féstəvəl]
n 축제, 잔치   a day or days when people celebrate a special event
I decided to open a bakery during the **festival**.
나는 축제 기간 동안 제과점을 열기로 했다.

key words
drop n 방울 / admire v 숭배하다, 찬양하다 / pluck v 잡아뜯다 / celebrate v 경축하다

🎧 Listen and repeat. Track 101

10 fist
[fist]
n 주먹   a hand when it is tightly closed
He struck the table with his **fist**.
그는 주먹으로 탁자를 쳤다.

11 flood
[flʌd]
n 홍수 / **v** 범람하다   to fill a place with water
The River Trent **floods** almost every year.
트렌트 강은 매년 범람한다.

12 hometown
[hóumtàun]
n 고향, 출생지   the place where you were born
Do you remember your **hometown**?
너는 고향을 기억하니?

13 homework
[hóumwə̀rk]
n 숙제   work that teachers give to pupils to do at home
Do you often have hard **homework**?
하기 힘든 과제가 자주 있습니까?

14 honest
[ánist]
a 정직한   always telling the truth
He is **honest** by nature.
그는 원래 정직한 사람이다.

15 honey
[hʌ́ni]
n 꿀   a sweet yellow substance made by bees
Honey is made by worker bees.
꿀은 일벌들에 의해서 만들어진다.

16 hoop
[hu:p]
n 테, 후프   a large ring of plastic or wood
The girl is playing with a **hoop**.
소녀가 훌라후프를 돌리고 있다.

17 however
[hauévər]
conj 하지만, 그러나   although something is true
He, **however**, has a different opinion.
하지만 그는 다른 의견을 가지고 있다.

18 litter
[lítər]
n 쓰레기   small pieces of rubbish / garbage
The men are picking up **litter**.
남자들이 쓰레기를 줍고 있다.

key words
pupil n 학생 / although conj 비록 ~일지라도 / rubbish n 쓰레기

Unit 34 171

Exercise

A. Complete the sentence.

1. The _____ are leaving the stadium.
   팬들이 경기장을 떠나고 있다.
2. I finally reached my _____ two hours late.
   나는 마침내 두 시간이나 늦게 목적지에 도착했다.
3. He struck the table with his _____.
   그는 주먹으로 탁자를 쳤다.
4. The worker uses a machine to _____ the hole.
   인부가 기계로 구멍을 파고 있다.
5. Do you often have hard _____?
   하기 힘든 과제가 자주 있습니까?
6. The _____ were sent by fax.
   세부적인 내용은 팩스로 보내졌다.
7. _____ is made by worker bees.
   꿀은 일벌들에 의해서 만들어진다.
8. I decided to open a bakery during the _____.
   나는 축제 기간 동안 제과점을 열기로 했다.
9. The men are picking up _____.
   남자들이 쓰레기를 줍고 있다.
10. Do you remember your _____?
    너는 고향을 기억하니?
11. The girl is playing with a _____.
    소녀가 훌라후프를 돌리고 있다.
12. If the sun shines, _____ goes away.
    태양이 빛나면 이슬은 사라진다.
13. He is _____ by nature.
    그는 원래 정직한 사람이다.
14. He is plucking _____ from a chicken.
    그는 닭의 깃털을 뽑고 있어요.
15. Throw the _____ to see who goes first.
    주사위를 던져서 누가 첫 번째인지 알아보자.
16. Could you _____ me to the Shilla Hotel?
    신라호텔까지 가는 길 좀 가르쳐주실래요?
17. The River Trent _____ almost every year.
    트렌트 강은 매년 범람한다.
18. He, _____, has a different opinion.
    하지만 그는 다른 의견을 가지고 있다.

Hint

| direct | honey | dice | fist | honest | fan | detail | flood | homework |
| feather | litter | destination | dew | however | hoop | festival | dig | hometown |

Unit 34

Exercise

B. Fill in the word and meaning.

	Word	Meaning
01	dew	
02	fan	
03	direct	
04	fist	
05	destination	
06	festival	
07	hometown	
08	honey	
09	detail	
10	homework	
11	litter	
12	hoop	
13	feather	
14	however	
15	dig	
16	honest	
17	flood	
18	dice	

	Meaning	Word
01	목적, 목적지	
02	상세, 세부	
03	이슬	
04	주사위	
05	파다	
06	길을 가리키다	
07	팬	
08	깃털	
09	축제, 잔치	
10	주먹	
11	홍수, 범람하다	
12	고향, 출생지	
13	숙제	
14	정직한	
15	꿀	
16	테, 후프	
17	하지만, 그러나	
18	쓰레기	

🎧 C. Listen, write the word and meaning. (Track 102)

	Word	Meaning		Word	Meaning
01			10		
02			11		
03			12		
04			13		
05			14		
06			15		
07			16		
08			17		
09			18		

Review 17

A. Read and fill in the word and meaning.

word	definition	meaning
	not excited, nervous or upset	
	very small organisms that can cause disease	
	an instrument for finding direction	
	to stay in a tent and live in it	
	a place where bread are made and sold	
	a long thin weapon which is sharp and pointed at one end	
	a planned set of activities over a period of time to achieve their aim	
	thinking about something / somebody carefully	
	a piece of a thin rod, used to help somebody to walk	
	to be joined together	
	money in the form of coins or bills	
	a business organization that makes money	
	a large building with thick, high walls that were built by kings	
	the grey or black powder that is left after something is burnt	
	all the people who live in a particular area	
	ordinary; not unusual	
	to have something inside or as part of itself	
	a person who supports somebody	

Hint

campaign   bacteria   contain   cane   assistant   common   arrow   cash   bakery
community   connect   ash   calm   compass   attention   castle   camp   company

B. Read and fill in the word and meaning.

word	definition	meaning
however	although something is true	
fan	a person who admires somebody	
litter	small pieces of rubbish / garbage	
destination	a place to which somebody / something is going	
hoop	a large ring of plastic or wood	
direct	to show somebody how to get to somewhere	
feather	one of the light, soft things that grow in a bird's skin	
hometown	the place where you were born	
festival	a day or days when people celebrate a special event	
detail	the small facts or features of something	
honest	always telling the truth	
fist	a hand when it is tightly closed	
dig	to make a hole in the ground	
honey	a sweet yellow substance made by bees	
dew	the very small drops of water that form on the ground	
flood	to fill a place with water	
homework	work that teachers give to pupils to do at home	
dice	a small square object with a different number of spots on each side	

Hint
direct honey dice fist honest fan detail flood homework
feather litter destination dew however hoop festival dig hometown

Unit 35

🎧 Listen and repeat. Track 103

01 lonely
[lóunli]
a 외로운, 고독한   unhappy because you have no friends
The problem is that I often feel **lonely** at night.
밤에 종종 외롭다는 것이 문제야.

02 lucky
[lʌ́ki]
a 행운의, 운 좋은   having good luck
He is **lucky** to be alive after an accident like that.
저런 사고에도 살아남다니 그는 운이 좋다.

03 magician
[mədʒíʃən]
n 마법사, 마술사   a person who performs magic tricks to entertain people
I promised her to become a great **magician**.
나는 그녀에게 훌륭한 마술사가 되겠다고 약속했어요.

04 manage
[mǽnidʒ]
v 다루다, 관리하다   control a business, system, people, etc.
He has **managed** a hotel for 10 years.
그는 10년간 호텔을 운영했다.

05 melt
[melt]
v 녹다   to change from a solid to a liquid
The snow has **melted** completely.
눈이 완전히 녹았다.

06 nature
[néitʃər]
n 자연   all the plants, animals and things that exist in the universe
We should protect **nature**.
우리는 자연을 보호해야 한다.

07 pack
[pæk]
v 싸다, 꾸리다   to put something into a container
There are many things to **pack** before he leaves.
그가 떠나기 전에 꾸려야 할 것들이 많다.

08 pain
[pein]
n 고통, 아픔   the feeling when you have been hurt
Headache is a **pain** in the inside part of your head.
두통은 당신 머리 안의 고통이다.

09 part
[paːrt]
n 일부, 부문   a section, piece of something
The first **part** of the concert is already over.
콘서트의 첫 부분은 이미 끝났어요.

key words
alive a 살아 있는 / solid n 고체 / universe n 우주

🎧 Listen and repeat. Track 104

10 past
[pæst]
n 과거　the time before the present
The word 'been' is the **past** participle of the verb 'be.'
been 이란 말은 be동사의 과거분사이다.

11 path
[pæθ]
n 작은 길, 보도　a way across a piece of land
There was a narrow **path** leading down the cliff.
절벽으로 이르는 좁고 작은 길이 있었어요.

12 peaceful
[píːsfəl]
a 평화로운　not wanting or involving war, violence
We have tried to find a **peaceful** solution.
우리는 평화로운 해결책을 찾기 위해 노력해 왔습니다.

13 recycle
[riːsáikəl]
v 재활용하다　to use the same ideas, methods, etc, again
Recycle cans and papers.
캔과 종이를 재활용 합시다.

14 rent
[rent]
v 빌리다, 임대하다　to pay money to somebody so that you can use something
I'd like to **rent** a compact car for four days.
나흘간 소형차를 빌리고 싶은데요.

15 require
[rikwáiəːr]
v 요구하다　to need something
Soccer **requires** teamwork more than individual skill.
축구는 개인기보다 팀워크를 더 요구한다.

16 respond
[rispánd]
v 응답하다, 반응하다　to react to something
I expect you to **respond** right away.
나는 당신이 즉시 응답하길 기대합니다.

17 rid
[rid]
v 제거하다　to succeed in removing something completely
You must get **rid** of bad habits.
당신은 나쁜 습관을 버려야 한다.

18 root
[ruːt]
n 뿌리　the part of a plant that grows under the ground
My uncle carefully pulled up a ginseng by its **roots**.
삼촌은 조심스럽게 인삼을 뿌리째 뽑았다.

key words
method n 방법 / compact a 소형인 / react v 반응을 나타내다

Exercise

A. Complete the sentence.

1. I promised her to become a great _____.
   나는 그녀에게 훌륭한 마술사가 되겠다고 약속했어요.

2. The first _____ of the concert is already over.
   콘서트의 첫 부분은 이미 끝났어요.

3. The snow has _____ completely.
   눈이 완전히 녹았다.

4. _____ cans and papers.
   캔과 종이를 재활용 합시다.

5. We should protect _____.
   우리는 자연을 보호해야 한다.

6. There are many things to _____ before he leaves.
   그가 떠나기 전에 꾸려야 할 것들이 많다.

7. He has _____ a hotel for 10 years.
   그는 10년간 호텔을 운영했다.

8. I expect you to _____ right away.
   나는 당신이 즉시 응답하길 기대합니다.

9. Headache is a _____ in the inside part of your head.
   두통은 당신 머리 안의 고통이다.

10. There was a narrow _____ leading down the cliff.
    절벽으로 이르는 좁고 작은 길이 있었어요.

11. We have tried to find a _____ solution.
    우리는 평화로운 해결책을 찾기 위해 노력해 왔습니다.

12. I'd like to _____ a compact car for four days.
    나흘간 소형차를 빌리고 싶은데요.

13. The problem is that I often feel _____ at night.
    밤에 종종 외롭다는 것이 문제야.

14. Soccer _____ teamwork more than individual skill.
    축구는 개인기보다 팀워크를 더 요구한다.

15. My uncle carefully pulled up a ginseng by its _____.
    삼촌은 조심스럽게 인삼을 뿌리째 뽑았다.

16. The word 'been' is the _____ participle of the verb 'be.'
    been이란 말은 be동사의 과거분사이다.

17. He is _____ to be alive after an accident like that.
    저런 사고에도 살아남다니 그는 운이 좋다.

18. You must get _____ of bad habits.
    당신은 나쁜 습관을 버려야 한다.

Hint

| root | pain | nature | manage | rid | pack | past | respond | lucky |
| lonely | path | magician | recycle | melt | part | rent | peaceful | require |

Exercise

B. Fill in the word and meaning.

	Word	Meaning
01	lucky	
02	pack	
03	manage	
04	part	
05	recycle	
06	path	
07	lonely	
08	respond	
09	pain	
10	rid	
11	magician	
12	root	
13	require	
14	past	
15	rent	
16	nature	
17	peaceful	
18	melt	

	Meaning	Word
01	외로운, 고독한	
02	행운의, 운좋은	
03	마법사, 마술사	
04	다루다, 관리하다	
05	녹다	
06	자연	
07	싸다, 꾸리다	
08	고통, 아픔	
09	일부, 부문	
10	과거	
11	작은 길, 보도	
12	평화로운	
13	재활용하다	
14	빌리다, 임대하다	
15	요구하다	
16	응답하다, 반응하다	
17	제거하다	
18	뿌리	

C. Listen, write the word and meaning. (Track 105)

	Word	Meaning		Word	Meaning
01			10		
02			11		
03			12		
04			13		
05			14		
06			15		
07			16		
08			17		
09			18		

Unit 36

🎧 Listen and repeat. Track 106

01 sharply [ʃáːrpli]
ad 날카롭게   having a very thin but strong edge or point
The road bends **sharply** to the left.
그 길은 왼쪽으로 날카롭게 굽어집니다.

02 shell [ʃel]
n 껍질, 등딱지   the hard outer part of eggs, some seeds, etc.
He's picking up a **shell** on the beach.
그는 바닷가에서 조개껍질을 줍고 있다.

03 shine [ʃain]
v 빛나다   to be bright
The sea is **shining** in the light of the moon.
바다가 달빛을 받아 빛나고 있다.

04 shy [ʃai]
a 수줍어하는   to be uncomfortable in the company of other people
Korean people are **shy** and polite.
한국 사람들은 수줍어하고 공손하다.

05 silent [sáilənt]
a 침묵을 지키는   not speaking, completely quiet
They were **silent** for several seconds.
그들은 몇 초 동안 침묵을 지켰다.

06 simple [símpəl]
a 간단한, 단순한   not complicated; easy to do
Many advertisers often use this **simple** fact.
많은 광고주들이 이 단순한 사실을 종종 이용한다.

07 swallow [swálou]
n 제비   a kind of small bird with pointed wings and a forked tail
One **swallow** does not make a summer.
제비 한 마리 봤다고 여름이 온 것이 아니다.

08 system [sístəm]
n 체제, 시스템   an organized set of ideas or rules
That's the way the **system** works.
그것이 그 시스템이 작동하는 방식이다.

09 tailor [téilər]
n 재봉사, 재단사   a person whose job is to make clothes
The man is looking for a **tailor**.
남자가 재단사를 찾고 있다.

key words
bend v 구부러지다 / uncomfortable a 불편한, 거북한 / complicated a 복잡한

🎧 Listen and repeat. (Track 107)

10 tale [teil]
n 이야기   an imaginative story
The **tale** is too long to hear.
그 이야기는 너무 길어서 들을 수 없다.

11 tap [tæp]
v 가볍게 두드리다   to hit somebody / something lightly
He **tapped** me on the shoulder.
그는 내 어깨를 가볍게 툭 쳤다.

12 tax [tæks]
n 세금, 조세   money that you have to pay to the government
We pay an income **tax**.
우리는 소득세를 낸다.

13 wallet [wάlit]
n 지갑   a small folding case made of leather or plastic
I'd like to buy the **wallet** at the store.
나는 그 상점에서 지갑을 사고 싶다.

14 wave [weiv]
n 파도, 물결   a raised line of water that moves across the surface of the sea
We watched the **waves** roll in and break on the shore.
우리는 파도가 해안으로 밀려들어와 부서지는 것을 봤다.

15 weather [wéðə:r]
n 날씨, 기후   the condition of the atmosphere in an area at a particular time
What is the **weather** like in December?
12월의 날씨는 어떠니?

16 wedding [wédiŋ]
n 결혼, 혼례   a marriage ceremony
100 guests were invited to the **wedding**.
100명의 손님이 결혼식에 초대되었다.

17 weed [wi:d]
n 잡초   a wild plant growing where it is not wanted
The girl pulled up the **weed** by its roots.
그 소녀는 그 잡초를 뿌리째 뽑았다.

18 weigh [wei]
v 무게를 달다   to measure how heavy something is
He **weighed** vegetables on a balance.
그는 야채를 저울에 달았다.

key words
imaginative a 상상의 / income n 소득 / atmosphere n 대기 / ceremony n 식

Exercise

A. Complete the sentence.

1. The _____ is too long to hear.
   그 이야기는 너무 길어서 들을 수 없다.
2. They were _____ for several seconds.
   그들은 몇 초 동안 침묵을 지켰다.
3. What is the _____ like in December?
   12월의 날씨는 어떠니?
4. That's the way the _____ works.
   그것이 그 시스템이 작동하는 방식이다.
5. The man is looking for a _____.
   남자가 재단사를 찾고 있다.
6. Korean people are _____ and polite.
   한국 사람들은 수줍어하고 공손하다.
7. He _____ me on the shoulder.
   그는 내 어깨를 가볍게 툭 쳤다.
8. One _____ does not make a summer.
   제비 한 마리 봤다고 여름이 온 것이 아니다.
9. We pay an income _____.
   우리는 소득세를 낸다.
10. The sea is _____ in the light of the moon.
    바다가 달빛을 받아 빛나고 있다.
11. I'd like to buy the _____ at the store.
    나는 그 상점에서 지갑을 사고 싶다.
12. The road bends _____ to the left.
    그 길은 왼쪽으로 날카롭게 굽어집니다.
13. We watched the _____ roll in and break on the shore.
    우리는 파도가 해안으로 밀려들어와 부서지는 것을 봤다.
14. 100 guests were invited to the _____.
    100명의 손님이 결혼식에 초대되었다.
15. He's picking up a _____ on the beach.
    그는 바닷가에서 조개 껍질을 줍고 있다.
16. The girl pulled up the _____ by its roots.
    그 소녀는 그 잡초를 뿌리째 뽑았다.
17. Many advertisers often use this _____ fact.
    많은 광고주들이 이 단순한 사실을 종종 이용한다.
18. He _____ vegetables on a balance.
    그는 야채를 저울에 달았다.

Hint

| wallet | silent | tailor | shine | tax | system | tap | sharply | weather |
| swallow | weigh | shell | wedding | shy | weed | simple | tale | wave |

Exercise

B. Fill in the word and meaning.

	Word	Meaning
01	shy	
02	tailor	
03	sharply	
04	tax	
05	wave	
06	simple	
07	weather	
08	system	
09	weed	
10	shine	
11	tap	
12	weigh	
13	silent	
14	wedding	
15	wallet	
16	swallow	
17	tale	
18	shell	

	Meaning	Word
01	날카롭게	
02	껍질, 등딱지	
03	빛나다	
04	수줍어하는	
05	침묵을 지키는	
06	간단한, 단순한	
07	제비	
08	체제, 시스템	
09	재봉사, 재단사	
10	이야기	
11	가볍게 두드리다	
12	세금, 조세	
13	지갑	
14	파도, 물결	
15	날씨, 기후	
16	결혼, 혼례	
17	잡초	
18	무게를 달다	

🎧 C. Listen, write the word and meaning. (Track 108)

	Word	Meaning		Word	Meaning
01			10		
02			11		
03			12		
04			13		
05			14		
06			15		
07			16		
08			17		
09			18		

Unit 36

Review 18

A. Read and fill in the word and meaning.

word	definition	meaning
	a way across a piece of land	
	unhappy because you have no friends	
	to pay money to somebody so that you can use something	
	a section, piece of something	
	to need something	
	the time before the present	
	having good luck	
	not wanting or involving war, violence	
	a person who performs magic tricks to entertain people	
	to use the same ideas, methods, etc, again	
	the feeling when you have been hurt	
	to react to something	
	control a business, system, people, etc.	
	the part of a plant that grows under the ground	
	to change from a solid to a liquid	
	to succeed in removing something completely	
	all the plants, animals and things that exist in the universe	
	to put something into a container	

Hint

root   pain   nature   manage   rid   pack   past   respond   lucky
lonely   path   magician   recycle   melt   part   rent   peaceful   require

B. Read and fill in the word and meaning.

word	definition	meaning
weigh	to measure how heavy something is	
system	an organized set of ideas or rules	
tailor	a person whose job is to make clothes	
sharply	having a very thin but strong edge or point	
weed	a wild plant growing where it is not wanted	
swallow	a kind of small bird with pointed wings and a forked tail	
tale	an imaginative story	
simple	not complicated; easy to do	
wedding	a marriage ceremony	
shell	the hard outer part of eggs, some seeds, etc.	
tap	to hit somebody / something lightly	
shine	to be bright	
wallet	a small folding case made of leather or plastic	
tax	money that you have to pay to the government	
shy	to be uncomfortable in the company of other people	
weather	the condition of the atmosphere in an area at a particular time	
silent	not speaking, completely quiet	
wave	a raised line of water that moves across the surface of the sea	

Hint
wallet　silent　tailor　shine　tax　system　tap　sharply　weather
swallow　weigh　shell　wedding　shy　weed　simple　tale　wave

Unit 37

🎧 Listen and repeat. Track 109

01 balance [bǽləns]
n 균형, 저울   a situation in which different things exist in equal
Suddenly, he lost his **balance** and fell down.
갑자기, 그는 균형을 잃고 쓰러졌다.

02 bargain [báːrgən]
n (싸게 산) 물건, 매매   a thing bought for less than the usual price
The shoppers were looking for **bargains**.
구매자들은 값싼 물건들을 찾고 있었다.

03 battery [bǽtəri]
n 건전지   a device that produces the electricity
When my **batteries** run low, I can't listen to music.
건전지가 다 떨어지면 음악을 듣지 못한다.

04 beard [biərd]
n 턱수염   hair that grows on the chin and cheeks
He is proud of his **beard**.
그는 그의 수염을 자랑스럽게 여긴다.

05 beg [beg]
v 빌다, 간청하다   to ask somebody for something in an anxious way
I **begged** and **begged** my friends to lend me a million won.
친구들에게 간청하고 간청해서 100만 원을 빌렸다.

06 bloom [bluːm]
n 꽃, 개화   producing flowers on a plant
The flowers are in full **bloom**.
꽃들이 만개했다.

07 careful [kɛ́ərfəl]
a 주의 깊은   thinking about what you are doing so that you do not make mistakes, etc
I'll need to give this matter some **careful** thought.
나는 이 문제에 대해 주의 깊게 생각해 봐야겠어.

08 cave [keiv]
n 동굴   a large hole in the side of a hill
I found him lying alone in the back of a **cave**.
나는 그가 동굴의 깊숙한 곳에 혼자 누워 있는 것을 발견했다.

09 cell [sel]
n 독방, 세포   the smallest living part of an animal or a plant
Cancer begins as a single **cell**.
암은 단일 세포에서 시작된다.

key words
device n 장치 / chin n 턱 / cancer n 암

🎧 Listen and repeat. Track 110

10 cereal
[síəriəl]
n 곡물, 곡물 음식   any type of grain that can be eaten; a food that is made from grain
Wheat, barley and rye are **cereals**.
밀, 보리 그리고 호밀은 곡물이다.

11 champion
[tʃǽmpiən]
n 챔피언   a person or team that has won a competition
He became the skating **champion** of the world.
그는 스케이트 세계 챔피언이 되었다.

12 chance
[tʃæns]
n 기회, 가망   a possibility of something happening
I had a **chance** to hear his music once.
나는 전에 그의 음악을 들을 기회가 있었어.

13 contest
[kántest]
n 경쟁, 콘테스트   a competition in which people try to win something
I have an important singing **contest** to go to.
나는 중요한 노래 경연 대회가 있어.

14 continue
[kəntínjuː]
v 계속하다   to keep doing something without stopping
Fierce fighting has **continued**.
격렬한 싸움이 계속되었다.

15 control
[kəntróul]
v 통제하다, 억제하다   to limit something
Police struggled to **control** the crowd.
경찰은 군중을 통제하기 위해 고군분투 했다.

16 conversation
[kànvərséiʃən]
n 대화, 회화   to talk with someone, usually in an informal situation
I happened to hear their **conversation**.
나는 우연히 그들의 대화를 듣게 되었다.

17 copyright
[kápiràit]
n 저작권   the legal right to publish a piece of writing or music
It might break **copyright** laws.
그것은 저작권법에 저촉될 수 있다.

18 cost
[kɔːst]
v 비용이 들다   to have the price to buy something
The meal **costs** 20 dollars per head.
식사는 한 사람당 20달러의 비용이 든다.

---

key words
barley n 보리 / rye n 호밀 / fierce a 격렬한 / limit v 제한하다

Unit 37   187

Exercise

A. Complete the sentence.

1. The meal _____ 20 dollars per head.
   식사는 한 사람당 20달러의 비용이 든다.

2. Cancer begins as a single _____.
   암은 단일 세포에서 시작된다.

3. Police struggled to _____ the crowd.
   경찰은 군중을 통제하기 위해 고군분투 했다.

4. Suddenly, he lost his _____ and fell down.
   갑자기, 그는 균형을 잃고 쓰러졌다.

5. I'll need to give this matter some _____ thought.
   나는 이 문제에 대해 주의 깊게 생각해 봐야겠어.

6. Fierce fighting has _____.
   격렬한 싸움이 계속되었다.

7. The shoppers were looking for _____.
   구매자들은 값싼 물건들을 찾고 있었다.

8. I have an important singing _____ to go to.
   나는 중요한 노래 경연 대회가 있어.

9. He became the skating _____ of the world.
   그는 스케이트 세계 챔피언이 되었다.

10. When my _____ run low, I can't listen to music.
    건전지가 다 떨어지면 음악을 듣지 못한다.

11. I had a _____ to hear his music once.
    나는 전에 그의 음악을 들을 기회가 있었어.

12. He is proud of his _____.
    그는 그의 수염을 자랑스럽게 여긴다.

13. I happened to hear their _____.
    나는 우연히 그들의 대화를 듣게 되었다.

14. I _____ and _____ my friends to lend me a million won.
    친구들에게 간청하고 간청해서 100만 원을 빌렸다.

15. It might break _____ laws.
    그것은 저작권법에 저촉될 수 있다.

16. The flowers are in full _____.
    꽃들이 만개했다.

17. I found him lying alone in the back of a _____.
    나는 그가 동굴의 깊숙한 곳에 혼자 누워 있는 것을 발견했다.

18. Wheat, barley and rye are _____.
    밀, 보리 그리고 호밀은 곡물이다.

Hint

| continue | beard | cave | bargain | copyright | careful | beg | cereal | control |
| balance | cell | cost | battery | chance | bloom | contest | champion | conversation |

Unit 37

Exercise

B. Fill in the word and meaning.

	Word	Meaning
01	careful	
02	chance	
03	bargain	
04	champion	
05	control	
06	balance	
07	conversation	
08	bloom	
09	cost	
10	cave	
11	beg	
12	cell	
13	copyright	
14	cereal	
15	continue	
16	beard	
17	contest	
18	battery	

	Meaning	Word
01	균형, 저울	
02	(싸게 산) 물건, 매매	
03	건전지	
04	턱수염	
05	빌다, 간청하다	
06	꽃, 개화	
07	주의 깊은	
08	동굴	
09	독방, 세포	
10	곡물, 곡물 음식	
11	챔피언	
12	기회, 가망	
13	경쟁, 콘테스트	
14	계속하다	
15	통제하다, 억제하다	
16	대화, 회화	
17	저작권	
18	비용이 들다	

🎧 C. Listen, write the word and meaning. (Track 111)

	Word	Meaning		Word	Meaning
01			10		
02			11		
03			12		
04			13		
05			14		
06			15		
07			16		
08			17		
09			18		

Unit 38

🎧 Listen and repeat. Track 112

01 delay [diléi]
v 늦추다, 미루다   not to do something until a later time
He wanted to **delay** his decision until morning.
그는 결정을 아침까지 미루고 싶어 했다.

02 discussion [diskʌ́ʃən]
n 토론   a conversation about somebody / something
Thank you all for joining the **discussion**.
토론에 참가해 주신 모든 분에게 감사드려요.

03 divide [diváid]
v 나누다   to separate something
When you **divide** 10 by 2, you get 5.
10을 2로 나누면 5가 된다.

04 documentary [dàkjəméntəri]
n 다큐멘터리   a film program giving facts about something
There was a fascinating **documentary** on TV last night.
어제 밤에 TV에서 재미있는 다큐멘터리가 방송됐어요.

05 double [dʌ́bəl]
a 두 배의, 두 겹의   twice as much or as many as usual
His income is **double** hers.
그는 그녀보다 두 배의 소득을 벌어.

06 dove [dʌv]
n 비둘기   a bird of the pigeon family
A **dove** is the emblem of peace.
비둘기는 평화의 상징이다.

07 flat [flæt]
a 편평한, 평탄한   smooth and level, with no parts that are higher than the rest
It is a **flat** round piece of dough.
그것은 편평하고 둥근 밀가루 반죽이다.

08 flour [flauər]
n 밀가루, 분말   a fine white powder made from grain
We mixed butter, sugar, milk and **flour** for a cake.
우리는 케이크를 만들기 위해 버터와 설탕, 우유, 그리고 밀가루를 섞었다.

09 fold [fould]
v 접다   to bend something so that one part lies on top of another part
Fold the paper in half again.
그 종이를 반으로 다시 접으세요.

key words
fascinating a 매혹적인 / pigeon n 비둘기 / emblem n 상징 / smooth a 매끄러운

🎧 Listen and repeat. (Track 113)

10 fond [fɑnd]
a 좋아하는, 다정한   liking a person or thing
I'm not very **fond** of getting up early.
나는 일찍 일어나는 것을 좋아하지 않아.

11 forward [fɔ́:rwərd]
ad 앞으로   towards a position that is in front
Take two paces **forward**.
두 걸음 앞으로 가거라.

12 frame [freim]
n 틀, 구조, 뼈대   a strong border or structure of wood, metal, etc.
The man is carrying a wood **frame**.
남자가 나무틀을 운반하고 있다.

13 hug [hʌg]
n 포옹 / v 껴안다   to put your arms around somebody
The mother **hugged** him for joy.
어머니는 기뻐서 그를 얼싸안았다.

14 hum [hʌm]
v 콧노래를 부르다   to sing a tune with your lips closed
He is **humming** a child to sleep.
그는 아이를 재우려고 콧노래를 부르고 있다.

15 human [hjú:mən]
a 인간의   connected with people rather than animals or machines
Animal life styles are different from **human** life styles.
동물들의 삶의 방식은 인간의 것과 다르다.

16 ice [ais]
n 얼음   water that has frozen
Ice and water are the same substance.
얼음과 물은 똑같은 물질이다.

17 idiom [ídiəm]
n 숙어, 관용구   an expression whose meaning is different from the meaning of the each word
The new edition includes the addition of new **idioms**.
새로 나온 판은 새로운 숙어들이 첨가되어 있다.

18 image [ímidʒ]
n 모습, 모양   a copy of somebody / something in the form of a picture
They only know your **image**.
그들은 단지 당신의 겉모습만 알 뿐이에요.

key words
tune n 곡 / freeze v 얼다 / edition n 판

Exercise

A. Complete the sentence.

1. _____ and water are the same substance.
   얼음과 물은 똑같은 물질이다.

2. He wanted to _____ his decision until morning.
   그는 결정을 아침까지 미루고 싶어 했다.

3. _____ the paper in half again.
   그 종이를 반으로 다시 접으세요.

4. Thank you all for joining the _____.
   토론에 참가해 주신 모든 분에게 감사드려요.

5. When you _____ 10 by 2, you get 5.
   10을 2로 나누면 5가 된다.

6. He is _____ a child to sleep.
   그는 아이를 재우려고 콧노래를 부르고 있다.

7. There was a fascinating _____ on TV last night.
   어제 밤에 TV에서 재미있는 다큐멘터리가 방송됐어요.

8. His income is _____ hers.
   그는 그녀보다 두 배의 소득을 벌어.

9. We mixed butter, sugar, milk and _____ for a cake.
   우리는 케이크를 만들기 위해 버터와 설탕, 우유, 그리고 밀가루를 섞었다.

10. They only know your _____.
    그들은 단지 당신의 겉모습만 알 뿐이에요.

11. I'm not very _____ of getting up early.
    나는 일찍 일어나는 것을 좋아하지 않아.

12. Take two paces _____.
    두 걸음 앞으로 가거라.

13. The man is carrying a wood _____.
    남자가 나무틀을 운반하고 있다.

14. It is a _____ round piece of dough.
    그것은 편평하고 둥근 밀가루 반죽이다.

15. The mother _____ him for joy.
    어머니는 기뻐서 그를 얼싸안았다.

16. Animal life styles are different from _____ life styles.
    동물들의 삶의 방식은 인간의 것과 다르다.

17. A _____ is the emblem of peace.
    비둘기는 평화의 상징이다.

18. The new edition includes the addition of new _____.
    새로 나온 판은 새로운 숙어들이 첨가되어 있다.

Hint

| dove | fond | ice | discussion | flat | image | flour | delay | frame |
| hum | divide | double | documentary | fold | forward | hug | human | idiom |

Exercise

B. Fill in the word and meaning.

	Word	Meaning
01	idiom	
02	forward	
03	delay	
04	fond	
05	divide	
06	flat	
07	frame	
08	image	
09	documentary	
10	flour	
11	ice	
12	dove	
13	hum	
14	fold	
15	double	
16	human	
17	discussion	
18	hug	

	Meaning	Word
01	늦추다, 미루다	
02	토론	
03	나누다	
04	다큐멘터리	
05	두 배의, 두 겹의	
06	비둘기	
07	편평한, 평탄한	
08	밀가루, 분말	
09	접다	
10	좋아하는, 다정한	
11	앞으로	
12	틀, 구조, 뼈대	
13	포옹, 껴안다	
14	콧노래를 부르다	
15	인간의	
16	얼음	
17	숙어, 관용구	
18	모습, 모양	

C. Listen, write the word and meaning. (Track 114)

	Word	Meaning		Word	Meaning
01			10		
02			11		
03			12		
04			13		
05			14		
06			15		
07			16		
08			17		
09			18		

Review 19

A. Read and fill in the word and meaning.

word	definition	meaning
	a competition in which people try to win something	
	a person or team that has won a competition	
	a situation in which different things exist in equal	
	a possibility of something happening	
	a thing bought for less than the usual price	
	to talk with someone, usually in an informal situation	
	to keep doing something without stopping	
	the legal right to publish a piece of writing or music	
	a device that produces the electricity	
	the smallest living part of an animal or a plant	
	producing flowers on a plant	
	to limit something	
	a large hole in the side of a hill	
	hair that grows on the chin and cheeks	
	to have the price to buy something	
	thinking about what you are doing so that you do not make mistakes, etc	
	to ask somebody for something in an anxious way	
	any type of grain that can be eaten; a food that is made from grain	

Hint
continue   beard   cave   bargain   copyright   careful   beg   cereal   control
balance   cell   cost   battery   chance   bloom   contest   champion   conversation

B. Read and fill in the word and meaning.

word	definition	meaning
	to put your arms around somebody	
	not to do something until a later time	
	to sing a tune with your lips closed	
	water that has frozen	
	a conversation about somebody / something	
	to bend something so that one part lies on top of another part	
	to separate something	
	connected with people rather than animals or machines	
	liking a person or thing	
	a film program giving facts about something	
	a fine white powder made from grain	
	an expression whose meaning is different from the meaning of the each word	
	towards a position that is in front	
	twice as much or as many as usual	
	smooth and level, with no parts that are higher than the rest	
	a copy of somebody / something in the form of a picture	
	a bird of the pigeon family	
	a strong border or structure of wood, metal, etc.	

Hint

dove   fond   ice   discussion   flat   image   flour   delay   frame
hum   divide   double   documentary   fold   forward   hug   human   idiom

Unit 39

🎧 Listen and repeat. Track 115

01 memory [méməri]
n 기억(력)   your ability to remember things
I'm very unhappy about my poor **memory**.
저는 제 나쁜 기억력 때문에 매우 속이 상해요.

02 mess [mes]
n 혼란, 어수선함   a dirty or untidy state
He has made a **mess** of my plans.
그가 나의 계획을 혼란스럽게 만들었다.

03 midnight [mídnàit]
n 한밤중, 자정   2 o'clock at night
They're open until **midnight**.
그곳은 자정까지 문이 열려 있다.

04 mind [maind]
n 마음, 정신   the part of your brain that thinks and remembers
The function of education is to develop the **mind**.
교육의 기능은 정신을 계발하는 것이다.

05 mission [míʃən]
n 임무, 특명   an important official job that a person is given to do
What is true about future **missions**?
앞으로의 임무에 대해서 무엇이 옳은 것일까?

06 model [mádl]
n 모형, 모델   a copy of something that is smaller than the real thing
I made a **model** to half size.
나는 1/2 크기의 모형을 만들었다.

07 period [píəriəd]
n 기간, 시대   a particular length of time
There are works of culture, history, and the arts of the Silla **period**.
그 곳엔 신라 시대의 문화와 역사, 그리고 미술 작품들이 있다.

08 photograph [fóutəgræf]
n 사진   a picture that is made by using a camera
The man is tacking a **photograph** to the wall.
남자가 사진을 벽에 붙이고 있다.

09 pill [pil]
n 알약   a small flat round piece of medicine
When should I take these **pills**?
언제 이 알약을 복용해야 합니까?

key words
remember v 기억하다 / untidy a 흐트러진 / scale n 규모 / length n 길이, 기간 / tack v 압정으로 고정시키다

🎧 Listen and repeat. Track 116

10 planet　　n 행성　　a large round object in space that moves around a star
[plǽnət]
When do you plan to visit the **planet**?
그 행성을 언제 방문할 계획입니까?

11 plastic　　n 플라스틱 / a 플라스틱의　　a light strong material that is produced by chemical processes
[plǽstik]
Gather **plastics** and paper bags.
플라스틱 제품이나 종이 봉지를 모아라.

12 plenty　　n 많음, 다수　　a lot
[plénti]
There is still **plenty** of time to get there.
도착할 때까지 아직 시간이 많이 있다.

13 reduce　　v 줄이다, 낮추다　　to make something less
[ridjúːs]
We should **reduce** dangerous wastes.
우리는 위험한 쓰레기들을 줄여야 한다.

14 response　　n 대답, 응답　　a spoken or written answer
[rispáns]
Our letters have never met with any **response**.
우리 편지에 대한 어떤 응답도 오지 않았다.

15 role　　n 역할, 배역　　the position that somebody has
[roul]
Doctors and lawyers can be good **role** models.
의사들과 변호사들은 훌륭한 역할 모델이 될 수 있다.

16 rope　　n 밧줄　　strong thick string made by twisting thinner strings or wires
[roup]
The **rope** is fastened to the post.
밧줄이 기둥에 묶여있다.

17 rough　　a 거친, 험악한　　not gentle or careful
[rʌf]
Part of the floor was covered with a **rough** mat.
마루의 일부에 거친 돗자리가 깔려 있었다.

18 row　　n 열, 줄　　a line of people or things
[rou]
The children were all standing in a **row**.
모든 아이들이 줄을 맞춰 서 있었어요.

key words
lawyer n 법률가 / twist v 꼬다, 비틀다 / fasten v 단단히 얽어매다

Exercise

A. Complete the sentence.

1. He has made a _____ of my plans.
   그가 나의 계획을 혼란스럽게 만들었다.

2. There is still _____ of time to get there.
   도착할 때까지 아직 시간이 많이 있다.

3. The function of education is to develop the _____.
   교육의 기능은 정신을 계발하는 것이다.

4. The _____ is fastened to the post.
   밧줄이 기둥에 묶여있다.

5. I made a _____ to half size.
   나는 1/2 크기의 모형을 만들었다.

6. When do you plan to visit the _____?
   그 행성을 언제 방문할 계획입니까?

7. Our letters have never met with any _____.
   우리 편지에 대한 어떤 응답도 오지 않았다.

8. There are works of culture, history, and the arts of the Silla _____.
   그 곳엔 신라 시대의 문화와 역사, 그리고 미술 작품들이 있다.

9. The children were all standing in a _____.
   모든 아이들이 줄을 맞춰 서 있었어요.

10. The man is tacking a _____ to the wall.
    남자가 사진을 벽에 붙이고 있다.

11. I'm very unhappy about my poor _____.
    저는 제 나쁜 기억력 때문에 매우 속이 상해요.

12. When should I take these _____?
    언제 이 알약을 복용해야 합니까?

13. They're open until _____.
    그곳은 자정까지 문이 열려 있다.

14. Gather _____ and paper bags.
    플라스틱 제품이나 종이 봉지를 모아라.

15. We should _____ dangerous wastes.
    우리는 위험한 쓰레기들을 줄여야 한다.

16. Doctors and lawyers can be good _____ models.
    의사들과 변호사들은 훌륭한 역할 모델이 될 수 있다.

17. What is true about future _____?
    앞으로의 임무에 대해서 무엇이 옳은 것일까?

18. Part of the floor was covered with a _____ mat.
    마루의 일부에 거친 돗자리가 깔려 있었다.

Hint

rough	model	response	role	mind	plastic	mess	memory	photograph
planet	period	midnight	row	mission	rope	pill	reduce	plenty

Unit 39

Exercise

B. Fill in the word and meaning.

	Word	Meaning
01	period	
02	memory	
03	plastic	
04	mess	
05	reduce	
06	photograph	
07	response	
08	role	
09	mission	
10	pill	
11	rope	
12	model	
13	planet	
14	rough	
15	row	
16	mind	
17	plenty	
18	midnight	

	Meaning	Word
01	기억(력)	
02	혼란, 어수선함	
03	한밤중, 자정	
04	마음, 정신	
05	임무, 특명	
06	모형, 모델	
07	기간, 시대	
08	사진	
09	알약	
10	행성	
11	플라스틱, 플라스틱의	
12	많음, 다수	
13	줄이다, 낮추다	
14	대답, 응답	
15	역할, 배역	
16	밧줄	
17	거친, 험악한	
18	열, 줄	

🎧 C. Listen, write the word and meaning. (Track 117)

	Word	Meaning		Word	Meaning
01			10		
02			11		
03			12		
04			13		
05			14		
06			15		
07			16		
08			17		
09			18		

Unit 40

🎧 Listen and repeat. (Track 118)

01 since [sins]
prep ~이래로   from a time in the past until a later time in the past
Since 1995, they've been living in Mexico.
1995년 이래로, 그들은 멕시코에 살고 있어.

02 sink [siŋk]
v 가라앉다   to go down below the surface
Suddenly, the boat began to **sink**.
갑자기 배가 가라앉기 시작했다.

03 skin [skin]
n 피부, 가죽   the layer of tissue that covers the body
The hunter got **skin** from a rabbit.
그 사냥꾼은 토끼 가죽을 구했다.

04 skip [skip]
v 가볍게 뛰다   to move forwards lightly making a little jump
He **skipped** along the street.
그는 길을 가볍게 뛰어갔다.

05 sleepy [slíːpi]
a 졸린   needing sleep
I already feel **sleepy** because I am so bored.
나는 너무나 지쳐서 벌써 졸리다.

06 smog [smag]
n 스모그, 연무   a form of air pollution that looks like a mixture of fog
London was a town full of hanging **smog**.
런던은 스모그가 심한 도시였다.

07 tear [tiəːr]
n 눈물   the drops of salty liquid that come out of your eyes
Most of the **tears** we make are to clean our eyes.
우리가 흘리는 눈물은 대부분 눈을 깨끗하게 하기 위한 것이다.

08 teenager [tíːnèidʒəːr]
n 10대의 소년(소녀)   a person who is between 13 and 19 years old
They can also have bad effects on **teenagers**.
그들은 10대들에게 나쁜 영향을 줄 수도 있다.

09 textile [tékstail]
n 직물 / a 직물의   any cloth made in a factory
The **textile** industry has been developing in the last five years.
지난 5년간 직물 산업이 발전해왔습니다.

key words
bored a 지루한 / mixture n 혼합물

🎧 Listen and repeat. Track 119

10 theater [θíːətər]
n 극장　a building where plays and entertainments are performed
Was the **theater** as big as the church?
그 극장은 교회만큼 컸니?

11 thief [θiːf]
n 도둑, 절도범　a person who steals something from another person
The policeman wasn't sure if he could catch a **thief**.
경찰은 도둑을 잡을 수 있을 지 확신할 수 없었다.

12 tin [tin]
n 주석, 양철 깡통　a chemical element that is a soft silver-white metal
Tin shines like silver but is softer and cheaper.
주석은 은처럼 빛나지만 은보다 부드럽고 값도 더 싸다.

13 wipe [waip]
v 닦다, 훔치다　to rub something's surface to remove dirt or liquid from it
The man is using a mop to **wipe** the walls.
남자가 긴 자루가 달린 걸레를 가지고 벽을 닦고 있다.

14 wire [waiər]
n 철사, 전선　metal in the form of thin thread
The repairman is on a ladder to work on the **wires**.
수리공이 전선을 수리하기 위해 사다리 위에 있다.

15 within [wiðín]
prep ~안에, ~이내에　in a period not longer than a particular length of time
The prisoner hopes to be freed **within** a few months.
그 죄수는 수개월 내에 석방되기를 희망한다.

16 without [wiðáut]
prep ~없이　not having
Without air no living thing could exist.
공기 없이는 어떠한 생물도 살 수 없다.

17 witness [wítnis]
n 목격자, 증인　a person who sees something happen
There were two **witnesses** to the accident.
그 사고를 본 두 명의 목격자가 있었다.

18 wrap [ræp]
v 싸다, 감싸다　to cover something completely
The doctor **wrapped** his leg in a bandage.
의사 선생님이 그의 다리를 붕대로 감았다.

key words
steal v 훔치다 / prisoner n 죄수 / bandage n 붕대

Exercise

A. Complete the sentence.

1. I already feel _____ because I am so bored.
   나는 너무나 지쳐서 벌써 졸리다.
2. Was the _____ as big as the church?
   그 극장은 교회만큼 컸니?
3. Suddenly, the boat began to _____.
   갑자기 배가 가라앉기 시작했다.
4. The hunter got _____ from a rabbit.
   그 사냥꾼은 토끼 가죽을 구했다.
5. Most of the _____ we make are to clean our eyes.
   우리가 흘리는 눈물은 대부분 눈을 깨끗하게 하기 위한 것이다.
6. They can also have bad effects on _____.
   그들은 10대들에게 나쁜 영향을 줄 수도 있다.
7. There were two _____ to the accident.
   그 사고를 본 두 명의 목격자가 있었다.
8. The policeman wasn't sure if he could catch a _____.
   경찰은 도둑을 잡을 수 있을 지 확신할 수 없었다.
9. _____ shines like silver but is softer and cheaper.
   주석은 은처럼 빛나지만 은보다 부드럽고 값도 더 싸다.
10. The man is using a mop to _____ the walls.
    남자가 긴 자루가 달린 걸레를 가지고 벽을 닦고 있다.
11. He _____ along the street.
    그는 길을 가볍게 뛰어갔다.
12. The _____ industry has been developing in the last five years.
    지난 5년간 직물 산업이 발전해왔습니다.
13. The repairman is on a ladder to work on the _____.
    수리공이 전선을 수리하기 위해 사다리 위에 있다.
14. _____ 1995, they've been living in Mexico.
    1995년 이래로, 그들은 멕시코에 살고 있어.
15. The prisoner hopes to be freed _____ a few months. .
    그 죄수는 수개월 내에 석방되기를 희망한다.
16. _____ air no living thing could exist.
    공기 없이는 어떠한 생물도 살 수 없다.
17. London was a town full of hanging _____.
    런던은 스모그가 심한 도시였다.
18. The doctor _____ his leg in a bandage.
    의사 선생님이 그의 다리를 붕대로 감았다.

Hint

| witness | sleepy | tin | skip | within | theater | sink | wrap | since |
| wire | teenager | without | skin | tear | smog | textile | wipe | thief |

Exercise

B. Fill in the word and meaning.

	Word	Meaning
01	sink	
02	teenager	
03	skin	
04	tin	
05	textile	
06	wipe	
07	since	
08	thief	
09	wire	
10	smog	
11	within	
12	skip	
13	theater	
14	wrap	
15	tear	
16	witness	
17	without	
18	sleepy	

	Meaning	Word
01	~이래로	
02	가라앉다	
03	피부, 가죽	
04	가볍게 뛰다	
05	졸린	
06	스모그, 연무	
07	눈물	
08	10대의 소년(소녀)	
09	직물, 직물의	
10	극장	
11	도둑, 절도범	
12	주석, 양철 깡통	
13	닦다, 훔치다	
14	철사, 전선	
15	~안에, ~이내에	
16	~없이	
17	목격자, 증인	
18	싸다, 감싸다	

🎧 C. Listen, write the word and meaning. (Track 120)

	Word	Meaning		Word	Meaning
01			10		
02			11		
03			12		
04			13		
05			14		
06			15		
07			16		
08			17		
09			18		

Review 20

A. Read and fill in the word and meaning.

word	definition	meaning
	to make something less	
	a light strong material that is produced by chemical processes	
	a spoken or written answer	
	your ability to remember things	
	a lot	
	the position that somebody has	
	a line of people or things	
	strong thick string made by twisting thinner strings or wires	
	a dirty or untidy state	
	a particular length of time	
	a copy of something that is smaller than the real thing	
	not gentle or careful	
	a small flat round piece of medicine	
	12 o'clock at night	
	a picture that is made by using a camera	
	an important official job that a person is given to do	
	a large round object in space that moves around a star	
	the part of your brain that thinks and remembers	

Hint

rough   model   response   role   mind   plastic   mess   memory   photograph
planet   period   midnight   row   mission   rope   pill   reduce   plenty

B. Read and fill in the word and meaning.

word	definition	meaning
	to rub something's surface to remove dirt or liquid from it	
	a chemical element that is a soft silver-white metal	
	from a time in the past until a later time in the past	
	metal in the form of thin thread	
	a person who steals something from another person	
	in a period not longer than a particular length of time	
	a building where plays and entertainments are performed	
	to go down below the surface	
	not having	
	the layer of tissue that covers the body	
	to cover something completely	
	a person who is between 13 and 19 years old	
	a person who sees something happen	
	to move forwards lightly making a little jump	
	the drops of salty liquid that come out of your eyes	
	a form of air pollution that looks like a mixture of fog	
	any cloth made in a factory	
	needing sleep	

Hint

witness　sleepy　　tin　　　skip　　within　theater　sink　　wrap　　since
wire　　　teenager　without　skin　　tear　　smog　　textile　wipe　　thief

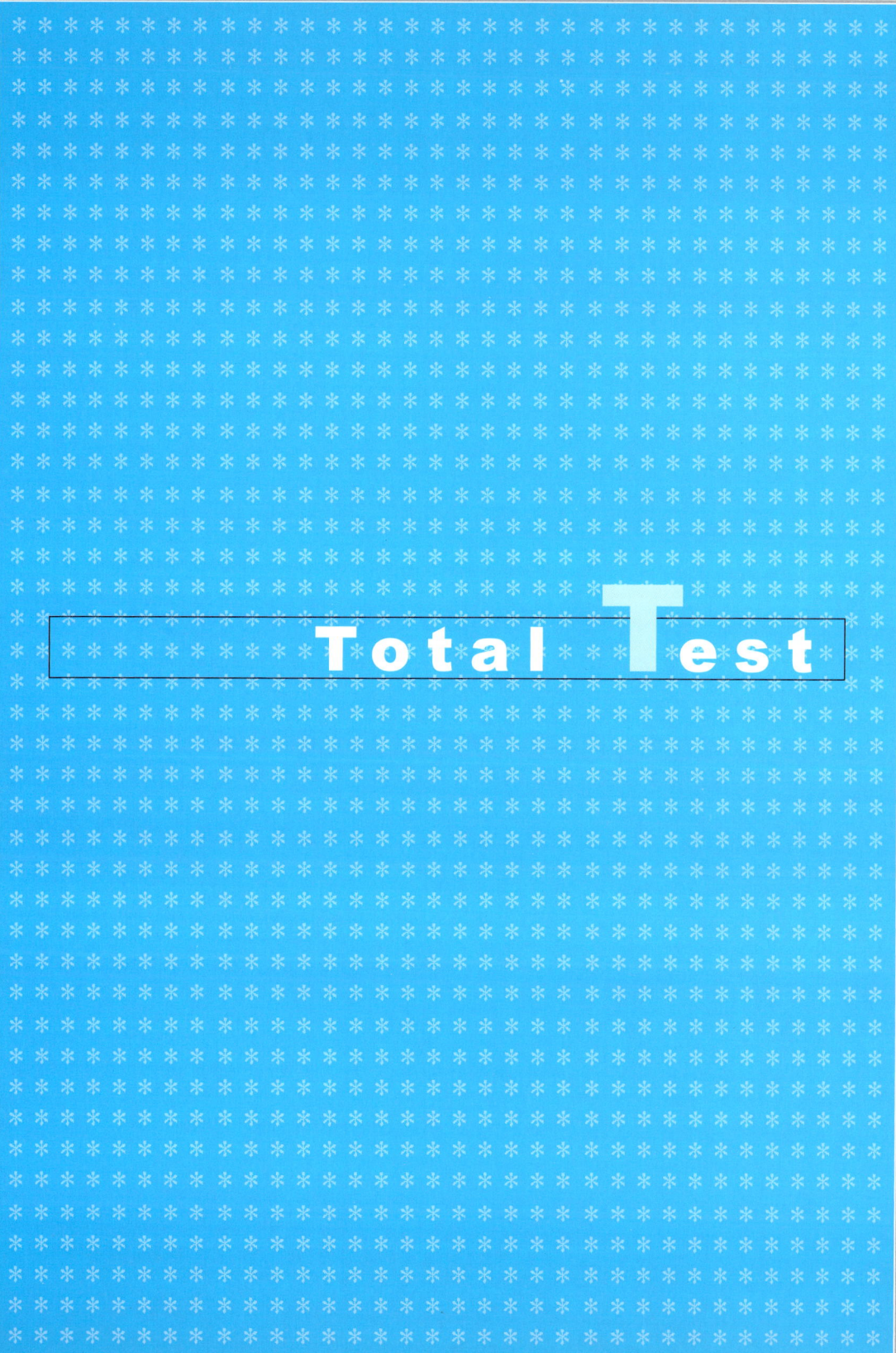

Test 1

Track 3

🎧 **Listen, write the word and meaning.**

	Word	Meaning
01		
02		
03		
04		
05		
06		
07		
08		
09		
10		
11		
12		
13		
14		
15		
16		
17		
18		

점수	점	확인	

Test 2

Track 6

🎧 **Listen, write the word and meaning.**

	Word	Meaning
01		
02		
03		
04		
05		
06		
07		
08		
09		
10		
11		
12		
13		
14		
15		
16		
17		
18		

점수	점	확인	

Test 3

Track 9

🎧 **Listen, write the word and meaning.**

	Word	Meaning
01		
02		
03		
04		
05		
06		
07		
08		
09		
10		
11		
12		
13		
14		
15		
16		
17		
18		

점수		점	확인	

Test 4

Track 12

🎧 **Listen, write the word and meaning.**

	Word	Meaning
01		
02		
03		
04		
05		
06		
07		
08		
09		
10		
11		
12		
13		
14		
15		
16		
17		
18		

점수		점	확인	

Test 5

Track 15

🎧 **Listen, write the word and meaning.**

	Word	Meaning
01		
02		
03		
04		
05		
06		
07		
08		
09		
10		
11		
12		
13		
14		
15		
16		
17		
18		

점수		확인	
	점		

Test 6

Track 18

🎧 **Listen, write the word and meaning.**

	Word	Meaning
01		
02		
03		
04		
05		
06		
07		
08		
09		
10		
11		
12		
13		
14		
15		
16		
17		
18		

점수		확인	
	점		

Test 7

Track 21

🎧 **Listen, write the word and meaning.**

	Word	Meaning
01		
02		
03		
04		
05		
06		
07		
08		
09		
10		
11		
12		
13		
14		
15		
16		
17		
18		

점수		점	확인	

Test 8

Track 24

🎧 **Listen, write the word and meaning.**

	Word	Meaning
01		
02		
03		
04		
05		
06		
07		
08		
09		
10		
11		
12		
13		
14		
15		
16		
17		
18		

점수		점	확인	

Test 9

Track 27

🎧 **Listen, write the word and meaning.**

	Word	Meaning
01		
02		
03		
04		
05		
06		
07		
08		
09		
10		
11		
12		
13		
14		
15		
16		
17		
18		

점수	점	확인	

Test 10

Track 30

🎧 **Listen, write the word and meaning.**

	Word	Meaning
01		
02		
03		
04		
05		
06		
07		
08		
09		
10		
11		
12		
13		
14		
15		
16		
17		
18		

점수	점	확인	

Test 11

Track 33

🎧 **Listen, write the word and meaning.**

	Word	Meaning
01		
02		
03		
04		
05		
06		
07		
08		
09		
10		
11		
12		
13		
14		
15		
16		
17		
18		

점수	점	확인	

Test 12

Track 36

🎧 **Listen, write the word and meaning.**

	Word	Meaning
01		
02		
03		
04		
05		
06		
07		
08		
09		
10		
11		
12		
13		
14		
15		
16		
17		
18		

점수	점	확인	

Test 13

Track 39

🎧 **Listen, write the word and meaning.**

	Word	Meaning
01		
02		
03		
04		
05		
06		
07		
08		
09		
10		
11		
12		
13		
14		
15		
16		
17		
18		

점수	점	확인	

Test 14

Track 42

🎧 **Listen, write the word and meaning.**

	Word	Meaning
01		
02		
03		
04		
05		
06		
07		
08		
09		
10		
11		
12		
13		
14		
15		
16		
17		
18		

점수	점	확인	

Test 15

Track 45

🎧 Listen, write the word and meaning.

	Word	Meaning
01		
02		
03		
04		
05		
06		
07		
08		
09		
10		
11		
12		
13		
14		
15		
16		
17		
18		

점수	점	확인	

Test 16

Track 48

🎧 Listen, write the word and meaning.

	Word	Meaning
01		
02		
03		
04		
05		
06		
07		
08		
09		
10		
11		
12		
13		
14		
15		
16		
17		
18		

점수	점	확인	

Test 17

Track 51

🎧 **Listen, write the word and meaning.**

	Word	Meaning
01		
02		
03		
04		
05		
06		
07		
08		
09		
10		
11		
12		
13		
14		
15		
16		
17		
18		

점수		점	확인	

Test 18

Track 54

🎧 **Listen, write the word and meaning.**

	Word	Meaning
01		
02		
03		
04		
05		
06		
07		
08		
09		
10		
11		
12		
13		
14		
15		
16		
17		
18		

점수		점	확인	

Test 19

Track 57

🎧 **Listen, write the word and meaning.**

	Word	Meaning
01		
02		
03		
04		
05		
06		
07		
08		
09		
10		
11		
12		
13		
14		
15		
16		
17		
18		

점수	점	확인	

Test 20

Track 60

🎧 **Listen, write the word and meaning.**

	Word	Meaning
01		
02		
03		
04		
05		
06		
07		
08		
09		
10		
11		
12		
13		
14		
15		
16		
17		
18		

점수	점	확인	

Test 21

(Track 63)

🎧 **Listen, write the word and meaning.**

	Word	Meaning
01		
02		
03		
04		
05		
06		
07		
08		
09		
10		
11		
12		
13		
14		
15		
16		
17		
18		

점수	점	확인	

Test 22

(Track 66)

🎧 **Listen, write the word and meaning.**

	Word	Meaning
01		
02		
03		
04		
05		
06		
07		
08		
09		
10		
11		
12		
13		
14		
15		
16		
17		
18		

점수	점	확인	

Test 23

Track 69

🎧 **Listen, write the word and meaning.**

	Word	Meaning
01		
02		
03		
04		
05		
06		
07		
08		
09		
10		
11		
12		
13		
14		
15		
16		
17		
18		

점수	점	확인	

Test 24

Track 72

🎧 **Listen, write the word and meaning.**

	Word	Meaning
01		
02		
03		
04		
05		
06		
07		
08		
09		
10		
11		
12		
13		
14		
15		
16		
17		
18		

점수	점	확인	

Test 25

Track 75

🎧 **Listen, write the word and meaning.**

	Word	Meaning
01		
02		
03		
04		
05		
06		
07		
08		
09		
10		
11		
12		
13		
14		
15		
16		
17		
18		

점수	점	확인	

Test 26

Track 78

🎧 **Listen, write the word and meaning.**

	Word	Meaning
01		
02		
03		
04		
05		
06		
07		
08		
09		
10		
11		
12		
13		
14		
15		
16		
17		
18		

점수	점	확인	

Test 27

Track 81

🎧 **Listen, write the word and meaning.**

	Word	Meaning
01		
02		
03		
04		
05		
06		
07		
08		
09		
10		
11		
12		
13		
14		
15		
16		
17		
18		

점수	점	확인

Test 28

Track 84

🎧 **Listen, write the word and meaning.**

	Word	Meaning
01		
02		
03		
04		
05		
06		
07		
08		
09		
10		
11		
12		
13		
14		
15		
16		
17		
18		

점수	점	확인

Test 29

Track 87

🎧 **Listen, write the word and meaning.**

	Word	Meaning
01		
02		
03		
04		
05		
06		
07		
08		
09		
10		
11		
12		
13		
14		
15		
16		
17		
18		

점수		점	확인	

Test 30

Track 90

🎧 **Listen, write the word and meaning.**

	Word	Meaning
01		
02		
03		
04		
05		
06		
07		
08		
09		
10		
11		
12		
13		
14		
15		
16		
17		
18		

점수		점	확인	

Test 31

Track 93

🎧 Listen, write the word and meaning.

	Word	Meaning
01		
02		
03		
04		
05		
06		
07		
08		
09		
10		
11		
12		
13		
14		
15		
16		
17		
18		

점수	점	확인	

Test 32

Track 96

🎧 Listen, write the word and meaning.

	Word	Meaning
01		
02		
03		
04		
05		
06		
07		
08		
09		
10		
11		
12		
13		
14		
15		
16		
17		
18		

점수	점	확인	

Test 33

Track 99

🎧 **Listen, write the word and meaning.**

	Word	Meaning
01		
02		
03		
04		
05		
06		
07		
08		
09		
10		
11		
12		
13		
14		
15		
16		
17		
18		

점수	점	확인	

Test 34

Track 102

🎧 **Listen, write the word and meaning.**

	Word	Meaning
01		
02		
03		
04		
05		
06		
07		
08		
09		
10		
11		
12		
13		
14		
15		
16		
17		
18		

점수	점	확인	

Test 35

Track 105

🎧 **Listen, write the word and meaning.**

	Word	Meaning
01		
02		
03		
04		
05		
06		
07		
08		
09		
10		
11		
12		
13		
14		
15		
16		
17		
18		

점수	점	확인	

Test 36

Track 108

🎧 **Listen, write the word and meaning.**

	Word	Meaning
01		
02		
03		
04		
05		
06		
07		
08		
09		
10		
11		
12		
13		
14		
15		
16		
17		
18		

점수	점	확인	

Test 37

Track 111

🎧 **Listen, write the word and meaning.**

	Word	Meaning
01		
02		
03		
04		
05		
06		
07		
08		
09		
10		
11		
12		
13		
14		
15		
16		
17		
18		

점수		점	확인	

Test 38

Track 114

🎧 **Listen, write the word and meaning.**

	Word	Meaning
01		
02		
03		
04		
05		
06		
07		
08		
09		
10		
11		
12		
13		
14		
15		
16		
17		
18		

점수		점	확인	

Test 39

Track 117

🎧 **Listen, write the word and meaning.**

	Word	Meaning
01		
02		
03		
04		
05		
06		
07		
08		
09		
10		
11		
12		
13		
14		
15		
16		
17		
18		

점수	점	확인

Test 40

Track 120

🎧 **Listen, write the word and meaning.**

	Word	Meaning
01		
02		
03		
04		
05		
06		
07		
08		
09		
10		
11		
12		
13		
14		
15		
16		
17		
18		

점수	점	확인

Answer Key

Unit 1

A
1. activity
2. chart
3. among
4. beauty
5. changing
6. basic
7. basis
8. because
9. challenges
10. chance
11. become
12. aching
13. believe
14. bright
15. chain
16. character
17. active
18. clear

B
1. 활동
2. 기초, 근거
3. 사슬
4. 빛나는, 맑은
5. 아픔, 아프다
6. ~이 되다
7. 우연, 기회
8. 활동적인
9. 믿다
10. 특성, 성격
11. 기본적인
12. 차트, 도표
13. 도전
14. ~ 때문에
15. 분명한, 맑은
16. ~의 사이에
17. 바꾸다
18. 아름다움

1. ache
2. active
3. activity
4. among
5. basic
6. basis
7. beauty
8. because
9. become
10. believe
11. bright
12. chain
13. challenge
14. chance
15. change
16. character
17. chart
18. clear

C
1. become ~이 되다
2. believe 믿다
3. because ~ 때문에
4. chain 사슬
5. ache 아픔, 아프다
6. bright 빛나는, 맑은
7. beauty 아름다움
8. challenge 도전
9. active 활동적인
10. chance 우연, 기회
11. basis 기초, 근거
12. change 바꾸다
13. activity 활동
14. character 특성, 성격
15. basic 기본적인
16. chart 차트, 도표
17. among ~의 사이에
18. clear 분명한, 맑은

Unit 2

A
1. custom
2. empty
3. diligent
4. dead
5. cultures
6. degrees
7. else
8. energy
9. fit
10. enough
11. entered
12. fighting
13. flu
14. dangerous
15. engineer
16. final
17. first
18. flicked

B
1. 죽은
2. 그밖에, 달리
3. 근면한, 부지런한
4. 최초의, 처음의
5. 충분한
6. 풍습, 관습
7. 에너지
8. 마지막의
9. 탁치다
10. 위험한
11. 들어가다
12. 독감
13. 속이 빈, 비어 있는
14. 건강이 좋은, 알맞은
15. 싸우다, 싸움
16. 문화, 교양
17. 기술자, 기사
18. 도, 정도, 계급

1. culture
2. custom
3. dangerous
4. dead
5. degree
6. diligent
7. else
8. empty
9. energy
10. engineer
11. enough
12. enter
13. fight
14. final
15. first
16. fit
17. flick
18. flu

C
1. degree 도, 정도, 계급
2. enter 들어가다
3. dead 죽은
4. enough 충분한
5. fight 싸우다, 싸움
6. dangerous 위험한
7. else 그밖에, 달리
8. diligent 근면한, 부러한
9. custom 풍습, 관습
10. final 마지막의
11. culture 문화, 교양
12. energy 에너지
13. flick 탁치다
14. first 최초의, 처음의
15. empty 속이 빈, 비어 있는
16. flu 독감
17. fit 건강이 좋은, 알맞은
18. engineer 기술자, 기사

Review 1

A
1. become ~이 되다
2. believe 믿다
3. because ~ 때문에
4. chain 사슬
5. ache 아픔, 아프다
6. bright 빛나는, 맑은
7. beauty 아름다움
8. challenge 도전
9. active 활동적인
10. chance 우연, 기회
11. basis 기초, 근거
12. change 바꾸다
13. activity 활동
14. character 특성, 성격
15. basic 기본적인
16. chart 차트, 도표
17. among ~의 사이에
18. clear 분명한, 맑은

B
1. degree 도, 정도, 계급
2. enter 들어가다
3. dead 죽은
4. enough 충분한
5. fight 싸우다, 싸움
6. dangerous 위험한
7. else 그밖에, 달리
8. diligent 근면한, 부지런한
9. custom 풍습, 관습
10. final 마지막의
11. culture 문화, 교양
12. energy 에너지
13. flick 탁치다
14. first 최초의, 처음의
15. empty 속이 빈, 비어 있는
16. flu 독감
17. fit 건강이 좋은, 알맞은
18. engineer 기술자, 기사

Unit 3

A
1. Olympics
2. heavy
3. hide
4. parents
5. hobby
6. order
7. hero
8. lose
9. happened
10. magazine
11. magic
12. If
13. main
14. packing
15. marry
16. own
17. mark
18. pair

B
1. 취미
2. 잡지
3. 자기 자신의
4. 무거운
5. 만약 ~라면
6. 한 쌍, 한 벌
7. 숨다, 숨기다
8. 싸다, 꾸리다
9. 잃다, 놓치다
10. 결혼하다
11. 부모
12. 일어나다
13. 주요한
14. 올림픽
15. 점수, 기호
16. 명령, 순서
17. 마법
18. 영웅

1. happen
2. heavy
3. hero
4. hide
5. hobby
6. if
7. lose
8. magazine
9. magic
10. main
11. mark
12. marry
13. Olympic
14. order
15. own
16. pack
17. pair
18. parents

C
1. pair
2. magic
3. pack
4. main
5. happen
6. magazine
7. own
8. heavy
9. mark
10. order
11. parents
12. if
13. marry
14. hero
15. Olympic
16. hobby
17. lose
18. hide

한 쌍, 한 벌
마법
싸다, 꾸리다
주요한
일어나다
잡지
자기 자신의
무거운
점수, 기호
명령, 순서
부모
만약 ~라면
결혼하다
영웅
올림픽
취미
잃다, 놓치다
숨다, 숨기다

Unit 4

A
1. sometimes
2. project
3. puzzle
4. quick
5. proud
6. toothpaste
7. race
8. shower
9. site
10. programmer
11. Tower
12. smart
13. touch
14. snowy
15. title
16. through
17. solve
18. topics

B
1. 퍼즐, 수수께끼
2. 경주, 레이스
3. 사이트, 장소
4. 프로그래머
5. 풀다, 해결하다
6. 빠른, 즉석의
7. 때때로
8. 자랑으로 여기는
9. 치약
10. 눈의, 눈이 내리는
11. ~을 통하여
12. 탑, 타워
13. 계획, 과제
14. 만지다
15. 영리한
16. 화제
17. 제목
18. 샤워, 소나기

1. programmer
2. project
3. proud
4. puzzle
5. quick
6. race
7. shower
8. site
9. smart
10. snowy
11. solve
12. sometimes
13. through
14. title
15. toothpaste
16. topic
17. touch
18. tower

C
1. snowy
2. programmer
3. touch
4. site
5. tower
6. smart
7. project
8. shower
9. topic
10. quick
11. race
12. solve
13. proud
14. toothpaste
15. sometimes
16. through
17. puzzle
18. title

눈의, 눈이 내리는
프로그래머
만지다
사이트, 장소
탑, 타워
영리한
계획, 과제
샤워, 소나기
화제
빠른, 즉석의
경주, 레이스
풀다, 해결하다
자랑으로 여기는
치약
때때로
~을 통하여
퍼즐, 수수께끼
제목

Review 2

A
1. pair
2. magic
3. pack
4. main
5. happen
6. magazine
7. own
8. heavy
9. mark
10. order
11. parents
12. if
13. marry
14. hero
15. Olympic
16. hobby
17. lose
18. hide

한 쌍, 한 벌
마법
싸다, 꾸리다
주요한
일어나다
잡지
자기 자신의
무거운
점수, 기호
명령, 순서
부모
만약 ~라면
결혼하다
영웅
올림픽
취미
잃다, 놓치다
숨다, 숨기다

B
1. snowy
2. programmer
3. touch
4. site
5. tower
6. smart
7. project
8. shower
9. topic
10. quick
11. race
12. solve
13. proud
14. toothpaste
15. sometimes
16. through
17. puzzle
18. title

눈의, 눈이 내리는
프로그래머
만지다
사이트, 장소
탑, 타워
영리한
계획, 과제
샤워, 소나기
화제
빠른, 즉석의
경주, 레이스
풀다, 해결하다
자랑으로 여기는
치약
때때로
~을 통하여
퍼즐, 수수께끼
제목

Unit 5

A
1. blowing
2. choose
3. choice
4. advice
5. agree
6. ahead
7. afraid
8. baking
9. blond
10. adults
11. Check
12. borrow
13. brave
14. cheer
15. Bricks
16. chat
17. aided
18. cheaply

B
1. 앞에, 전방에
2. 금발의
3. 두려워하는
4. 잡담, 잡담하다
5. (빵 등을) 굽다
6. 격려, 환호
7. 용감한
8. 성인, 어른
9. 빌리다
10. 싸게, 값싸게
11. 원조하다, 돕다
12. 고르다, 선택하다
13. 동의하다
14. 벽돌
15. 선택
16. (바람이) 불다
17. 체크하다, 점검하다
18. 충고, 조언

1. adult
2. advice
3. afraid
4. agree
5. ahead
6. aid
7. bake
8. blond
9. blow
10. borrow
11. brave
12. brick
13. chat
14. cheaply
15. check
16. cheer
17. choice
18. choose

C
1. brick — 벽돌
2. aid — 원조하다, 돕다
3. chat — 잡담, 잡담하다
4. bake — (빵 등을) 굽다
5. adult — 성인, 어른
6. cheaply — 싸게, 값싸게
7. advice — 충고, 조언
8. cheer — 격려, 환호
9. blond — 금발의
10. ahead — 앞에, 전방에
11. brave — 용감한
12. check — 체크하다, 점검하다
13. blow — (바람이) 불다
14. afraid — 두려워하는
15. choice — 선택
16. borrow — 빌리다
17. choose — 고르다, 선택하다
18. agree — 동의하다

Unit 6

A
1. die
2. delicious
3. diary
4. focus
5. department
6. foreign
7. dentist
8. envelope
9. foolish
10. envy
11. destination
12. forest
13. erasing
14. escape
15. environment
16. even
17. Follow
18. fuse

B
1. 죽다
2. 부러워하다
3. 맛있는
4. 초점
5. 달아나다
6. 봉투
7. 외국의
8. 치과의사
9. 어리석은
10. 목적지
11. ~조차도
12. 숲, 산림
13. 부서, 부문
14. 도화선
15. 환경
16. 따라가다
17. 지우다
18. 일기

1. delicious
2. dentist
3. department
4. destination
5. diary
6. die
7. envelope
8. environment
9. envy
10. erase
11. escape
12. even
13. focus
14. follow
15. foolish
16. foreign
17. forest
18. fuse

C
1. focus — 초점
2. destination — 목적지
3. escape — 달아나다
4. follow — 따라가다
5. delicious — 맛있는
6. foolish — 어리석은
7. envy — 부러워하다
8. foreign — 외국의
9. erase — 지우다
10. dentist — 치과의사
11. forest — 숲, 산림
12. environment — 환경
13. fuse — 도화선
14. department — 부서, 부문
15. envelope — 봉투
16. diary — 일기
17. even — ~조차도
18. die — 죽다

Review 3

A
1. brick — 벽돌
2. aid — 원조하다, 돕다
3. chat — 잡담, 잡담하다
4. bake — (빵 등을) 굽다
5. adult — 성인, 어른
6. cheaply — 싸게, 값싸게
7. advice — 충고, 조언
8. cheer — 격려, 환호
9. blond — 금발의
10. ahead — 앞에, 전방에
11. brave — 용감한
12. check — 체크하다, 점검하다
13. blow — (바람이) 불다
14. afraid — 두려워하는
15. choice — 선택
16. borrow — 빌리다
17. choose — 고르다, 선택하다
18. agree — 동의하다

B
1. focus — 초점
2. destination — 목적지
3. escape — 달아나다
4. follow — 따라가다
5. delicious — 맛있는
6. foolish — 어리석은
7. envy — 부러워하다
8. foreign — 외국의
9. erase — 지우다
10. dentist — 치과의사
11. forest — 숲, 산림
12. environment — 환경
13. fuse — 도화선
14. department — 부서, 부문
15. envelope — 봉투
16. diary — 일기
17. even — ~조차도
18. die — 죽다

Unit 7

A
1. homeless
2. horn
3. pattern
4. hurry
5. Maybe
6. print
7. means
8. hope
9. medicine
10. hockey
11. Memorial
12. moment
13. hunt
14. Pat
15. perfect
16. matter
17. pet
18. Practice

B
1. 경적, 뿔
2. 문제, 일
3. 서두르다, 매우 급함
4. 기념의, 기념물(관)
5. 가볍게 치다
6. 하키
7. 순간, 잠깐
8. 애완동물
9. 아마
10. 연습하다, 연습
11. 집없는
12. 약, 약물
13. 인쇄하다
14. 바라다
15. 완전한
16. 의미하다
17. 도안, 모형
18. 사냥하다

1. hockey
2. homeless
3. hope
4. horn
5. hunt
6. hurry
7. matter
8. maybe
9. mean
10. medicine
11. memorial
12. moment
13. pat
14. pattern
15. perfect
16. pet
17. practice
18. print

C
1. matter — 문제, 일
2. print — 인쇄하다
3. homeless — 집없는
4. practice — 연습하다, 연습
5. hurry — 서두르다, 매우 급함
6. maybe — 아마
7. hockey — 하키
8. pet — 애완동물
9. mean — 의미하다
10. perfect — 완전한
11. hope — 바라다
12. pattern — 도안, 모형
13. medicine — 약, 약물
14. horn — 경적, 뿔
15. pat — 가볍게 치다
16. memorial — 기념의, 기념물(관)
17. hunt — 사냥하다
18. moment — 순간, 잠깐

Unit 8

A
1. trip
2. really
3. repeat
4. respond
5. report
6. unfair
7. refrigerator
8. sound
9. unit
10. sour
11. travel
12. space
13. soon
14. spaghetti
15. remember
16. special
17. triangle
18. type

B
1. 곧, 이내
2. 여행하다
3. 냉장고
4. 스파게티
5. (짧은) 여행
6. 공간
7. 반복하다
8. 불공평한, 부당한
9. 진짜로, 정말로
10. 소리, 음
11. 단위, 단원
12. 보고, 기사
13. 신, 시큼한
14. 삼각형
15. 기억하다
16. 특별한
17. 형, 타입
18. 응답하다, 반응하다

1. really
2. refrigerator
3. remember
4. repeat
5. report
6. respond
7. soon
8. sound
9. sour
10. space
11. spaghetti
12. special
13. travel
14. triangle
15. trip
16. type
17. unfair
18. unit

C
1. travel — 여행하다
2. really — 진짜로, 정말로
3. triangle — 삼각형
4. special — 특별한
5. refrigerator — 냉장고
6. trip — (짧은) 여행
7. spaghetti — 스파게티
8. remember — 기억하다
9. type — 형, 타입
10. space — 공간
11. repeat — 반복하다
12. unfair — 불공평한, 부당한
13. soon — 곧, 이내
14. report — 보고, 기사
15. sour — 신, 시큼한
16. unit — 단위, 단원
17. respond — 응답하다, 대답하다
18. sound — 소리, 음

Review 4

A
1. matter — 문제, 일
2. print — 인쇄하다
3. homeless — 집없는
4. practice — 연습하다, 연습
5. hurry — 서두르다, 매우 급함
6. maybe — 아마
7. hockey — 하키
8. pet — 애완동물
9. mean — 의미하다
10. perfect — 완전한
11. hope — 바라다
12. pattern — 도안, 모형
13. medicine — 약, 약물
14. horn — 경적, 뿔
15. pat — 가볍게 치다
16. memorial — 기념의, 기념물(관)
17. hunt — 사냥하다
18. moment — 순간, 잠깐

B
1. travel — 여행하다
2. really — 진짜로, 정말로
3. triangle — 삼각형
4. special — 특별한
5. refrigerator — 냉장고
6. trip — (짧은) 여행
7. spaghetti — 스파게티
8. remember — 기억하다
9. type — 형, 타입
10. space — 공간
11. repeat — 반복하다
12. unfair — 불공평한, 부당한
13. soon — 곧, 이내
14. report — 보고, 기사
15. sour — 신, 시큼한
16. unit — 단위, 단원
17. respond — 응답하다, 대답하다
18. sound — 소리, 음

Unit 9

A
1. aisle
2. alone
3. airport
4. blanks
5. bucket
6. almost
7. bug
8. click
9. closet
10. build
11. alarm
12. busy
13. campus
14. along
15. classical
16. clerk
17. clinic
18. business

B
1. 자명종, 경보
2. 짓다, 세우다
3. 교정, 학교 마당
4. 공항
5. 점원, 사무원
6. 양동이
7. 전문병원, 진료소
8. 복도, 통로
9. 바쁜
10. 홀로, 단독으로
11. 벌레, 곤충
12. 벽장
13. 거의
14. 딸깍(하는 소리)
15. 빈, 빈 곳
16. 고전적인
17. 직업, 사업
18. ~을 따라

1. airport
2. aisle
3. alarm
4. almost
5. alone
6. along
7. blank
8. bucket
9. bug
10. build
11. business
12. busy
13. campus
14. classical
15. clerk
16. click
17. clinic
18. closet

C
1. bug — 벌레, 곤충
2. airport — 공항
3. clinic — 전문병원, 진료소
4. closet — 벽장
5. bucket — 양동이
6. click — 딸깍하는 소리
7. build — 짓다, 세우다
8. aisle — 복도, 통로
9. along — ~을 따라
10. business — 직업, 사업
11. alarm — 자명종, 경보
12. clerk — 점원, 사무원
13. blank — 빈, 빈 곳
14. almost — 거의
15. busy — 바쁜
16. classical — 고전적인
17. alone — 홀로, 단독으로
18. campus — 교정, 학교 마당

Unit 10

A
1. expensive
2. district
3. event
4. difficult
5. director
6. fur
7. discuss
8. fresh
9. diet
10. exam
11. differences
12. excited
13. forget-me-not
14. form
15. excellent
16. function
17. exchange
18. funny

B
1. 감독, 지도자
2. 사건
3. 털, 모피
4. 어려운
5. 값비싼
6. 다이어트, 규정식
7. 기능, 구실
8. 뛰어난
9. 물망초
10. 다름, 차이
11. 흥분시키다
12. 우스운, 재미있는
13. 토론하다, 의논하다
14. 교환하다
15. 형식, 모양
16. 시험
17. 신선한, 새로운
18. 지역, 지구

1. diet
2. difference
3. difficult
4. director
5. discuss
6. district
7. event
8. exam
9. excellent
10. exchange
11. excite
12. expensive
13. forget-me-not
14. form
15. fresh
16. function
17. funny
18. fur

C
1. difference — 다름, 차이
2. function — 기능, 구실
3. excite — 흥분시키다
4. funny — 우스운, 재미있는
5. diet — 다이어트, 규정식
6. exchange — 교환하다
7. fresh — 신선한, 새로운
8. excellent — 뛰어난
9. fur — 털, 모피
10. difficult — 어려운
11. form — 형식, 모양
12. exam — 시험
13. forget-me-not — 물망초
14. director — 감독, 지도자
15. event — 사건
16. discuss — 토론하다, 의논하다
17. expensive — 값비싼
18. district — 지역, 지구

Review 5

A
1. bug — 벌레, 곤충
2. airport — 공항
3. clinic — 전문병원, 진료소
4. closet — 벽장
5. bucket — 양동이
6. click — 딸깍(하는 소리)
7. build — 짓다, 세우다
8. aisle — 복도, 통로
9. along — ~을 따라
10. business — 직업, 사업
11. alarm — 자명종, 경보
12. clerk — 점원, 사무원
13. blank — 빈, 빈 곳
14. almost — 거의
15. busy — 바쁜
16. classical — 고전적인
17. alone — 홀로, 단독으로
18. campus — 교정, 학교 마당

B
1. difference — 다름, 차이
2. function — 기능, 구실
3. excite — 흥분시키다
4. funny — 우스운, 재미있는
5. diet — 다이어트, 규정식
6. exchange — 교환하다
7. fresh — 신선한, 새로운
8. excellent — 뛰어난
9. fur — 털, 모피
10. difficult — 어려운
11. form — 형식, 모양
12. exam — 시험
13. forget-me-not — 물망초
14. director — 감독, 지도자
15. event — 사건
16. discuss — 토론하다, 의논하다
17. expensive — 값비싼
18. district — 지역, 지구

Unit 11

A
1. interested
2. iguana
3. pictures
4. important
5. Internet
6. playground
7. island
8. meal
9. mini
10. Mix
11. moon
12. picnic
13. metal
14. pass
15. middle
16. places
17. imagined
18. Plants

B
1. 금속
2. 상상하다
3. 소형의
4. 달
5. 섬
6. 중앙, 한가운데
7. 지나다
8. 이구아나
9. 그림, 사진
10. 운동장, 놀이터
11. 중요한
12. 식물, 풀
13. 식사
14. 곳, 장소
15. 인터넷
16. 소풍, 피크닉
17. 섞다, 혼합하다
18. 관심을 끌다

1. iguana
2. imagine
3. important
4. interest
5. Internet
6. island
7. meal
8. metal
9. middle
10. mini
11. mix
12. moon
13. pass
14. picnic
15. picture
16. place
17. plant
18. playground

C
1. mini — 소형의
2. iguana — 이구아나
3. plant — 식물, 풀
4. middle — 중앙, 한가운데
5. place — 곳, 장소
6. mix — 섞다, 혼합하다
7. imagine — 상상하다
8. moon — 달
9. important — 중요한
10. pass — 지나다
11. island — 섬
12. metal — 금속
13. interest — 관심을 끌다
14. picnic — 소풍, 피크닉
15. playground — 운동장, 놀이터
16. Internet — 인터넷
17. meal — 식사
18. picture — 그림, 사진

Unit 12

A
1. rocks
2. steak
3. row
4. sale
5. situation
6. speed
7. village
8. round
9. storm
10. war
11. straight
12. usual
13. vacation
14. rushed
15. view
16. stick
17. waste
18. still

B
1. 판매
2. 보통의, 평소의
3. 둥근, 원형의
4. 스테이크
5. 열, 줄
6. 휴가, 방학
7. 상황
8. 마을
9. 아직도, 여전히
10. 돌진하다
11. 폭풍
12. 낭비하다
13. 속도, 속력
14. 전쟁
15. 전망, 풍경
16. 곧장, 곧은
17. 바위
18. 찌르다, 붙이다

1. rock
2. round
3. row
4. rush
5. sale
6. situation
7. speed
8. steak
9. stick
10. still
11. storm
12. straight
13. usual
14. vacation
15. view
16. village
17. war
18. waste

C
1. still — 아직도, 여전히
2. war — 전쟁
3. stick — 찌르다, 붙이다
4. village — 마을
5. rock — 바위
6. view — 전망, 풍경
7. steak — 스테이크
8. vacation — 휴가, 방학
9. round — 둥근, 원형의
10. straight — 곧장, 곧은
11. speed — 속도, 속력
12. usual — 보통의, 평소의
13. row — 열, 줄
14. waste — 낭비하다
15. situation — 상황
16. storm — 폭풍
17. rush — 돌진하다
18. sale — 판매

Review 6

A
1. mini — 소형의
2. iguana — 이구아나
3. plant — 식물, 풀
4. middle — 중앙, 한가운데
5. place — 곳, 장소
6. mix — 섞다, 혼합하다
7. imagine — 상상하다
8. moon — 달
9. important — 중요한
10. pass — 지나다
11. island — 섬
12. metal — 금속
13. interest — 관심을 끌다
14. picnic — 소풍, 피크닉
15. playground — 운동장, 놀이터
16. Internet — 인터넷
17. meal — 식사
18. picture — 그림, 사진

B
1. still — 아직도, 여전히
2. war — 전쟁
3. stick — 찌르다, 붙이다
4. village — 마을
5. rock — 바위
6. view — 전망, 풍경
7. steak — 스테이크
8. vacation — 휴가, 방학
9. round — 둥근, 원형의
10. straight — 곧장, 곧은
11. speed — 속도, 속력
12. usual — 보통의, 평소의
13. row — 열, 줄
14. waste — 낭비하다
15. situation — 상황
16. storm — 폭풍
17. rush — 돌진하다
18. sale — 판매

Unit 13

A
1. connecting
2. angry
3. care
4. another
5. base
6. concert
7. calendar
8. cape
9. capital
10. also
11. captain
12. altogether
13. carved
14. Collect
15. comic
16. concept
17. angel
18. congratulations

B
1. 천사
2. 선장, 장
3. 만화, 희극의
4. 또한, 역시
5. 모으다
6. 개념
7. 아주, 전부
8. 조각하다
9. 기초
10. 잇다, 연결하다
11. 달력
12. 성난
13. 돌봄, 주의, 걱정
14. 콘서트, 음악회
15. 망토
16. 축하
17. 또 하나의, 다른
18. 수도, 대문자

1. also
2. altogether
3. angel
4. angry
5. another
6. base
7. calendar
8. cape
9. capital
10. captain
11. care
12. carve
13. collect
14. comic
15. concept
16. concert
17. congratulation
18. connect

C
1. cape — 망토
2. collect — 모으다
3. another — 또 하나의, 다른
4. base — 기초
5. calendar — 달력
6. connect — 잇다, 연결하다
7. angry — 성난
8. capital — 수도, 대문자
9. concept — 개념
10. comic — 만화, 희극의
11. captain — 선장, 장
12. altogether — 아주, 전부
13. concert — 콘서트, 음악회
14. carve — 조각하다
15. angel — 천사
16. care — 돌봄, 주의, 걱정
17. congratulation — 축하
18. also — 또한, 역시

Unit 14

A
1. dots
2. gentle
3. doughnuts
4. Electric
5. double
6. germs
7. different
8. fell
9. false
10. gained
11. famous
12. drama
13. genius
14. gift
15. Express
16. extend
17. ghosts
18. driving

B
1. 점, 규정시각
2. 거짓의, 틀린
3. 전기의
4. 얻다, 획득하다
5. 다른, 상이한
6. 부드러운
7. 도넛
8. 유령
9. 표현하다
10. 선물
11. 세균, 병원균
12. 극, 드라마
13. 천재
14. 연장하다
15. 유명한
16. 운전하다, 몰다
17. 떨어지다, 넘어지다
18. 배로 늘다, 두 배

1. different
2. dot
3. double
4. doughnut
5. drama
6. drive
7. electric
8. express
9. extend
10. fall
11. false
12. famous
13. gain
14. genius
15. gentle
16. germ
17. ghost
18. gift

C
1. gain — 얻다, 획득하다
2. famous — 유명한
3. genius — 천재
4. different — 다른, 상이한
5. fall — 떨어지다, 넘어지다
6. dot — 점, 규정시각
7. false — 거짓의, 틀린
8. extend — 연장하다
9. double — 배로 늘다, 두 배
10. gentle — 부드러운
11. gift — 선물
12. drama — 극, 드라마
13. electric — 전기의
14. drive — 운전하다, 몰다
15. germ — 세균, 병원균
16. doughnut — 도넛
17. express — 표현하다
18. ghost — 유령

Review 7

A
1. cape — 망토
2. collect — 모으다
3. another — 또 하나의, 다른
4. base — 기초
5. calendar — 달력
6. connect — 잇다, 연결하다
7. angry — 성난
8. capital — 수도, 대문자
9. concept — 개념
10. comic — 만화, 희극의
11. captain — 선장, 장
12. altogether — 아주, 전부
13. concert — 콘서트, 음악회
14. carve — 조각하다
15. angel — 천사
16. care — 돌봄, 주의, 걱정
17. congratulation — 축하
18. also — 또한, 역시

B
1. gain — 얻다, 획득하다
2. famous — 유명한
3. genius — 천재
4. different — 다른, 상이한
5. fall — 떨어지다, 넘어지다
6. dot — 점, 규정시각
7. false — 거짓의, 틀린
8. extend — 연장하다
9. double — 배로 늘다, 두 배
10. gentle — 부드러운
11. gift — 선물
12. drama — 극, 드라마
13. electric — 전기의
14. drive — 운전하다, 몰다
15. germ — 세균, 병원균
16. doughnut — 도넛
17. express — 표현하다
18. ghost — 유령

Unit 15

A
1. mathematics
2. introduced
3. pleasure
4. jar
5. police station
6. judge
7. Most
8. interesting
9. mountain
10. narrow
11. plate
12. more
13. pole
14. pollution
15. joined
16. museum
17. invention
18. poll

B
1. 발명, 발명품
2. 대부분의
3. 막대기, 장대
4. 흥미가 있는
5. 기쁨, 즐거움
6. 수학
7. 여론조사, 투표
8. 박물관
9. 소개하다
10. 기쁨, 즐거움
11. 항아리, 단지
12. 폭이 좁은
13. 더 많은, 여분의
14. 오염
15. 심판, 판단하다
16. 경찰서
17. 산
18. 가입하다, 결합하다

1. interesting
2. introduce
3. invention
4. jar
5. join
6. judge
7. mathematics
8. more
9. most
10. mountain
11. museum
12. narrow
13. plate
14. pleasure
15. pole
16. police station
17. poll
18. pollution

C
1. most 대부분의
2. pollution 오염
3. mountain 산
4. interesting 흥미가 있는
5. more 더 많은, 여분의
6. pole 막대기, 장대
7. introduce 소개하다
8. plate 접시
9. mathematics 수학
10. narrow 폭이 좁은
11. invention 발명, 발명품
12. museum 박물관
13. judge 심판, 판단하다
14. pleasure 기쁨, 즐거움
15. jar 항아리, 단지
16. police station 경찰서
17. join 가입하다, 결합하다
18. pool 여론조사, 투표

Unit 16

A
1. save
2. usually
3. thirsty
4. science
5. seasons
6. weak
7. second
8. whispered
9. strange
10. straw
11. wise
12. strike
13. thick
14. seeds
15. thousand
16. while
17. scissors
18. will

B
1. 짚
2. 계절
3. 두꺼운
4. 보통, 일반적으로
5. 과학
6. 약한
7. 치다, 때리다
8. 구하다, 절약하다
9. 속삭이다
10. ~할 것이다
11. 둘째의
12. 현명한, 신중한
13. ~하는 동안에
14. 씨앗
15. 목마른
16. 이상한
17. 천
18. 가위

1. save
2. science
3. scissors
4. season
5. second
6. seed
7. strange
8. straw
9. strike
10. thick
11. thirsty
12. thousand
13. usually
14. weak
15. while
16. whisper
17. will
18. wise

C
1. weak 약한
2. science 과학
3. usually 보통, 일반적으로
4. scissors 가위
5. thousand 천
6. while ~하는 동안에
7. save 구하다, 절약하다
8. whisper 속삭이다
9. strike 치다, 때리다
10. will ~할 것이다
11. thirsty 목마른
12. season 계절
13. wise 현명한, 신중한
14. seed 씨앗
15. straw 짚
16. second 둘째의
17. thick 두꺼운
18. strange 이상한

Review 8

A
1. most 대부분의
2. pollution 오염
3. mountain 산
4. interesting 흥미가 있는
5. more 더 많은, 여분의
6. pole 막대기, 장대
7. introduce 소개하다
8. plate 접시
9. mathematics 수학
10. narrow 폭이 좁은
11. invention 발명, 발명품
12. museum 박물관
13. judge 심판, 판단하다
14. pleasure 기쁨, 즐거움
15. jar 항아리, 단지
16. police station 경찰서
17. join 가입하다, 결합하다
18. pool 여론조사, 투표

B
1. weak 약한
2. science 과학
3. usually 보통, 일반적으로
4. scissors 가위
5. thousand 천
6. while ~하는 동안에
7. save 구하다, 절약하다
8. whisper 속삭이다
9. strike 치다, 때리다
10. will ~할 것이다
11. thirsty 목마른
12. season 계절
13. wise 현명한, 신중한
14. seed 씨앗
15. straw 짚
16. second 둘째의
17. thick 두꺼운
18. strange 이상한

Unit 17

A
1. ceiling
2. artist
3. Chop
4. autumn
5. cart
6. channels
7. cause
8. crowd
9. bat
10. cartoon
11. attack
12. cough
13. century
14. couple
15. coupon
16. advise
17. bathtub
18. course

B
1. 방망이, 박쥐
2. 충고하다, 조언하다
3. 세기
4. 손수레, 카트
5. 채널
6. 미술가, 예술가
7. 기침
8. 만화
9. 강의, 진로
10. 베다, 자르다
11. 군중
12. 가을
13. 쿠폰, 우대권
14. 원인, 이유
15. 한 쌍, 커플
16. 욕조
17. 천장
18. 공격, 공격하다

1. advise
2. artist
3. attack
4. autumn
5. bat
6. bathtub
7. cart
8. cartoon
9. cause
10. ceiling
11. century
12. channel
13. chop
14. cough
15. couple
16. coupon
17. course
18. crowd

C
1. chop
2. couple
3. century
4. cough
5. channel
6. advise
7. ceiling
8. crowd
9. coupon
10. cause
11. bathtub
12. artist
13. cart
14. course
15. attack
16. cartoon
17. bat
18. autumn

베다, 자르다
한 쌍, 커플
세기
기침
채널
충고하다, 조언하다
천장
군중
쿠폰, 우대권
원인, 이유
욕조
미술가, 예술가
손수레, 카트
강의, 진로
공격, 공격하다
만화
방망이, 박쥐
가을

Unit 18

A
1. Either
2. glue
3. during
4. electricity
5. dull
6. fare
7. greetings
8. fashions
9. groups
10. fault
11. grand
12. expression
13. favorite
14. guess
15. feed
16. earth
17. fever
18. grade

B
1. 전기
2. 과실, 잘못
3. 접착제, 접착하다
4. ~ 동안에
5. 열
6. 운임, 통행료
7. 인사, 인사말
8. 둔한, 무딘
9. 좋아하는
10. 집단
11. 지구
12. (음식을) 먹이다
13. 추측하다
14. 표현, 표정
15. 웅대한, 당당한
16. 유행, 방식
17. 학년, 등급
18. (둘 중) 어느 한쪽

1. dull
2. during
3. earth
4. either
5. electricity
6. expression
7. fare
8. fashion
9. fault
10. favorite
11. feed
12. fever
13. glue
14. grade
15. grand
16. greeting
17. group
18. guess

C
1. feed
2. dull
3. fever
4. earth
5. glue
6. during
7. grade
8. expression
9. fare
10. group
11. grand
12. either
13. fashion
14. guess
15. electricity
16. fault
17. favorite
18. greeting

(음식을) 먹이다
둔한, 무딘
열
지구
접착제, 접착하다
~ 동안에
학년, 등급
표현, 표정
운임, 통행료
집단
웅대한, 당당한
(둘 중) 어느 한쪽
유행, 방식
추측하다
전기
과실, 잘못
좋아하는
인사, 인사말

Review 9

A
1. chop
2. couple
3. century
4. cough
5. channel
6. advise
7. ceiling
8. crowd
9. coupon
10. cause
11. bathtub
12. artist
13. cart
14. course
15. attack
16. cartoon
17. bat
18. autumn

베다, 자르다
한 쌍, 커플
세기
기침
채널
충고하다, 조언하다
천장
군중
쿠폰, 우대권
원인, 이유
욕조
미술가, 예술가
손수레, 카트
강의, 진로
공격, 공격하다
만화
방망이, 박쥐
가을

B
1. feed
2. dull
3. fever
4. earth
5. glue
6. during
7. grade
8. expression
9. fare
10. group
11. grand
12. either
13. fashion
14. guess
15. electricity
16. fault
17. favorite
18. greeting

(음식을) 먹이다
둔한, 무딘
열
지구
접착제, 접착하다
~ 동안에
학년, 등급
표현, 표정
운임, 통행료
집단
웅대한, 당당한
(둘 중) 어느 한쪽
유행, 방식
추측하다
전기
과실, 잘못
좋아하는
인사, 인사말

Unit 19

A
1. leadership
2. neighbors
3. lilacs
4. power
5. loud
6. powder
7. luck
8. president
9. necklace
10. present
11. lie
12. noise
13. novel
14. price
15. language
16. office
17. Nobody
18. pot

B
1. 목걸이
2. 드러눕다
3. 아무도 ~않다
4. 사무실, 임무
5. 가루, 분말
6. 지도(력), 지휘
7. 힘, 능력
8. 언어
9. 가격
10. 이웃사람
11. 대통령, 장
12. 라일락
13. 소리, 소음
14. 선물
15. 행운, 운
16. 그릇, 단지
17. 소설
18. 시끄러운

1. leadership
2. language
3. lie
4. lilac
5. loud
6. luck
7. necklace
8. neighbor
9. nobody
10. noise
11. novel
12. office
13. pot
14. powder
15. power
16. present
17. president
18. price

C
1. neighbor — 이웃사람
2. luck — 행운, 운
3. price — 가격
4. leadership — 지도(력), 지휘
5. necklace — 목걸이
6. president — 대통령, 장
7. nobody — 아무도 ~않다
8. present — 선물
9. language — 언어
10. noise — 소리, 소음
11. pot — 그릇, 단지
12. power — 힘, 능력
13. lie — 드러눕다
14. novel — 소설
15. loud — 시끄러운
16. office — 사무실, 임무
17. lilac — 라일락
18. powder — 가루, 분말

Unit 20

A
1. series
2. yet
3. shape
4. sharp
5. wish
6. shocked
7. wrong
8. shouted
9. worrying
10. stupid
11. terrible
12. sure
13. text
14. symbol
15. temple
16. wondered
17. scientist
18. write

B
1. 시리즈, 연속
2. 절, 신전
3. 바라다
4. 모양, 형상
5. 의아하게 여기다
6. 상징, 기호
7. 잘못된, 틀린
8. 과학자
9. 본문, 원문
10. 어리석은
11. 아직 ~않다
12. 날카로운
13. 쓰다
14. 확신하고 있는
15. 걱정하다
16. 깜짝 놀라게 하다
17. 심한, 지독한
18. 소리치다

1. scientist
2. series
3. shape
4. sharp
5. shock
6. shout
7. stupid
8. sure
9. symbol
10. temple
11. terrible
12. text
13. wish
14. wonder
15. worry
16. write
17. wrong
18. yet

C
1. scientist — 과학자
2. symbol — 상징, 기호
3. temple — 절, 신전
4. wish — 바라다
5. series — 시리즈, 연속
6. terrible — 심한, 지독한
7. shape — 모양, 형상
8. sure — 확신하고 있는
9. text — 본문, 원문
10. sharp — 날카로운
11. wonder — 의아하게 여기다
12. stupid — 어리석은
13. shock — 깜짝 놀라게 하다
14. yet — 아직 ~않다
15. worry — 걱정하다
16. wrong — 잘못된, 틀린
17. shout — 소리치다
18. write — 쓰다

Review 10

A
1. neighbor — 이웃사람
2. luck — 행운, 운
3. price — 가격
4. leadership — 지도(력), 지휘
5. necklace — 목걸이
6. president — 대통령, 장
7. nobody — 아무도 ~않다
8. present — 선물
9. language — 언어
10. noise — 소리, 소음
11. pot — 그릇, 단지
12. power — 힘, 능력
13. lie — 드러눕다
14. novel — 소설
15. loud — 시끄러운
16. office — 사무실, 임무
17. lilac — 라일락
18. powder — 가루, 분말

B
1. scientist — 과학자
2. symbol — 상징, 기호
3. temple — 절, 신전
4. wish — 바라다
5. series — 시리즈, 연속
6. terrible — 심한, 지독한
7. shape — 모양, 형상
8. sure — 확신하고 있는
9. text — 본문, 원문
10. sharp — 날카로운
11. wonder — 의아하게 여기다
12. stupid — 어리석은
13. shock — 깜짝 놀라게 하다
14. yet — 아직 ~않다
15. worry — 걱정하다
16. wrong — 잘못된, 틀린
17. shout — 소리치다
18. write — 쓰다

Unit 21

A
1. blind
2. actor
3. bit
4. chimney
5. art
6. Chapter
7. avoid
8. Bend
9. cartoonist
10. bit / bit
11. chief
12. bombs
13. abroad
14. bow
15. add
16. chew
17. best
18. chips

B
1. 굽히다, 구부리다
2. 굴뚝
3. 물린 상처, 물다
4. 외국으로
5. 최고의, 최상의
6. (책, 논문의) 장
7. 배우
8. 소량, 조금
9. 씹다
10. 토막, 얇은 조각
11. 더하다, 추가하다
12. 눈 먼
13. 주요한
14. 폭탄, 폭격하다
15. 만화가
16. 피하다, 막다
17. 고개를 숙이다
18. 예술, 미술

1. abroad
2. actor
3. add
4. art
5. avoid
6. bend
7. best
8. bit
9. bite
10. blind
11. bomb
12. bow
13. cartoonist
14. chapter
15. chew
16. chief
17. chimney
18. chip

C
1. cartoonist — 만화가
2. bend — 굽히다, 구부리다
3. chapter — (책, 논문의) 장
4. avoid — 피하다, 막다
5. bite — 물린 상처, 물다
6. art — 예술, 미술
7. best — 최고의, 최상의
8. bow — 고개를 숙이다
9. abroad — 외국으로
10. chew — 씹다
11. bit — 소량, 조금
12. chimney — 굴뚝
13. actor — 배우
14. blind — 눈 먼
15. chief — 주요한
16. add — 더하다, 추가하다
17. chip — 토막, 얇은 조각
18. bomb — 폭탄, 폭격하다

Unit 22

A
1. eager
2. couch
3. gained
4. courageous
5. download
6. crocodiles
7. drain
8. fume
9. crab
10. edge
11. courts
12. furniture
13. couple
14. dyeing
15. gallery
16. duties
17. garage
18. includes

B
1. 다운로드하다
2. 가구
3. 한 쌍, 둘
4. 배수, 배수관
5. 얻다, 늘리다
6. 용기 있는, 용감한
7. 포함하다
8. 차고
9. 법정, 안뜰
10. 의무
11. 간절히 바라는
12. 게
13. 염색하다
14. 화랑, 미술관
15. 악어
16. 가장자리, 모서리
17. 노발대발하다, 증기
18. 침상, 소파

1. couch
2. couple
3. courageous
4. court
5. crab
6. crocodile
7. download
8. drain
9. duty
10. dye
11. eager
12. edge
13. fume
14. furniture
15. gain
16. gallery
17. garage
18. include

C
1. garage — 차고
2. couch — 침상, 소파
3. gain — 얻다, 늘리다
4. furniture — 가구
5. gallery — 화랑, 미술관
6. couple — 한 쌍, 둘
7. include — 포함하다
8. courageous — 용기 있는, 용감한
9. duty — 의무
10. eager — 간절히 바라는
11. court — 법정, 안뜰
12. dye — 염색하다
13. download — 다운로드하다
14. edge — 가장자리, 모서리
15. crab — 게
16. fume — 노발대발하다, 증기
17. drain — 배수, 배수관
18. crocodile — 악어

Review 11

A
1. cartoonist — 만화가
2. bend — 굽히다, 구부리다
3. chapter — (책, 논문의) 장
4. avoid — 피하다, 막다
5. bite — 물린 상처, 물다
6. art — 예술, 미술
7. best — 최고의, 최상의
8. bow — 고개를 숙이다
9. abroad — 외국으로
10. chew — 씹다
11. bit — 소량, 조금
12. chimney — 굴뚝
13. actor — 배우
14. blind — 눈 먼
15. chief — 주요한
16. add — 더하다, 추가하다
17. chip — 토막, 얇은 조각
18. bomb — 폭탄, 폭격하다

B
1. garage — 차고
2. couch — 침상, 소파
3. gain — 얻다, 늘리다
4. furniture — 가구
5. gallery — 화랑, 미술관
6. couple — 한 쌍, 둘
7. include — 포함하다
8. courageous — 용기 있는, 용감한
9. duty — 의무
10. eager — 간절히 바라는
11. court — 법정, 안뜰
12. dye — 염색하다
13. download — 다운로드하다
14. edge — 가장자리, 모서리
15. crab — 게
16. fume — 노발대발하다, 증기
17. drain — 배수, 배수관
18. crocodile — 악어

Unit 23

A
1. poison
2. insects
3. link
4. poems
5. instead
6. interested
7. loaned
8. possible
9. monster
10. proverb
11. moods
12. muscle
13. neat
14. information
15. plum
16. popular
17. mule
18. rate

B
1. 관심이 있는
2. 괴물
3. 곤충
4. 깔끔한, 단정한
5. 서양자두
6. 대신에
7. 인기 있는, 대중적인
8. 노새
9. 가능한
10. 빌려주다
11. 비율, 요금
12. 독
13. 속담
14. 정보
15. 근육, 힘줄
16. 시, 운문
17. 잇다, 관련 짓다
18. 기분, 분위기

1. information
2. insect
3. instead
4. interested
5. link
6. loan
7. monster
8. mood
9. mule
10. muscle
11. neat
12. plum
13. poem
14. poison
15. popular
16. possible
17. proverb
18. rate

C
1. information 정보
2. muscle 근육, 힘줄
3. neat 깔끔한, 단정한
4. mule 노새
5. plum 서양자두
6. insect 곤충
7. poem 시, 운문
8. rate 비율, 요금
9. poison 독
10. instead 대신에
11. popular 인기 있는, 대중적인
12. mood 기분, 분위기
13. interested 관심이 있는
14. monster 괴물
15. possible 가능한
16. loan 빌려주다
17. proverb 속담
18. link 잇다, 관련 짓다

Unit 24

A
1. sort
2. rubber
3. surveyed
4. rug
5. Safety
6. soil
7. treat
8. speech
9. rude
10. tombs
11. tools
12. rub
13. smooth
14. trade
15. solution
16. traffic
17. sparkle
18. trash

B
1. 매끄러운
2. 불꽃, 번쩍임
3. 비비다, 문지르다
4. 조사하다
5. 고무, 고무줄
6. 연설, 말
7. 거래하다, 무역
8. 버릇없는, 무례한
9. 교통
10. 흙, 토양
11. 쓰레기
12. 깔개, 융단
13. 다루다, 대우하다
14. 해결, 용해
15. 도구, 연장
16. 종류
17. 무덤, 묘
18. 안전, 무사

1. rub
2. rubber
3. rude
4. rug
5. safety
6. smooth
7. soil
8. solution
9. sort
10. sparkle
11. speech
12. survey
13. tomb
14. tool
15. trade
16. traffic
17. trash
18. treat

C
1. safety 안전, 무사
2. tomb 무덤, 묘
3. rug 깔개, 융단
4. survey 조사하다
5. tool 도구, 연장
6. smooth 매끄러운
7. rubber 고무, 고무줄
8. trade 거래하다, 무역
9. soil 흙, 토양
10. traffic 교통
11. solution 해결, 용해
12. rub 비비다, 문지르다
13. trash 쓰레기
14. sparkle 불꽃, 번쩍임
15. treat 다루다, 대우하다
16. sort 종류
17. rude 버릇없는, 무례한
18. speech 연설, 말

Review 12

A
1. information 정보
2. muscle 근육, 힘줄
3. neat 깔끔한, 단정한
4. mule 노새
5. plum 서양자두
6. insect 곤충
7. poem 시, 운문
8. rate 비율, 요금
9. poison 독
10. instead 대신에
11. popular 인기 있는, 대중적인
12. mood 기분, 분위기
13. interested 관심이 있는
14. monster 괴물
15. possible 가능한
16. loan 빌려주다
17. proverb 속담
18. link 잇다, 관련 짓다

B
1. safety 안전, 무사
2. tomb 무덤, 묘
3. rug 깔개, 융단
4. survey 조사하다
5. tool 도구, 연장
6. smooth 매끄러운
7. rubber 고무, 고무줄
8. trade 거래하다, 무역
9. soil 흙, 토양
10. traffic 교통
11. solution 해결, 용해
12. rub 비비다, 문지르다
13. trash 쓰레기
14. sparkle 불꽃, 번쩍임
15. treat 다루다, 대우하다
16. sort 종류
17. rude 버릇없는, 무례한
18. speech 연설, 말

Unit 25

A
1. clown
2. allow
3. bottom
4. already
5. clay
6. boil
7. accident
8. border
9. clapped
10. alike
11. brain
12. agreement
13. choice
14. cigarette
15. bones
16. alcohol
17. coach
18. bored

B
1. 동의, 협정
2. 뼈
3. 어릿광대
4. 바닥, 밑바닥
5. 허락하다
6. 뇌, 두뇌
7. 알코올, 술
8. 담배
9. 끓다, 끓이다
10. 찰흙, 점토
11. 똑같은
12. (손뼉을)치다
13. 지도자
14. 이미, 벌써
15. 선택
16. 지루한, 싫증나는
17. 사고, 재난
18. 국경, 경계

1. accident
2. agreement
3. alcohol
4. alike
5. allow
6. already
7. boil
8. bone
9. border
10. bored
11. bottom
12. brain
13. choice
14. cigarette
15. clap
16. clay
17. clown
18. coach

C
1. alike — 똑같은
2. bored — 지루한, 싫증나는
3. coach — 지도자
4. alcohol — 알코올, 술
5. clown — 어릿광대
6. border — 국경, 경계
7. accident — 사고, 재난
8. clay — 찰흙, 점토
9. choice — 선택
10. bottom — 바닥, 밑바닥
11. cigarette — 담배
12. bone — 뼈
13. agreement — 동의, 협정
14. clap — (손뼉을)치다
15. brain — 뇌, 두뇌
16. already — 이미, 벌써
17. boil — 끓다, 끓이다
18. allow — 허락하다

Unit 26

A
1. crown
2. giant
3. curly
4. guard
5. equal
6. curve
7. greenhouse
8. cube
9. cure
10. goose
11. crops
12. Elegance
13. error
14. escape
15. especially
16. general
17. escalator
18. goal

B
1. 입방체, 정육면체
2. 우아함, 고상
3. 곡선, 커브
4. 에스컬레이터
5. 수확, 농작물
6. 거인, 거대한
7. 잘못, 실수
8. 온실
9. 지키다, 경계하다
10. 왕관
11. 특히, 특별히
12. 거위
13. 목적
14. 달아나다
15. 곱슬머리의
16. 같은, 동등한
17. 일반, 일반의
18. 치료, 치료하다

1. crop
2. crown
3. cube
4. cure
5. curly
6. curve
7. elegance
8. equal
9. error
10. escalator
11. escape
12. especially
13. general
14. giant
15. goal
16. goose
17. greenhouse
18. guard

C
1. error — 잘못, 실수
2. crown — 왕관
3. escape — 달아나다
4. crop — 수확, 농작물
5. escalator — 에스컬레이터
6. cure — 치료, 치료하다
7. giant — 거인, 거대한
8. equal — 같은, 동등한
9. cube — 입방체, 정육면체
10. general — 일반, 일반의
11. curve — 곡선, 커브
12. especially — 특히, 특별히
13. goal — 목적
14. elegance — 우아함, 고상
15. greenhouse — 온실
16. curly — 곱슬머리의
17. goose — 거위
18. guard — 지키다, 경계하다

Review 13

A
1. alike — 똑같은
2. bored — 지루한, 싫증나는
3. coach — 지도자
4. alcohol — 알코올, 술
5. clown — 어릿광대
6. border — 국경, 경계
7. accident — 사고, 재난
8. clay — 찰흙, 점토
9. choice — 선택
10. bottom — 바닥, 밑바닥
11. cigarette — 담배
12. bone — 뼈
13. agreement — 동의, 협정
14. clap — (손뼉을)치다
15. brain — 뇌, 두뇌
16. already — 이미, 벌써
17. boil — 끓다, 끓이다
18. allow — 허락하다

B
1. error — 잘못, 실수
2. crown — 왕관
3. escape — 달아나다
4. crop — 수확, 농작물
5. escalator — 에스컬레이터
6. cure — 치료, 치료하다
7. giant — 거인, 거대한
8. equal — 같은, 동등한
9. cube — 입방체, 정육면체
10. general — 일반, 일반의
11. curve — 곡선, 커브
12. especially — 특히, 특별히
13. goal — 목적
14. elegance — 우아함, 고상
15. greenhouse — 온실
16. curly — 곱슬머리의
17. goose — 거위
18. guard — 지키다, 경계하다

Unit 27

A
1. pride
2. noodles
3. invented
4. items
5. jewels
6. interview
7. nodded
8. prison
9. nonstop
10. ostrich
11. portable
12. iron
13. needle
14. pouring
15. powerful
16. noisy
17. jog
18. present

B
1. 조깅하다
2. 발명하다
3. 휴대용의
4. 끄덕임, 끄덕이다
5. 철, 철제
6. 강한, 강력한
7. 직행의
8. 품목, 조항
9. 감옥, 교도소
10. 시끄러운
11. 출석한
12. 보석
13. 타조
14. 자랑, 자만심
15. 바늘
16. 쏟다, 따르다
17. 국수
18. 면접

1. interview
2. invent
3. iron
4. item
5. jewel
6. jog
7. needle
8. nod
9. noisy
10. nonstop
11. noodle
12. ostrich
13. portable
14. pour
15. powder
16. present
17. pride
18. prison

C
1. ostrich — 타조
2. nonstop — 직행의
3. portable — 휴대용의
4. interview — 면접
5. pour — 쏟다, 따르다
6. noisy — 시끄러운
7. invent — 발명하다
8. noodle — 국수
9. prison — 감옥, 교도소
10. iron — 철, 철제
11. jewel — 보석
12. item — 품목, 조항
13. needle — 바늘
14. powerful — 강한, 강력한
15. jog — 조깅하다
16. present — 출석한
17. nod — 끄덕임, 끄덕이다
18. pride — 자랑, 자만심

Unit 28

A
1. salmons
2. seashore
3. spins
4. university
5. spiders
6. stadium
7. stomach
8. union
9. stranger
10. tray
11. salty
12. treasure
13. seconds
14. troubles
15. Seek
16. trousers
17. stream
18. scene

B
1. 위, 배
2. 연어
3. 쟁반
4. 장면, 현장
5. 대학교
6. (몇) 초
7. 결합, 단결
8. 짠, 소금기가 있는
9. 시내, 개울
10. 실을 내다, 잣다
11. 낯선 사람
12. 바지
13. 해변, 바닷가
14. 경기장
15. 고생, 근심
16. 찾다, 추구하다
17. 보물
18. 거미

1. salmon
2. salty
3. scene
4. seashore
5. second
6. seek
7. spider
8. spin
9. stadium
10. stomach
11. stranger
12. stream
13. tray
14. treasure
15. trouble
16. trousers
17. union
18. university

C
1. salmon — 연어
2. trousers — 바지
3. stadium — 경기장
4. trouble — 고생, 근심
5. salty — 짠, 소금기가 있는
6. stomach — 위, 배
7. union — 결합, 단결
8. seek — 찾다, 추구하다
9. university — 대학교
10. spider — 거미
11. scene — 장면, 현장
12. treasure — 보물
13. spin — 실을 내다, 잣다
14. seashore — 해변, 바닷가
15. tray — 쟁반
16. second — (몇) 초
17. stranger — 낯선 사람
18. stream — 시내, 개울

Review 14

A
1. ostrich — 타조
2. nonstop — 직행의
3. portable — 휴대용의
4. interview — 면접
5. pour — 쏟다, 따르다
6. noisy — 시끄러운
7. invent — 발명하다
8. noodle — 국수
9. prison — 감옥, 교도소
10. iron — 철, 철제
11. jewel — 보석
12. item — 품목, 조항
13. needle — 바늘
14. powerful — 강한, 강력한
15. jog — 조깅하다
16. present — 출석한
17. nod — 끄덕임, 끄덕이다
18. pride — 자랑, 자만심

B
1. salmon — 연어
2. trousers — 바지
3. stadium — 경기장
4. trouble — 고생, 근심
5. salty — 짠, 소금기가 있는
6. stomach — 위, 배
7. union — 결합, 단결
8. seek — 찾다, 추구하다
9. university — 대학교
10. spider — 거미
11. scene — 장면, 현장
12. treasure — 보물
13. spin — 실을 내다, 잣다
14. seashore — 해변, 바닷가
15. tray — 쟁반
16. second — (몇) 초
17. stranger — 낯선 사람
18. stream — 시내, 개울

Unit 29

A
1. anxious
2. collect
3. appearance
4. bullet
5. area
6. behaved
7. broadcasted
8. bubbles
9. Coast
10. affair
11. butterflies
12. buzz
13. cabbage
14. apart
15. bar
16. coal
17. argue
18. college

B
1. 떨어져서
2. 술집, 막대기
3. 양배추
4. 걱정스러운
5. 해안, 연안
6. 방송하다
7. (윙윙)울리는 소리
8. 외관, 출현
9. 거품
10. 규범, 암호
11. 행동하다
12. 일, 사건
13. 단과대학
14. 나비
15. 논하다, 논쟁하다
16. 석탄
17. 탄알
18. 구역, 지역

1. affair
2. anxious
3. apart
4. appearance
5. area
6. argue
7. bar
8. behave
9. broadcast
10. bubble
11. bullet
12. butterfly
13. buzz
14. cabbage
15. coal
16. coast
17. code
18. college

C
1. bullet 탄알
2. affair 일, 사건
3. college 단과대학
4. broadcast 방송하다
5. anxious 걱정스러운
6. bubble 거품
7. cabbage 양배추
8. code 규범, 암호
9. behave 행동하다
10. appearance 외관, 출현
11. butterfly 나비
12. argue 논하다, 논쟁하다
13. buzz (윙윙)울리는 소리
14. apart 떨어져서
15. coal 석탄
16. coast 해안, 연안
17. bar 술집, 막대기
18. area 구역, 지역

Unit 30

A
1. history
2. desert
3. comedy
4. Hang
5. creatures
6. decide
7. excited
8. colored
9. herbs
10. Express
11. handkerchief
12. extra
13. Factories
14. knowledge
15. fail
16. fairy
17. healthy
18. hosts

B
1. 피조물, 생물
2. 표현하다, 나타내다
3. 공장
4. 채색된, ~색의
5. 걸다, 매달다
6. 희극, 코미디
7. 요정
8. 손수건
9. 여분의, 임시의
10. 약용식물, 풀잎
11. 지식
12. 결정하다, 결심하다
13. 역사
14. 흥분한
15. 주인
16. 건강한
17. 실패하다, 떨어지다
18. 사막

1. colored
2. comedy
3. creature
4. decide
5. desert
6. excited
7. express
8. extra
9. factory
10. fail
11. fairy
12. handkerchief
13. hang
14. healthy
15. herb
16. history
17. host
18. knowledge

C
1. host 주인
2. desert 사막
3. excited 흥분한
4. history 역사
5. colored 채색된, ~색의
6. decide 결정하다, 결심하다
7. express 표현하다, 나타내다
8. herb 약용식물, 풀잎
9. comedy 희극, 코미디
10. knowledge 지식
11. fail 실패하다, 떨어지다
12. creature 피조물, 생물
13. handkerchief 손수건
14. healthy 건강한
15. factory 공장
16. extra 여분의, 임시의
17. fairy 요정
18. hang 걸다, 매달다

Review 15

A
1. bullet 탄알
2. affair 일, 사건
3. college 단과대학
4. broadcast 방송하다
5. anxious 걱정스러운
6. bubble 거품
7. cabbage 양배추
8. code 규범, 암호
9. behave 행동하다
10. appearance 외관, 출현
11. butterfly 나비
12. argue 논하다, 논쟁하다
13. buzz (윙윙)울리는 소리
14. apart 떨어져서
15. coal 석탄
16. coast 해안, 연안
17. bar 술집, 막대기
18. area 구역, 지역

B
1. host 주인
2. desert 사막
3. excited 흥분한
4. history 역사
5. colored 채색된, ~색의
6. decide 결정하다, 결심하다
7. express 표현하다, 나타내다
8. herb 약용식물, 풀잎
9. comedy 희극, 코미디
10. knowledge 지식
11. fail 실패하다, 떨어지다
12. creature 피조물, 생물
13. handkerchief 손수건
14. healthy 건강한
15. factory 공장
16. extra 여분의, 임시의
17. fairy 요정
18. hang 걸다, 매달다

Unit 31

A
1. least
2. ocean
3. Most
4. kindergarten
5. raw
6. level
7. nut
8. oneself
9. keyboard
10. ladder
11. operated
12. quarters
13. opinion
14. quite
15. reasons
16. officer
17. kicks
18. receive

B
1. 사다리
2. 견과
3. 스스로, 자기 자신을
4. 자판
5. 의견, 견해
6. 수준
7. 아주, 완전히
8. 대양, 바다
9. 생것의, 날것의
10. 유치원
11. 이유, 까닭
12. 장교, 공무원
13. 받다, 맞이하다
14. 최소, 최저
15. 4분의 1
16. 대부분의
17. 작동하다, 움직이다
18. 차다

1. keyboard
2. kick
3. kindergarten
4. ladder
5. least
6. level
7. most
8. nut
9. ocean
10. officer
11. oneself
12. operate
13. opinion
14. quarter
15. quite
16. raw
17. reason
18. receive

C
1. reason
2. receive
3. keyboard
4. ocean
5. raw
6. kick
7. quite
8. officer
9. kindergarten
10. nut
11. oneself
12. ladder
13. operate
14. level
15. quarter
16. least
17. opinion
18. most

이유, 까닭
받다, 맞이하다
자판
대양, 바다
생것의, 날것의
차다
아주, 완전히
장교, 공무원
유치원
견과
스스로, 자기 자신을
사다리
작동하다, 움직이다
수준
4분의 1
최소, 최저
의견, 견해
대부분의

Unit 32

A
1. sentence
2. Senior
3. value
4. sense
5. voice
6. serve
7. sweep
8. traces
9. Shake
10. stress
11. stuff
12. valley
13. voted
14. suit
15. surprise
16. seminar
17. success
18. vet

B
1. 성공
2. 연상의, 선배의
3. 자취, 흔적, 발자국
4. 흔들다
5. 어울리다, 한 벌
6. 계곡, 골짜기
7. 세미나
8. 청소하다, 쓸다
9. 목소리, 음성
10. 압박, 스트레스
11. 투표, 투표하다
12. 감각, 직감
13. 수의사
14. 채우다, 메우다
15. 가치, 가격
16. (음식을)차려 내다, 봉사하다
17. 놀람, 놀라게 하다
18. 문장

1. seminar
2. senior
3. sense
4. sentence
5. serve
6. shake
7. stress
8. stuff
9. success
10. suit
11. surprise
12. sweep
13. trace
14. valley
15. value
16. vet
17. voice
18. voice

C
1. sweep
2. sense
3. success
4. trace
5. seminar
6. surprise
7. valley
8. senior
9. value
10. suit
11. sentence
12. stuff
13. vet
14. serve
15. stress
16. voice
17. shake
18. vote

청소하다, 쓸다
감각, 직감
성공
자취, 흔적, 발자국
세미나
놀람, 놀라게 하다
계곡, 골짜기
연상의, 선배의
가치, 가격
어울리다, 한 벌
문장
채우다, 메우다
수의사
(음식을)차려 내다, 봉사 하다
압박, 스트레스
목소리, 음성
흔들다
투표, 투표하다

Review 16

A
1. reason
2. receive
3. keyboard
4. ocean
5. raw
6. kick
7. quite
8. officer
9. kindergarten
10. nut
11. oneself
12. ladder
13. operate
14. level
15. quarter
16. least
17. opinion
18. most

이유, 까닭
받다, 맞이하다
자판
대양, 바다
생것의, 날것의
차다
아주, 완전히
장교, 공무원
유치원
견과
스스로, 자기 자신을
사다리
작동하다, 움직이다
수준
4분의 1
최소, 최저
의견, 견해
대부분의

B
1. sweep
2. sense
3. success
4. trace
5. seminar
6. surprise
7. valley
8. senior
9. value
10. suit
11. sentence
12. stuff
13. vet
14. serve
15. stress
16. voice
17. shake
18. vote

청소하다, 쓸다
감각, 직감
성공
자취, 흔적, 발자국
세미나
놀람, 놀라게 하다
계곡, 골짜기
연상의, 선배의
가치, 가격
어울리다, 한 벌
문장
채우다, 메우다
수의사
(음식을)차려내다, 봉사하다
압박, 스트레스
목소리, 음성
흔들다
투표, 투표하다

Unit 33

A
1. common
2. bakery
3. arrow
4. contains
5. compass
6. assistants
7. castle
8. attention
9. community
10. bacteria
11. calm
12. camped
13. campaign
14. ash
15. cane
16. cash
17. company
18. connecting

B
1. 세균, 박테리아
2. 화살
3. 지팡이
4. 제과점
5. 현금, 현찰
6. 지역사회
7. 잇다, 연결하다
8. 보조자
9. 포함하다
10. 나침반, 컴퍼스
11. 회사, 교제
12. 주의, 돌봄
13. 평범한, 보통의
14. 야영하다
15. 캠페인, 선거운동
16. 성, 성곽
17. 고요한, 잔잔한
18. 재, 화산재

1. arrow
2. ash
3. assistant
4. attention
5. bacteria
6. bakery
7. calm
8. camp
9. campaign
10. cane
11. cash
12. castle
13. common
14. community
15. company
16. compass
17. connect
18. contain

C
1. calm 고요한, 잔잔한
2. bacteria 세균, 박테리아
3. compass 나침반, 컴퍼스
4. camp 야영하다
5. bakery 제과점
6. arrow 화살
7. campaign 캠페인, 선거운동
8. attention 주의, 돌봄
9. cane 지팡이
10. connect 잇다, 연결하다
11. cash 현금, 현찰
12. company 회사, 교제
13. castle 성, 성곽
14. ash 재, 화산재
15. community 지역사회
16. common 평범한, 보통의
17. contain 포함하다
18. assistant 보조자

Unit 34

A
1. fans
2. destination
3. fist
4. dig
5. homework
6. details
7. Honey
8. festival
9. litter
10. hometown
11. hoop
12. dew
13. honest
14. feathers
15. dice
16. direct
17. floods
18. however

B
1. 이슬
2. 팬
3. 길을 가리키다
4. 주먹
5. 목적, 목적지
6. 축제, 잔치
7. 고향, 출생지
8. 꿀
9. 상세, 세부
10. 숙제
11. 쓰레기
12. 테, 후프
13. 깃털
14. 하지만, 그러나
15. 파다
16. 정직한
17. 홍수, 범람하다
18. 주사위

1. destination
2. detail
3. dew
4. dice
5. dig
6. direct
7. fan
8. feather
9. festival
10. fist
11. flood
12. hometown
13. homework
14. honest
15. honey
16. hoop
17. however
18. litter

C
1. however 하지만, 그러나
2. fan 팬
3. litter 쓰레기
4. destination 목적, 목적지
5. hoop 테, 후프
6. direct 길을 가리키다
7. feather 깃털
8. hometown 고향, 출생지
9. festival 축제, 잔치
10. detail 상세, 세부
11. honest 정직한
12. fist 주먹
13. dig 파다
14. honey 꿀
15. dew 이슬
16. flood 홍수, 범람하다
17. homework 숙제
18. dice 주사위

Review 17

A
1. calm 고요한, 잔잔한
2. bacteria 세균, 박테리아
3. compass 나침반, 컴퍼스
4. camp 야영하다
5. bakery 제과점
6. arrow 화살
7. campaign 캠페인, 선거운동
8. attention 주의, 돌봄
9. cane 지팡이
10. connect 잇다, 연결하다
11. cash 현금, 현찰
12. company 회사, 교제
13. castle 성, 성곽
14. ash 재, 화산재
15. community 지역사회
16. common 평범한, 보통의
17. contain 포함하다
18. assistant 보조자

B
1. however 하지만, 그러나
2. fan 팬
3. litter 쓰레기
4. destination 목적, 목적지
5. hoop 테, 후프
6. direct 길을 가리키다
7. feather 깃털
8. hometown 고향, 출생지
9. festival 축제, 잔치
10. detail 상세, 세부
11. honest 정직한
12. fist 주먹
13. dig 파다
14. honey 꿀
15. dew 이슬
16. flood 홍수, 범람하다
17. homework 숙제
18. dice 주사위

Unit 35

A
1. magician
2. part
3. melted
4. Recycle
5. nature
6. pack
7. managed
8. respond
9. pain
10. path
11. peaceful
12. rent
13. lonely
14. requires
15. roots
16. past
17. lucky
18. rid

B
1. 행운의, 운좋은
2. 싸다, 꾸리다
3. 다루다, 관리하다
4. 일부, 부문
5. 재활용하다
6. 작은 길, 보도
7. 외로운, 고독한
8. 응답하다, 반응하다
9. 고통, 아픔
10. 제거하다
11. 마법사, 마술사
12. 뿌리
13. 요구하다
14. 과거
15. 빌리다, 임대하다
16. 자연
17. 평화로운
18. 녹다

1. lonely
2. lucky
3. magician
4. manage
5. melt
6. nature
7. pack
8. pain
9. part
10. past
11. path
12. peaceful
13. recycle
14. rent
15. require
16. respond
17. rid
18. root

C
1. path — 작은 길, 보도
2. lonely — 외로운, 고독한
3. rent — 빌리다, 임대하다
4. part — 일부, 부문
5. require — 요구하다
6. past — 과거
7. lucky — 행운의, 운좋은
8. peaceful — 평화로운
9. magician — 마법사, 마술사
10. recycle — 재활용하다
11. pain — 고통, 아픔
12. respond — 응답하다, 반응하다
13. manage — 다루다, 관리하다
14. root — 뿌리
15. melt — 녹다
16. rid — 제거하다
17. nature — 자연
18. pack — 싸다, 꾸리다

Unit 36

A
1. tale
2. silent
3. weather
4. system
5. tailor
6. shy
7. tapped
8. swallow
9. tax
10. shining
11. wallet
12. sharply
13. waves
14. wedding
15. shell
16. weed
17. simple
18. weighed

B
1. 수줍어하는
2. 재봉사, 재단사
3. 날카롭게
4. 세금, 조세
5. 파도, 물결
6. 간단한, 단순한
7. 날씨, 기후
8. 체제, 시스템
9. 잡초
10. 빛나다
11. 가볍게 두드리다
12. 무게를 달다
13. 침묵을 지키다
14. 결혼, 혼례
15. 지갑
16. 제비
17. 이야기
18. 껍질, 등딱지

1. sharply
2. shell
3. shine
4. shy
5. silent
6. simple
7. swallow
8. system
9. tailor
10. tale
11. tap
12. tax
13. wallet
14. wave
15. weather
16. wedding
17. weed
18. weigh

C
1. weigh — 무게를 달다
2. system — 체제, 시스템
3. tailor — 재봉사, 재단사
4. sharply — 날카롭게
5. weed — 잡초
6. swallow — 제비
7. tale — 이야기
8. simple — 간단한, 단순한
9. wedding — 결혼, 혼례
10. shell — 껍질, 등딱지
11. tap — 가볍게 두드리다
12. shine — 빛나다
13. wallet — 지갑
14. tax — 세금, 조세
15. shy — 수줍어하는
16. weather — 날씨, 기후
17. silent — 침묵을 지키는
18. wave — 파도, 물결

Review 18

A
1. path — 작은 길, 보도
2. lonely — 외로운, 고독한
3. rent — 빌리다, 임대하다
4. part — 일부, 부문
5. require — 요구하다
6. past — 과거
7. lucky — 행운의, 운좋은
8. peaceful — 평화로운
9. magician — 마법사, 마술사
10. recycle — 재활용하다
11. pain — 고통, 아픔
12. respond — 응답하다, 반응하다
13. manage — 다루다, 관리하다
14. root — 뿌리
15. melt — 녹다
16. rid — 제거하다
17. nature — 자연
18. pack — 싸다, 꾸리다

B
1. weigh — 무게를 달다
2. system — 체제, 시스템
3. tailor — 재봉사, 재단사
4. sharply — 날카롭게
5. weed — 잡초
6. swallow — 제비
7. tale — 이야기
8. simple — 간단한, 단순한
9. wedding — 결혼, 혼례
10. shell — 껍질, 등딱지
11. tap — 가볍게 두드리다
12. shine — 빛나다
13. wallet — 지갑
14. tax — 세금, 조세
15. shy — 수줍어하는
16. weather — 날씨, 기후
17. silent — 침묵을 지키는
18. wave — 파도, 물결

Unit 37

A
1. costs
2. cell
3. control
4. balance
5. careful
6. continued
7. bargains
8. contest
9. champion
10. batteries
11. chance
12. beard
13. conversation
14. begged / begged
15. copyright
16. bloom
17. cave
18. cereals

B
1. 주의 깊은
2. 기회, 가망
3. (싸게 산) 물건, 매매
4. 챔피언
5. 통제하다, 억제하다
6. 균형, 저울
7. 대화, 회화
8. 꽃, 개화
9. 비용이 들다
10. 동굴
11. 빌다, 간청하다
12. 독방, 세포
13. 저작권
14. 곡물, 곡물 음식
15. 계속하다
16. 턱수염
17. 경쟁, 콘테스트
18. 건전지

1. balance
2. bargain
3. battery
4. beard
5. beg
6. bloom
7. careful
8. cave
9. cell
10. cereal
11. champion
12. chance
13. contest
14. continue
15. control
16. conversation
17. copyright
18. cost

C
1. contest   경쟁, 콘테스트
2. champion   챔피언
3. balance   균형, 저울
4. chance   기회, 가망
5. bargain   (싸게 산) 물건, 매매
6. conversation   대화, 회화
7. continue   계속하다
8. copyright   저작권
9. battery   건전지
10. cell   독방, 세포
11. bloom   꽃, 개화
12. control   통제하다, 억제하다
13. cave   동굴
14. beard   턱수염
15. cost   비용이 들다
16. careful   주의 깊은
17. beg   빌다, 간청하다
18. cereal   곡물, 곡물 음식

Unit 38

A
1. Ice
2. delay
3. Fold
4. discussion
5. divide
6. humming
7. documentary
8. double
9. flour
10. image
11. fond
12. forward
13. frame
14. flat
15. hugged
16. humans
17. dove
18. idioms

B
1. 숙어, 관용구
2. 앞으로
3. 늦추다, 미루다
4. 좋아하는, 다정한
5. 나누다
6. 편평한, 평탄한
7. 틀, 구조, 뼈대
8. 모습, 모양
9. 다큐멘터리
10. 밀가루, 분말
11. 얼음
12. 비둘기
13. 콧노래를 부르다
14. 접다
15. 두 배의, 두 겹의
16. 인간의
17. 토론
18. 포옹, 껴안다

1. delay
2. discussion
3. divide
4. documentary
5. double
6. dove
7. flat
8. flour
9. fold
10. fond
11. forward
12. frame
13. hug
14. hum
15. human
16. ice
17. idiom
18. image

C
1. hug   포옹, 껴안다
2. delay   늦추다, 미루다
3. hum   콧노래를 부르다
4. ice   얼음
5. discussion   토론
6. fold   접다
7. divide   나누다
8. human   인간의
9. fond   좋아하는 다정한
10. documentary   다큐멘터리
11. flour   밀가루, 분말
12. idiom   숙어, 관용구
13. forward   앞으로
14. double   두 배의, 두 겹의
15. flat   편평한, 평탄한
16. image   모습, 모양
17. dove   비둘기
18. frame   틀, 구조, 뼈대

Review 19

A
1. contest   경쟁, 콘테스트
2. champion   챔피언
3. balance   균형, 저울
4. chance   기회, 가망
5. bargain   (싸게 산) 물건, 매매
6. conversation   대화, 회화
7. continue   계속하다
8. copyright   저작권
9. battery   건전지
10. cell   독방, 세포
11. bloom   꽃, 개화
12. control   통제하다, 억제하다
13. cave   동굴
14. beard   턱수염
15. cost   비용이 들다
16. careful   주의 깊은
17. beg   빌다, 간청하다
18. cereal   곡물, 곡물 음식

B
1. hug   포옹, 껴안다
2. delay   늦추다, 미루다
3. hum   콧노래를 부르다
4. ice   얼음
5. discussion   토론
6. fold   접다
7. divide   나누다
8. human   인간의
9. fond   좋아하는 다정한
10. documentary   다큐멘터리
11. flour   밀가루, 분말
12. idiom   숙어, 관용구
13. forward   앞으로
14. double   두 배의, 두 겹의
15. flat   편평한, 평탄한
16. image   모습, 모양
17. dove   비둘기
18. frame   틀, 구조, 뼈대

Unit 39

A
1. mess
2. plenty
3. mind
4. rope
5. model
6. planet
7. response
8. period
9. row
10. photograph
11. memory
12. pills
13. midnight
14. plastics
15. reduce
16. role
17. missions
18. rough

B
1. 기간, 시대
2. 기억(력)
3. 플라스틱, 플라스틱의
4. 혼란, 어수선함
5. 줄이다, 낮추다
6. 사진
7. 대답, 응답
8. 역할, 배역
9. 임무, 특병
10. 알약
11. 밧줄
12. 모형, 모델
13. 행성
14. 거친, 험악한
15. 열, 줄
16. 마음, 정신
17. 많음, 다수
18. 한밤중, 자정

1. memory
2. mess
3. midnight
4. mind
5. mission
6. model
7. period
8. photograph
9. pill
10. planet
11. plastic
12. plenty
13. reduce
14. response
15. role
16. rope
17. rough
18. row

C
1. reduce — 줄이다, 낮추다
2. plastic — 플라스틱, 플라스틱의
3. response — 대답, 응답
4. memory — 기억(력)
5. plenty — 많음, 다수
6. role — 역할, 배역
7. row — 열, 줄
8. rope — 밧줄
9. mess — 혼란, 어수선함
10. period — 기간, 시대
11. model — 모형, 모델
12. rough — 거친, 험악한
13. pill — 알약
14. midnight — 한밤중, 자정
15. photograph — 사진
16. mission — 임무, 특병
17. planet — 행성
18. mind — 마음, 정신

Unit 40

A
1. sleepy
2. theater
3. sink
4. skin
5. tears
6. teenagers
7. witnesses
8. thief
9. Tin
10. wipe
11. skipped
12. textile
13. wires
14. Since
15. within
16. Without
17. smog
18. wrapped

B
1. 가라앉다
2. 10대의 소년(소녀)
3. 피부, 가죽
4. 주석, 양철 깡통
5. 직물, 직물의
6. 닦다, 훔치다
7. ~이래로
8. 도둑, 절도범
9. 철사, 전선
10. 스모그, 연무
11. ~안에, ~이내에
12. 가볍게 뛰다
13. 극장
14. 싸다, 감싸다
15. 눈물
16. 목격자, 증인
17. ~없이
18. 졸린

1. since
2. sink
3. skin
4. skip
5. sleepy
6. smog
7. tear
8. teenager
9. textile
10. theater
11. thief
12. tin
13. wipe
14. wire
15. within
16. without
17. witness
18. wrap

C
1. wipe — 닦다, 훔치다
2. tin — 주석, 양철 깡통
3. since — ~이래로
4. wire — 철사, 전선
5. thief — 도둑, 절도범
6. within — ~안에, ~이내에
7. theater — 극장
8. sink — 가라앉다
9. without — ~없이
10. skin — 피부, 가죽
11. wrap — 싸다, 감싸다
12. teenager — 10대의 소년(소녀)
13. witness — 목격자, 증인
14. skip — 가볍게 뛰다
15. tear — 눈물
16. smog — 스모그, 연무
17. textile — 직물, 직물의
18. sleepy — 졸린

Review 20

A
1. reduce — 줄이다, 낮추다
2. plastic — 플라스틱, 플라스틱의
3. response — 대답, 응답
4. memory — 기억(력)
5. plenty — 많음, 다수
6. role — 역할, 배역
7. row — 열, 줄
8. rope — 밧줄
9. mess — 혼란, 어수선함
10. period — 기간, 시대
11. model — 모형, 모델
12. rough — 거친, 험악한
13. pill — 알약
14. midnight — 한밤중, 자정
15. photograph — 사진
16. mission — 임무, 특병
17. planet — 행성
18. mind — 마음, 정신

B
1. wipe — 닦다, 훔치다
2. tin — 주석, 양철 깡통
3. since — ~이래로
4. wire — 철사, 전선
5. thief — 도둑, 절도범
6. within — ~안에, ~이내에
7. theater — 극장
8. sink — 가라앉다
9. without — ~없이
10. skin — 피부, 가죽
11. wrap — 싸다, 감싸다
12. teenager — 10대의 소년(소녀)
13. witness — 목격자, 증인
14. skip — 가볍게 뛰다
15. tear — 눈물
16. smog — 스모그, 연무
17. textile — 직물, 직물의
18. sleepy — 졸린

Total Test — 해당 Unit별 Exercise 3번 문제의 정답과 일치

 MEMO